A COLLECTION FOR ELEMENTARY EDUCATORS

A Year of Inquiry

A COLLECTION FOR ELEMENTARY EDUCATORS

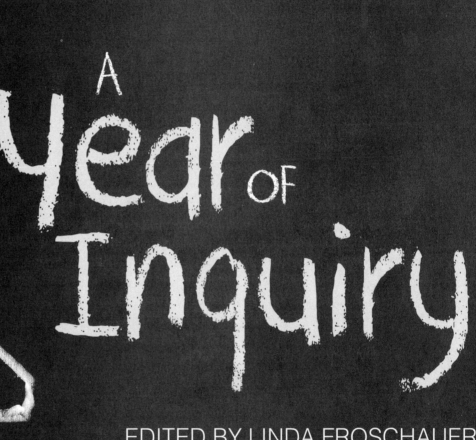

A Year OF Inquiry

EDITED BY LINDA FROSCHAUER

NSTApress
National Science Teachers Association
Arlington, Virginia

National Science Teachers Association

Claire Reinburg, Director
Jennifer Horak, Managing Editor
Andrew Cooke, Senior Editor
Wendy Rubin, Associate Editor
Agnes Bannigan, Associate Editor
Amy America, Book Acquisitions Coordinator

ART AND DESIGN
Will Thomas Jr., Director, cover and interior design

PRINTING AND PRODUCTION
Catherine Lorrain, Director

NATIONAL SCIENCE TEACHERS ASSOCIATION
Gerald F. Wheeler, Executive Director
David Beacom, Publisher
1840 Wilson Blvd., Arlington, VA 22201
www.nsta.org/store
For customer service inquiries, please call 800-277-5300.

NSTA is committed to publishing material that promotes the best in inquiry-based science education. However, conditions of actual use may vary, and the safety procedures and practices described in this book are intended to serve only as a guide. Additional precautionary measures may be required. NSTA and the authors do not warrant or represent that the procedures and practices in this book meet any safety code or standard of federal, state, or local regulations. NSTA and the authors disclaim any liability for personal injury or damage to property arising out of or relating to the use of this book, including any of the recommendations, instructions, or materials contained therein.

PERMISSIONS
Book purchasers may photocopy, print, or e-mail up to five copies of an NSTA book chapter for personal use only; this does not include display or promotional use. Elementary, middle, and high school teachers may reproduce forms, sample documents, and single NSTA book chapters needed for classroom or noncommercial, professional-development use only. E-book buyers may download files to multiple personal devices but are prohibited from posting the files to third-party servers or websites, or from passing files to non-buyers. For additional permission to photocopy or use material electronically from this NSTA Press book, please contact the Copyright Clearance Center (CCC) (*www.copyright.com*; 978-750-8400). Please access *www.nsta.org/permissions* for further information about NSTA's rights and permissions policies.

Library of Congress Cataloging-in-Publication Data
A year of inquiry : a collection for elementary educators / edited by Linda Froschauer.
    p. cm.
 Includes bibliographical references and index.
 ISBN 978-1-936959-34-1
 1. Science--Study and teaching (Elementary) 2. Science teachers. 3. Inquiry-based learning. 4. Effective teaching. I. Froschauer, Linda.
 LB1585.Y46 2012
 372.35'044--dc23

                    2012024304

 eISBN 978-1-936959-65-5

Contents

Introduction vii

What Does a Scientist Do? 1

CHAPTER 1   *A Powerful Way to Learn*, Norman G. Lederman...2
CHAPTER 2   *Supporting Ideas With Evidence*, Susan Gomez-Zwiep and David Harris..........5
CHAPTER 3   *Sound Science*, Aaron J. Sickel, Michele H. Lee, and Enrique M. Pareja..........10
CHAPTER 4   *Dig Deeply*, Sharon Owings and Barbara Merino 16

Process Skills...23

CHAPTER 5   *Inquiry, Process Skills, and Thinking in Science*, Mike Padilla 24
CHAPTER 6   *Inference or Observation?* Kevin D. Finson 27
CHAPTER 7   *Nature's Palette*, Brooke B. McBride and Carol A. Brewer 32
CHAPTER 8   *Beyond Predictions*, Dennis W. Smithenry and Jenny Kim 37

Science Notebooks 45

CHAPTER 9   *A Foolproof Tool*, Linda Froschauer 46
CHAPTER 10 *A Menu of Options*, Valerie Joyner...48
CHAPTER 11 *Interactive Reflective Logs*, Cynthia Minchew Deaton, Benjamin E. Deaton,
             and Katina Leland 54
CHAPTER 12 *Reuse That Notebook!* Elizabeth Lener 60

Investigable Questions 65

CHAPTER 13 *Sparks That Ignite Inquiry*, Lawrence F. Lowery..66
CHAPTER 14 *A Quest to Improve*, Azza Sharkawy..69
CHAPTER 15 *Personalized Inquiry*, Patricia Simpson 75
CHAPTER 16 *Picture This!* Leslie Bradbury, Lisa Gross, Jeff Goodman, and William Straits 81

Data Collection and Representation...87

CHAPTER 17 *Helping Young Learners Make Sense of Data: A 21st-Century Capability*, Joseph Krajcik ...88
CHAPTER 18 *Early Primary Invasion Scientists*, Katie V. Spellman and Christine P. Villano 91
CHAPTER 19 *Measure Lines*, Sally Crissman...97
CHAPTER 20 *No Duck Left Behind*, Sandi Cooper, Julie Thomas, and Tammy Motley............102

Contents

Selecting an Inquiry Experience 109

CHAPTER 21 *Pathways to Inquiry*, Lynn Rankin 110

CHAPTER 22 *Inquiry Into the Heart of a Comet*, Whitney Cobb, Maura Rountree-Brown, Lucy McFadden,
and Elizabeth Warner 113

CHAPTER 23 *Thinking Inside the Box*, Carolyn Jeffries 118

CHAPTER 24 *Concept-Based Learning*, Bethany Schill and Linda Howell 124

Switching From Cookbook Labs to Full Inquiry 133

CHAPTER 25 *Inquiry Is Essential*, Rodger W. Bybee 134

CHAPTER 26 *Five Strategies to Support All Teachers*, Paula A. Magee and Ryan Flessner 137

CHAPTER 27 *Fire Up the Inquiry*, Kimberly Lott 142

CHAPTER 28 *Water Pressure in Depth*, Mary Jean Lynch and John Zenchak 149

Sharing Research Results 155

CHAPTER 29 *What a Copper-Plated Nail Taught Me About Sharing Research Results*, Linda Shore 156

CHAPTER 30 *A Standards-Based Science Fair*, Peter Rillero 158

CHAPTER 31 *Living or Nonliving?* Britt Legaspi and William Straits 164

CHAPTER 32 *Claims, Evidence, and Reasoning*, Katherine L. McNeill and Dean M. Martin 170

Assessing Inquiry 177

CHAPTER 33 *The Changing Landscape of Assessment*, Richard A. Duschl 178

CHAPTER 34 *Feed Up, Feedback, and Feed Forward*, Douglas Fisher and Nancy Frey 181

CHAPTER 35 *Capitalizing on Curiosity*, Adam Devitt 188

CHAPTER 36 *Whoooo Knew?* Ellen Schiller and Jacque Melin 193

Index 203

Introduction

Designing *A Year of Inquiry: A Collection for Elementary Educators*

Over the years, the *Science and Children* (*S&C*) editorial team has received a significant number of manuscripts that focus on inquiry. Many of these manuscripts have been quickly accepted and published in *S&C* issues. But no matter how many articles we publish on the topic, the interest in inquiry has not diminished. In fact, our readers have clamored for more. These manuscript submissions reveal a huge diversity in the understanding of what inquiry is and the role it can and should play in the elementary curriculum. With interest high and an understanding essential, we designed *A Year of Inquiry: A Collection for Elementary Educators*: a book structured around an entire year of support, instruction, and learning through inquiry.

A Year of Inquiry highlights 10 months' worth of inquiry articles from *S&C* issues published in 2010–2011, which are separated into the book's sections and chapters. Each section opens with a brief, introductory chapter followed by four related chapters, all focusing on a particular theme. The first theme, for example, is What Does a Scientist Do? and starts with a chapter by the *S&C* contributing author Norman Lederman titled "A Powerful Way to Learn." In selecting the theme for each section to be published during the year of inquiry, we considered those inquiry-supporting components that teachers frequently express an interest in learning more about, as well as topics that lead to a greater understanding of science practices. The first theme, or topic, supports teachers' interest in and need for a greater understanding of what a scientist does. Topics for the rest of the book include process skill development; record keeping in science notebooks; structuring investigable questions; collecting, representing, and analyzing data; and sharing research results. The theme topics then go on to support teaching by providing information concerning the selection of an inquiry experience, switching from cookbook labs to full inquiry, and assessing student work.

In each section's opening chapter, experts in our field provide clear descriptions of the theme. These chapters serve as an introduction to each theme-specific section and set the stage for the section's articles. As we designed the book and began identifying these leaders in science education for inclusion in our full year of inquiry, we realized that many elementary classroom teachers could benefit from the variety of ideas being shared by *S&C* authors. Without hesitation, we began selecting articles from each *S&C* issue that would provide a broad spectrum of ideas to support grades preK–6 teachers as they create inquiry teaching and learning opportunities. The selected articles, which are the book's chapters, provide a balance of science core content as well as grade levels.

Introduction

Most of the chapters are developed around specific disciplinary core ideas, but you will find that many of them provide suggestions for strategies that can be implemented within many content areas. Similarly, the grade levels designated by the authors serve as a guideline and modifications for providing more rigor or slicing back on content can easily be accomplished. We hope the entire collection will serve as a source of ideas and springboard for developing your own strategies.

Although the collection features four chapters in each section, the response was unprecedented in the quantity and quality of manuscript submissions for each theme. To see additional materials that appeared in each theme issue go to *http://www.nsta.org/ elementaryschool/yearofinquiry.aspx*.

Inquiry and *A Framework for K–12 Science Education*

Inquiry has been a part of our view of quality science education since its introduction during the 1960s science reform movement. It was this reform and the subsequent NSF projects—including Science a Process Approach (SAPA), Elementary Science Study (ESS), and Science Curriculum Improvement Study (SCIS)—that brought inquiry to the attention of elementary teachers. The "alphabet soup" projects emphasized doing science and removed our reliance on memorization, textbooks, and lecture for developing science literacy. The emphasis on developing the processes of science also moved us away from the scientific method (indicating only one type of scientific method), moving us into exploration for learning. *Benchmarks for Science Literacy* (AAAS 1993) and the *National Science Education Standards* (NRC 1996) brought more attention to inquiry. The result has been an increase in what has been called hands-on (some have included minds-on in this explanation) science including investigations, laboratories, projects, and activities linked to real-life problems.

Inquiry will continue to be an important component in our arsenal of strategies that support student learning. The recently released *A Framework for K–12 Science Education: Practices, Crosscutting Concepts, and Core Ideas* (NRC 2011) highlights the importance of practices.

Rodger Bybee said it best when he explained the role of inquiry within the new *Framework* in his December *S&C* editorial (2011).

> Science teachers have asked—Why use the term *practices*? Why not continue using *inquiry*? These are reasonable questions .... scientific inquiry has not been implemented as widely as expected ....
>
> Scientific inquiry is one form of scientific practice. So, the perspective presented in the Framework is not one of replacing inquiry; rather, it is one of expanding and enriching the teaching and learning of science. Notice the emphasis on teaching strategies aligned with science practices. When students engage in scientific practices, activities become the basis for learning about experiments, data and evidence, social discourse, models and tools, mathematics, and the ability to evaluate knowledge claims, conduct empirical investigations, and develop explanations. (pp. 13–14)

How Students Learn: Science in the Classroom (Donovan and Bransford 2005) also provides insight to the role of the processes and inquiry. *Taking Science to School* (NRC 2007) and *Ready, Set, Science!* (NRC 2008) add to that knowledge base and inform the reader about strategies to use in developing student scientific literacy. Subsequently, the research base supporting the concepts explained in *Taking Science to School* and *Ready, Set, Science!* are frequently referenced and provide major contributions to the *Framework*. *Ready, Set, Science!* specifically addresses the inclusion of inquiry in science practices:

> Throughout this book, we talk about "scientific practices" and refer to the kind of teaching that integrates the four strands as "science as practice." Why not use the term "inquiry" instead? Science practice involves doing something and learning something in such a way that the doing and learning cannot really be separated. Thus, "practice" as used in this book, encompasses several of the different dictionary definitions of the term. It refers to doing something repeatedly in order to become proficient (as in practicing the trumpet). It refers to learning something so thoroughly that it becomes second nature (as in practicing thrift). And it refers to using one's knowledge to meet an objective (as in practicing law or practicing teaching).
>
> A particularly important form of scientific practice is scientific inquiry. The term "inquiry" has come to have different meanings as the concept has been implemented in curriculum frameworks, textbooks, and individual classrooms in recent years. To reflect this diversity and to broaden the discussion of effective science teaching and learning, the Committee on Science Learning, Kindergarten Through Eighth Grade chose to emphasize scientific practices rather than the specific practice of inquiry. This decision has several benefits. What we say about scientific practice applies to inquiry as well as to many other activities that take place in science classrooms. Focusing on practices also places inquiry in a broader context that can reveal when and why inquiry is effective. (p. 34)

With this definition of inquiry in mind, we could have called this theme year The Year of Practices. The themes identify and elaborate on several of the practices that are critical in helping students understand and learn science.

Integrating Inquiry With Core Content

We would like to remind you that the practices identified in *A Year of Inquiry: A Collection for Elementary Educators* should be integrated with the core concepts you are teaching. They should also be complimentary to the crosscutting concepts and be used in a variety of contexts when addressing those concepts. The notion of teaching a practice without these connections does not hold the same value in student learning as it does if taught within the context of content—the conceptual understanding you want to develop. *A Framework for K–12 Science Education: Practices, Crosscutting Concepts, and Core Ideas* is specific. Science practices should not be taught in isolation of the core content:

Introduction

Our view is that this perspective [seeing science as set of practices] is an improvement over previous approaches, in several ways. First, it minimizes the tendency to reduce scientific practice to a single set of procedures, such as identifying and controlling variables, classifying entities, and identifying sources of error. This tendency overemphasizes experimental investigation at the expense of other practices, such as modeling, critique, and communication. In addition, when such procedures are taught in isolation from science content, they become the aims of instruction in and of themselves rather than a means of developing a deeper understanding of the concepts and purposes of science.

Second, a focus on practices (in the plural) avoids the mistaken impression that there is one distinctive approach common to all science—a single "scientific method"—or that uncertainty is a universal attribute of science. In reality, practicing scientists employ a broad spectrum of methods, and although science involves many areas of uncertainty as knowledge is developed, there are now many aspects of scientific knowledge that are so well established as to be unquestioned foundations of the culture and its technologies. It is only through engagement in the practices that students can recognize how such knowledge comes about and why some parts of scientific theory are more firmly established than others.

Third, attempts to develop the idea that science should be taught through a process of inquiry have been hampered by the lack of a commonly accepted definition of its constituent elements. Such ambiguity results in widely divergent pedagogic objectives—an outcome that is counterproductive to the goal of common standards. (p. 3-43)

We consider eight practices to be essential elements of the K–12 science and engineering curriculum:

1. Asking questions (for science) and defining problems (for engineering)

2. Developing and using models

3. Planning and carrying out investigations

4. Analyzing and interpreting data

5. Using mathematics, information and computer technology, and computational thinking

6. Constructing explanations (for science) and designing solutions (for engineering)

7. Engaging in argument from evidence

8. Obtaining, evaluating, and communicating information (p. 3-49)

You will find examples of all of these practices included in *A Year of Inquiry: A Collection for Elementary Educators*.

In Closing

We hope you will find this collection helpful to you as you consider infusing inquiry into your curriculum. The collection can serve as one reference point for you as you construct valuable learning experiences for your students. Using these suggestions is the highest form of flattery; our authors would be thrilled to hear how you have implemented their ideas and incorporate them into the curriculum you are developing based on the *Framework* and the forthcoming *Next Generation Science Standards*.

Finally, a special thank you goes out to all of those who generously share their expertise, ideas, and enthusiasm for science teaching with the readers of *Science and Children*.

Best wishes for continued science education success,

The *Science and Children* Editorial Team
Linda Froschauer, Field Editor
Valynda Mayes, Managing Editor
Stephanie Andersen, Associate Editor

References

American Association for the Advancement of Science (AAAS). 1993. *Benchmarks for science literacy.* New York: Oxford University Press.

Bybee, R. 2011. *Scientific and engineering practices in K–12 classrooms: Understanding a framework for K–12 science education.* Science and Children 49 (4): 10–16. Arlington, VA: NSTA.

Donovan, S., and J. Bransford. 2005. *How students learn: Science in the classroom.* Washington, DC: The National Academies Press.

National Research Council (NRC). 1996. *National science education standards.* Washington, DC: The National Academies Press.

National Research Council (NRC). 2007. *Taking science to school: Learning and teaching science in grades K–8.* Washington, DC: National Academies Press.

National Research Council (NRC). 2008. *Ready, set, science! Putting research to work in K–8 science classrooms.* Washington, DC: The National Academies Press.

National Research Council (NRC). 2011. *A framework for K–12 science education: Practices, crosscutting concepts, and core ideas.* Washington, DC: The National Academies Press.

CHAPTER 1

A Powerful Way to Learn

By Norman G. Lederman

Science education has placed a renewed emphasis on inquiry, which in reform documents is described from three different perspectives: the teacher's approach, the abilities for students to develop, and the knowledge about what scientists do. The latter two perspectives are subject matter to be mastered by students and comprise what students should know as well as be able to do—and they are clearly delineated in the *Benchmarks for Science Literacy* (AAAS 1993), National Research Council's guide to inquiry (NRC 2000), and *National Science Education Standards* (NRC 1996).

In terms of abilities, students are expected to develop scientists' skills as they do their work (e.g., the ability to ask questions, design investigations to answer their questions, collect and analyze data, draw inferences and conclusions from the analysis of data). Students are also expected to know about inquiry. Students should know, for example, that

- all investigations begin with a question but do not necessarily involve the testing of a hypothesis,
- there is no single scientific method,
- scientists performing the same procedures do not always get the same results,
- research questions guide research procedures, and
- research procedures may influence results.

In short, it is believed that students will do inquiry better if they have an understanding of what they are doing and why they are doing it. In the end, current reforms are focusing on students' ability to do inquiry and their knowledge about inquiry.

Because of how scientists develop scientific knowledge (e.g., theories, laws, concepts), the resulting information possesses certain unavoidable characteristics. The characteristics of scientific knowledge are often referred to as "Nature of Science," or more appropriately "Nature of Scientific Knowledge." These characteristics, for example, include the recognition that scientific knowledge is always subject to change. This does not mean that the knowledge is not durable or that it has little supportive evidence. It simply means that, either as a consequence of additional data or reinterpretation of existing data, scientists may change their explanations of natural phenomena. Scientists used to think the Earth was the center of our solar system; we now think that the Sun is at the center.

Because scientists are human beings, subjectivity and individual creativity are unavoidable components of all scientific knowledge. Objectivity is a goal, but subjectivity is unavoidable and can be extremely beneficial. Scientists, like all human beings, come to every situation with different backgrounds, knowledge, perceptions, and biases that influence their interpretation of data. There are numerous instances in the history of science in which one individual viewed the existing data in different ways than the rest of the scientific community (e.g., Watson and Crick's views on the structure of DNA).

Scientific knowledge is at least partially based on empirical data (quantitative and qualitative) gathered through scientific investigations. The necessity for an empirical base is one of the distinguishing characteristics of science from other ways of knowing (e.g., history, art, and mathematics). However, scientists are limited to their senses—and extensions of their senses (e.g., technology)—in the collection of data. Consequently, all data are not readily observable, and scientists must combine inferences with observations to make sense of the natural world. For example, the picture of the atom in your science book was never actually observed. It is an inference developed from observations. The layers of the Earth pictured in your science book were not directly observed. Again, observations were combined with inferences in the development of scientists' knowledge of the structure of the Earth. The inferences that were made were influenced by scientists' subjectivity and creativity, which circle back to why scientific knowledge is always subject to change. Although less likely to be linked to the content in your classes, scientific laws and scientific theories are simply more sophisticated versions of observations and inferences. It is important for students to know that all scientific knowledge is partly a function of both observations and inferences.

If our classroom instruction is to truly reflect what scientists do, it is important to put students in situations in which they are expected to ask questions about the natural world, design investigations to answer these questions, collect data, and draw conclusions based on their analysis of the data. Organizing instruction in this manner is often described as using an inquiry-oriented teaching approach. Through such a teaching approach, students will come to understand what scientists do. Engaging students in conversations about what they have done in these investigations and discussing why they made the decisions they did will help students to develop a more in-depth knowledge about inquiry. It is important that you make explicit connections to the knowledge about inquiry previously discussed, such as the idea that there is no one single set or sequence of steps that all scientific investigations follow (e.g., the scientific method).

Finally, after students have designed and completed investigations and have reflected on what they have done, students should be engaged in discussions about the knowledge and conclusions they have constructed. If the investigation was repeated, is it possible that students might change their conclusions? Is this the same as what happens in the scientific community? Did the students use any creativity in the interpretation of the data collected? Can they identify what observations were made and what inferences were made? Discussions around questions such as these will help students develop an accurate view of the nature of scientific knowledge. It will help students realize that when two scientists disagree about why dinosaurs became extinct or why scientists often disagree about environmental issues, it is not a weakness of science but rather an example of science in action. Science and scientific knowledge are ever changing and dynamic; it is for this reason that science is such a powerful way of learning about the natural world.

References

American Association for the Advancement of Science. (AAAS). 1993. *Benchmarks for science literacy: A Project 2061 report.* New York: Oxford University Press.

National Research Council (NRC). 1996. *National science education standards.* Washington, DC: National Academies Press.

National Research Council (NRC). 2000. *Inquiry and the national science education standards.* Washington, DC: National Academies Press.

CHAPTER 2

Supporting Ideas With Evidence

A Framework for Helping Students Approach Inquiry as Scientists Do

By Susan Gomez-Zwiep and David Harris

We often hear about the value of critical thinking and problem solving in science, but what does that really mean in the elementary classroom? When students answer our questions (e.g., what do plants need?) quickly or with limited responses (e.g., dirt, sunlight), their thinking isn't visible. Although we ask students to collect data and to tell us what the data means, students do not always find it easy to make connections or explain the reasoning behind their conclusions.

One way to help elementary students see connections more easily and to make their thinking more visible is to teach them to approach scientific investigation and problem solving as scientists do—from the framework of "finding evidence to support claims." In this article, we begin by introducing students to the concept of evidence, then build on that idea by introducing the concepts of cause and effect and the need for accuracy in evidence (i.e., measurement), and finally by introducing the ideas of variables and control in an investigation. When students develop understanding of each of these concepts, they will be able to approach any inquiry investigation as scientists do. Students will understand the importance of evidence and how evidence can be used to explain the reasoning behind scientific ideas, which will be useful as they move to more independent investigations in their later school years.

Evidence

For many children, all ideas are equally plausible (Bransford, Brown, and Cocking 1999; Driver et al. 2000). Our goal as science teachers is to teach students that explanations with evidence are stronger than explanations alone. We need to first clearly define evidence. One way to do this is to ask students a series of questions based on a statement about something familiar. Choose a well-known subject matter so the focus is on evidence and not on trying to understand a new science concept. For example, we present a statement about whether the color of a shoe affects how fast you can run:

- "I read an article that said 'red tennis shoes make you run faster than any other color of shoe.' Do we believe that?" (*Yes, some shoes make me faster than other shoes. No, the color doesn't have anything to do with it.*)
- Whether your students believe the statement is not as important as their response to your follow-up question, "What would make you believe that this claim is true?" (*I might believe it if I saw a track star running in red shoes. I would have to run fast in the shoes myself.*)

After you discuss students' ideas, redirect them to think about what would convince them to believe that red shoes do help one run faster. Ask the following:

- "Is the fact that the statement is in the newspaper good enough?" (*No, it could be a lie. Yes, because the newspaper does not just print anything.*)
- "What could we do to find out more about shoes and color?" (*We could ask people with different color shoes to run and see who is faster. We could interview runners about what they look for in a running shoe.*)

Explain to students that when we test these ideas, we are gathering information as scientists do. This information is called evidence. Once we have enough evidence, we can decide if a statement is supported. If we don't have any evidence, our statement is not as strong. So, the statement "red shoes make you run fast" is not a strong statement because we do not have any evidence to support it.

For primary students, the conversation could end here. For upper elementary students, the conversation could extend into more sophisticated discussions of evidence. Ask the following:

- What would we need to do to prove that *some* shoes help you run faster?
- How many people or shoes would you accept as "enough" data?
- What type of data would be more persuasive than others?

For any of these questions, students might answer that they would need to "see" something or they would need to set up some type of situation to test shoes. Either way, they are talking about evidence, and that is what is important at first. Student comments should reflect that they understand "saying" something does not mean it necessarily is "true." Through these conversations, students will begin to recognize that claims supported with evidence are stronger than those without, and that evidence is integral to the process of answering questions convincingly.

Cause and Effect

Once students understand the need for supporting claims with evidence, refine this idea by introducing the concept of cause and effect. Often when students consider conducting an investigation, they think of many ideas to test, but have a difficult time understanding that they need to look for a specific result. Typically, students want to change many things at once and have not thought about what they will look for as a result. Help build students' understanding of cause and effect by having them observe a discrepant event, an experience in which the outcome does not match with prior understanding or expectations. This causes the student to wonder and question why the event happened as it did. For the purposes of helping students to recognize the concept of cause and effect, the particular discrepant event observed is not important. As was the case with the earlier inquiry described, it may be easier for students to grasp this aspect of the nature of science if the conversation is not dependent on their understanding of a particular science concept. One possible discrepant event is described below:

Show students 5 ml of oil with four to five drops of food coloring added. Students will observe a yellow liquid with dark-colored balls. Add this to a cup of water and after a few minutes you will get a fantastic display of water "fireworks" in the cup. Streaks of yellow, blue, red, and green will pop out of the oil layer into the water, eventually mixing into a blend of colored water. After the observation, ask students to describe what happened. (*At first the food coloring didn't mix. It just sat on top of the water in little balls. After some time, the food coloring shot out in color streaks into the water. Eventually the colors got all mixed up in the cup and made one dark color.*)

Once you have checked that students understood the sequence of events, have a conversation about possible investigations. Ask the following:

- "What could we do to affect what happened in the cup?"
- "What change could we make in our actions?"

Students will likely have many ideas (e.g., *make the water hot, add more drops of food coloring, mix it up faster/slower*). Write down all of their ideas on a piece of chart paper. Don't worry if they offer an idea that you wouldn't do in class. Chart all ideas and title the list, "Things We Can Change."

Sometimes, students may steer off course and start to talk about possible effects, such as *the colors will come out faster, or the colors will mix slower.* If that is the case, start a second chart and title it, "Things That Might Happen." Bring students back to the discussion with questions such as, "Is that something you can do differently, or is it something you think might happen because we did something different?"

Once you have a list of possible things to change, identify the ideas you will pursue further. Circle the student choices that will work well in your class and let each group of students test a different variable, or you can do the tests as demonstrations for students to observe. It is important to point out that in science investigations only one change is made at a time. This is because scientists want to make sure they know that if something different happens, it is because of the change they made.

This is a good time to specifically introduce the usefulness of a sample in which no change has been made, to compare to the changed sample. This is called a comparison group. Ask, "Do we remember exactly what happened? How can we be sure we didn't miss something? What if we had the first example to look at again? Would that make it easier to tell if there was a difference?" Whatever discrepant event you choose to use, it should be one that will allow students to test a comparison group. As data is collected, chart data under the categories "What We Did" and "What Happened." Eventually, as students become confident with which data

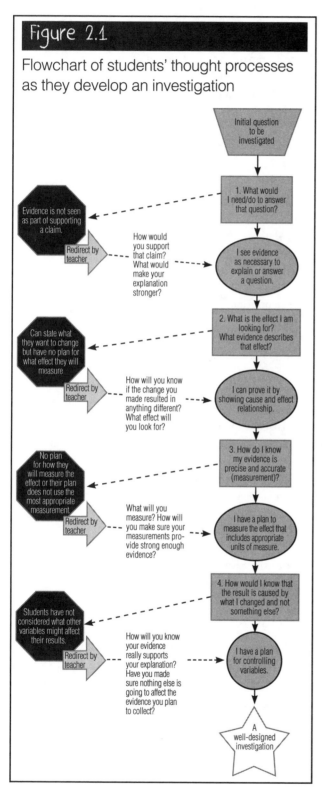

Figure 2.1

Flowchart of students' thought processes as they develop an investigation

fits into each column, the terms *cause* and *effect* can replace the original table headings.

For upper elementary students this model of "cause" and "effect" can provide the connection to more academic language through translation into hypothesis statements: "If (I cause this change), then (this effect) will/will not happen. " As they prepare to show or quantify the described effect, the quality changed can be labeled as the independent variable and the quality affected can be labeled as the dependent variable.

Measurement

Once students understand the connections between cause and effect in an investigation, they can move on to the idea that change needs to be quantified for comparison, and the way to achieve this is through measurement.

So far in our activities, students have discussed the effect of shoe color on performance and they have discussed speed or the color movement in water due to temperature. The questions were about effect. What was described? The speed I ran did not change when I changed shoe color; the color moved faster, the water was hotter. In science, however, such descriptions often require a comparison. Sometimes it is simply existence—color/no color; other times it is subtler—light red, dark red. In any case, there is a scale and units on that scale that help us describe our evidence. Whether centimeters, degrees Celsius, or clarity of water, measurement is the tool for describing and comparing the evidence gathered by quantifying the evidence. Evidence is made stronger by showing how much effect (change in dependent variable) resulted from a certain amount of cause (change to independent variable).

Variable Control

We can further extend students' understanding of supporting claims with evidence by introducing the topic of variable control. How do I know the evidence I collect is only affected by the cause I put into place? Getting back to the red shoes, whatever change

I put into place, there were other things I could have changed. One idea is to ask students to consider all the possible things they could change before conducting the experiment; let them brainstorm a list. As students select a change to use for the investigation (i.e., the independent variable) all the other changes are labeled "Things I Will Not Change." As students collect their data, remind them about those things they chose to keep constant. Controlling variables allows you to state with increased confidence that the effect you measured is the result of the change you made.

Making Thinking Visible

When we ask students to make an observation or conduct an investigation, they often see the role of the "data" collected as the answer or proof that they followed the steps outlined by the teacher. But with a cause-and-effect question in mind, gathering data can be seen as the means to support or refute a possible argument. In other words, we do investigations to gather evidence to strengthen our explanation. When students fail to support their explanations with evidence, we don't really know how they have made their conclusions. Are their explanations fueled by the activity or from preconceived notions? Investigations can help make critical thinking visible.

Figure 2.1 describes the thought process students typically go through as they develop an investigation. Each question is a point of critical reflection for a student. Initially, the teachers ask the questions. Eventually, however, students move from question to question toward a plan for investigation, moving straight down the flowchart on their own. For primary grades, students can learn to move through the first two "stop signs." The teacher's role is to be prepared for these points of hesitation with questions that redirect students. This foundational thinking lays the groundwork for the next two stop signs for upper elementary students. If a student considers a good answer to be one with evidence and can state cause-and-effect relationships, the details of setting up an investigation (e.g., measurement, controlling for variables) are just a matter of being more convincing in your argument.

It is through feedback that focuses on evidence that we can support the development of scientific thinking. As students mature, incorporating this evidence framework provides the ability to apply higher-order thinking strategies as students attempt to solve new problems. These critical-thinking skills allow students to change these "stop signs" into decision points that do not require the teacher's help to keep moving forward.

References

Bransford, J. D., A. L. Brown, and R. R. Cocking, eds. 1999. *How people learn: Brain, mind, experience, and school.* Washington, DC: National Academies Press.

Driver, R., A. Squires, P. Rushworth, and V. Wood-Robinson. 2000. *Making sense of secondary science: Research into children's ideas.* London: Routledge Falmer.

NSTA Connection
Download a copy of the flowchart in Figure 2.1 at at *www.nsta.org/ elementaryschool/connections/201009YearOfInquiryFig2.pdf*.

CHAPTER 3

Sound Science

An Approach to Teaching Content, Inquiry Skills, and the Nature of Science

By Aaron J. Sickel, Michele H. Lee, and
Enrique M. Pareja

As we teach, it is important not only to focus on science concepts and inquiry skills, but also to help children understand that science is a human endeavor to make sense of the world. Just as scientists seek to understand the world by gathering empirical evidence, elementary students can learn to make observations and develop explanations based on data and scientific understandings.

Using the metaphor of science being a three-legged stool, Weinburgh (2003) suggests science instruction rests on three "legs"—science content, inquiry processes and skills, and the nature of science. Together, the three can provide students with a balanced understanding of science. Through our classroom experiences, we have realized teaching two legs—science concepts and inquiry skills—is not enough to help students understand science as a human endeavor. Student acquisition of scientific knowledge and skills does not necessarily translate into an understanding of the nature of science or how science itself works (AAAS 1993).

How can a teacher simultaneously teach science concepts through inquiry while helping students learn about the nature of science? After pondering this question in our own teaching, we developed a BSCS 5E Learning Model lesson (Bybee et al. 2006) that concurrently embeds opportunities for fourth-grade students to (a) learn a science concept, (b) develop an inquiry skill, and (c) learn about scientific inquiry (an aspect of the nature of science). We specifically set out to help students understand that sound is produced by vibrating objects (science concept), help students make and use observations to construct an explanation (inquiry skill), and help students understand that scientific explanations are evidence-based (understanding *about* scientific inquiry). We have collaborated to teach this lesson to fourth-grade students both in public school classrooms and at a summer science camp.

Engage

To stimulate students' interest and draw out their initial ideas about sound, data collection, and scientific explanations, we begin the lesson by casually creating sounds with everyday objects (e.g., bike horn, toy rattle, guitar) and asking what the objects have in common. Students are quick to note that the objects all make sounds. We then prompt students to brainstorm examples of other things that make sound. We ask students to consider questions like "What do you think causes these things to make sound?" and "What do you already know about sound?" During class discussion, students often reveal common misconceptions and knowledge gaps. For example, when asked about sound production, some suggest sound waves or vibrations but are not always able to explain what these terms mean (Brown and Boehringer 2007). Others associate sound with a force (often human-induced) such as hitting or plucking.

To assess what students know about making scientific explanations and observations, we ask, "How did you come up with these explanations about sound?" and "What helped you figure out how sound is produced?" Students commonly mention observations or experiences—like watching someone play guitar—to support how they came to a conclusion. When asked, "How do scientists develop explanations?" students typically say that scientists make observations, experiment, or look for the answers in books. Because students will observe various sounds during the next lesson phase, we expand on their notion of "looking to see what happens" to ensure they recognize that observations can be collected using different senses. The following questions guide the conversation:

Hearing: "How might you know if someone is talking?"
Sight: "How might you know if someone is talking if your ears were plugged?"
Touch: "How might you know whether someone moving his/her lips is actually talking or not?" (Students will suggest touching their throat while talking.)

Explore

Armed with their senses and a science notebook, students are ready to investigate what causes sound. There are multiple approaches to exploring sound, and this phase provides wonderful opportunities to explore music from other cultures or have students play musical instruments. We choose to set up different stations where students can make various sounds (see NSTA Connection for descriptions of sound stations).

At the stations, students document what they hear, see, or feel while (a) plucking rubber bands, (b) striking and placing tuning forks in water, (c) flicking the tip of a ruler at the edge

Plucking guitar string

of a desk, (d) blowing bubbles in a cup of water, and (e) plucking guitar strings. Safety note: Require safety goggles at the ruler-flicking and rubber band stations, and be sure to check for latex allergies. At the bubble-blowing station, we make sure each student gets a separate cup with fresh water and a clean straw.

During this lesson phase, we encourage students to collect information using multiple senses and record their notes and drawings because their observations serve as an important basis for understanding sound production and how scientists use evidence to develop explanations. Each of these five observation stations has investigation prompts for students to consider as they collect data and start sense-making about what might cause sound to be produced. For example, at the rubber band station we ask, "If you couldn't hear, how would you know if the plucked rubber band was making a sound or not?" Students observe hearing a sound or feeling vibrations only when they see the rubber band moving.

Explain

After students create and observe various sounds, we convene for a class discussion and ask for their current ideas about sound production. Within this social forum, students share and consider their data to develop an explanation. To facilitate discussion, we encourage students to provide data from their science notebooks while we ask questions about their observations. For example, "What happened to the ruler when you flicked it? What observations did you record in your notebook from other stations?" This strategy of cueing students to refer to their science notebook encourages them to use and share data as they develop a scientific explanation. We also encourage students to return to the stations and demonstrate what they observed and to focus on using evidence when developing explanations. Many students easily relate the vibrating ruler to quivering rubber bands and guitar strings and suggest vibration as the commonality. We ask students to share observations collected through the sense of touch. Students often point out feeling the tuning fork shiver after striking it or feeling the plastic cup shake as they blew bubbles in water. When students introduce the term *vibration*, we seek clarification and consensus on the meaning. It helps to have students kinesthetically act it out by asking, "Can you show what a vibration is?" As students depict vibrations (waving hands, pencils, or bodies), we lead them to note the back-and-forth motion. After students discuss similarities and patterns across the different phenomena, we ask them to consider the evidence as they answer the prompt *I think sound is caused by ...* in their notebooks.

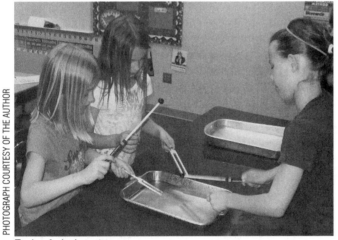

PHOTOGRAPH COURTESY OF THE AUTHOR

Tuning forks in water

As students share their explanations, we ask how they came up with them. This provides an opportunity to discuss the importance of using data. We say that the data they have collected serves as *evidence* (a new term introduced) and provides a reason to use or not use an explanation. However, a consensus explanation does not magically happen. We encourage students to note similarities (many use the terms *vibration* or *sound waves*) and differences (hitting, plucking, striking) so that the class condenses everyone's explanations into a few succinct statements. Writing ideas on the board and grouping them helps this process. Our students often suggest explanations such as

- sound is caused by vibrations, and
- sound is caused by hitting, plucking, or striking something.

This discussion provides an opportunity for students to defend their explanations. Students readily refer to their observations, showing what they drew or wrote in their notebooks, and we discuss how the observations help them explain sound production. Because there are usually several competing explanations, we have students vote (independently) for one explanation on a ballot and then tally and report the results (Abell, Anderson, and Chezem 2000). Though we recognize that scientists do not rely on voting to resolve disagreements, we purposefully engage students in this exercise so they commit to an explanation, consider alternative explanations, and determine which one is the most plausible using evidence. One explanation will typically receive more votes than the others, so we ask the class for their thoughts on which explanation to accept. Students will often say that one explanation is right because it received the most votes. We then point out that scientists decide based on evidence, not consensus, so how can we know which explanation is the one we should accept? How can we resolve our disagreement about the different scientific explanations? Some students suggest we collect more evidence or go through the stations again, providing a perfect segue into the next phase of the lesson.

Elaborate

In this phase, students test their explanations for sound in a new context and gather more data to add to their understanding about sound production. Determining the "new context" is dependent on students' misunderstandings. Because students often think sound is caused by people or objects physically hitting, plucking, or striking something, we choose an activity that purposefully introduces them to a sound produced without a visible force. The demonstration involves stretching a section of rubber balloon across the open end of a metal can and then pouring salt onto the balloon surface. Next, we play music through a stereo speaker next to the balloon surface (only turn the volume up to the point that the salt begins moving). Students make observations by using a magnifying glass to look at the salt and by feeling the speaker as the music plays. Students will note the salt "dancing" up and down and the feeling of vibrations through the speaker. We ask students to explain the dancing salt and encourage them to refer back to the possible explanations they generated in the Explain phase. Evidence moves the class to consensus that vibrations coming from inside the speaker caused the salt to move without any physical force from humans. We then ask students to apply the explanation that sound is caused by vibrations to the data they collected from the observation stations. One by one, students are able to recall evidence of vibrations for each station. Eventually we re-ask the question, "How do you think scientists come up with their explanations?" We focus again on how students used their collected data to construct their explanations. They begin to say things like *we observed sound and talked about it.* This dialogue allows us to discuss more explicitly that scientists develop their explanations from thinking about observations and continually collecting data to use as evidence just like we did.

Evaluate

Throughout the lesson, we informally assess students' ideas about sound, data collection, and scientific explanations through class discussions and review of their science notebooks. At the conclusion of the lesson, we assess students' understandings in relation to the goals of our lesson. One useful way to assess students' understandings is to embed questions in scenarios (Figure 3.1). For the science content goal, we ask students to commit to an explanation about how sound is produced and use their data to support their answers. We address our goal for developing inquiry skills with two assessments. Because students are making observations and developing explanations throughout the lesson, we review their science notebooks as a performance assessment of their ability to do inquiry. Also, the summative scenario for this goal asks

Figure 3.1

Linking learning expectations, lesson goals, and summative assessment scenarios

Learning expectations	Lesson goals	Assessment scenarios
Understand a science concept	Sound is produced by vibrating objects.	Dina and Steve are discussing their ideas about sound. Dina says, "I think all sounds are caused by vibrations." Steve says, "I think all sounds are caused when you hit or strike something." They turn to you and ask what you think. I agree with (circle your answer) Dina Steve Both Neither Using the observations collected in your journal, write down the reasons for choosing your answer.
Develop inquiry skills	Record observations of sound. Use collected data to construct an explanation about what produces sound.	When Shonda plays her drum, it makes a sound. Yet she is not sure whether the sound is caused by vibrations. What would you tell her to do in order to figure out whether the drum sounds are caused by vibrations? Write down the steps that she should take.
Develop understandings about scientific inquiry	Scientists develop explanations using observations (evidence) and what they know about the world (scientific knowledge).	John and Brandi are discussing how scientists develop explanations. John says, "Scientists use evidence to make explanations." Brandi says, "Scientists use what they know about the world to make explanations." They turn to you and ask what you think. I agree with (circle your answer) John Brandi Both Neither Based on your investigation about what causes sound to be produced, write down the reasons for choosing your answer.

students to list the steps necessary to develop an explanation of sound being produced from a drum. We are checking to see if students recognize the role of collecting and thinking about data to develop explanations. Last, we address the thinking about inquiry goal by asking students to consider how scientists develop explanations. If students argue that scientists use evidence and what they know about the world to develop explanations, it demonstrates a mastery level of understanding about this aspect of the nature of science.

Blowing bubbles in a cup of water with a straw

Balancing Three Legs of Science

This lesson shows that students can simultaneously learn science content and do inquiry while learning how scientists construct their knowledge claims. Establishing lesson goals for the three facets of science instruction allows teachers to balance the learning of science knowledge and skills with understandings about the human aspects of doing science. If students engage in an inquiry, we can capitalize on their experiences by having them develop scientific explanations using data they have collected themselves. As students construct explanations, teachers can easily help students see how their actions are similar to what scientists do. Though not every lesson may be conducive for blending the three legs of science instruction, we believe the balanced approach can work, and in this lesson it is particularly useful to help students think like scientists.

References

Abell, S. K., G. Anderson, and J. Chezem. 2000. Science as argument and explanation: Exploring concepts of sound in third grade. In *Inquiring into inquiry learning and teaching in science,* eds. J. Minstrell and E. van Zee, 65–79. Washington, DC: American Association for the Advancement of Science.

American Association for the Advancement of Science (AAAS). 1993. *Benchmarks for science literacy.* New York: Oxford University Press.

Brown, T., and K. Boehringer. 2007. Breaking the sound barrier: Finally some hands-on learning centers that teach about sound. *Science and Children* 44 (5): 35–39.

Bybee, R. W., J. Taylor, A. Gardner, P. van Scotter, J. Powell, A. Westbrook, and N. Landes. 2006. *The BSCS 5E instructional model: Origins, effectiveness, and applications.* Colorado Springs, CO: BSCS.

Weinburgh, M. 2003. A leg (or three) to stand on. *Science and Children* 40 (6): 28–30.

NSTA Connection
Download descriptions of the sound stations at *www.nsta.org/SC1009*.

CHAPTER 4
Dig Deeply

A Gardening Project With Peas Engages Second- and Third-Grade Students in Thinking, Acting, and Writing Like Scientists

By Sharon Owings and Barbara Merino

Most children enjoy being in gardens. Our school garden is just outside the classroom, so students can go in during recess under my supervision. Although students had participated in several gardening projects, I wanted them to dig deeply and cultivate more than just plants. Building on my second- and third-grade students' enthusiasm for gardening, I designed a pea project in which they would discover how plants grow under different conditions while also developing observation and nonfiction writing skills.

Though my students enjoyed writing fiction and dialogues, they were less capable nonfiction writers. To assess their expository writing skills, I gave them a purposely vague writing prompt: "Write about what you have been doing in your garden. You may have as much time as you need." I collected these writing samples for comparison with later writing. To develop their writing, I taught them to use data recording sheets and journals. Throughout the project, I emphasized scientific discourse using scientific terms.

From the exciting discovery of the first sprout until the last pod was harvested, I reiterated that botanists observe plants carefully to create accurate drawings and that labels make illustrations more informative. My young botanists confidently used thermometers and moisture meters to collect data and cared for their plants diligently; they took pride in recording their plants' progress and growth. Most important, the attention to detail showed in their writing.

Getting Started

Snow peas (*Pisum sativum*) are excellent subjects for student projects. Most children enjoy the mild taste and crunchy pods and are enthusiastic about growing them. Pea seeds are large enough for small hands to manage, germinate promptly even in cool weather, and will grow in all but the poorest soil. The parts of the plant are distinct and easily recognizable. Furthermore, peas' short life cycle permits students to experience all stages of the plant's growth in a few months.

I launched the project by telling students that they would become *botanists*, scientists who work with plants. I explained that each botanist would be responsible for planting and caring for six pea seeds. Two seeds would be planted outside. Two more would be planted beside the first two, but would be covered with a *cloche* (a bell-shaped covering used to protect plants). We used the top third of a clear plastic two-liter bottle. The last two seeds would be planted in containers (the bottom two-thirds of a two-liter bottle) and grown inside.

Because scientists need to keep careful records of their experiments, each botanist would maintain a binder that contained plant growth records and documentations of plant care procedures. Each student received a new observation sheet each day. They used their observation sheets

Observing a pea plant under the cloche

PHOTOGRAPHS COURTESY OF THE AUTHOR

as journal pages, writing notes, observations, questions, and comments in the margins or on the backs of their sheets. Binder paper was available if they needed more writing space.

I gathered a large collection of fiction and nonfiction books about plants and gardens and put them on display in the classroom. Throughout the project, I read aloud from these books, using them to guide discussions and focus instruction. As scientific terms emerged in the reading, I highlighted them for the students. If the text did not provide adequate explanation of the term's meaning, we used dictionaries. We added the words to our gardening word wall, which remained in place throughout the project. Once a term had been added to the word wall, students were expected to incorporate this "focus word" into their speaking vocabularies, use it appropriately, and spell it correctly in their journals.

Introduce Scientific Drawing

On the first day, I conducted a demonstration using dried lima beans. I first modeled making an accurately sized, labeled drawing of a dry bean and supervised students' efforts to make their own drawings. These lima beans were enormous, so it was possible for the children to trace around them for accurately sized and shaped drawings. Less conveniently sized or shaped seeds can be more accurately drawn if

Using instruments to measure climatic and soil conditions

the students use graph paper. Then, we added two cups of water to one cup of dry beans and let them soak overnight.

The next day, the beans had absorbed most of the water and had doubled in size, making it easy for the botanists to understand that seeds need water to grow. I modeled drawing a soaked bean near the picture of the dried bean to show changes in size and appearance. The meaning of *dicot* was introduced when students split a soaked bean into two congruent parts and discovered the bean's embryonic root, stem, and leaf. I told them that *di* is a prefix that means *two*, and I showed them that the two parts of the bean are symmetrical. I contrasted *dicot* with *monocot* and gave them examples of monocots (e.g., corn, other grasses). I explained that botanists can examine a plant's seed to help identify, classify, or group the plant. This reminded them that they had spent time earlier in the year comparing different leaves and talking about their various functions. I included the information that the first pair of leaves (seed leaves) that come from dicot seed emerge as a pair, whereas a blade emerges from a monocot seed. Emphasizing the importance of labels in scientific illustrations, I modeled drawing and labeling the bean's visible plant parts. I stressed the importance of learning scientific terms so that we could discuss and share information without any misunderstandings. Students drew the beans and added the pages to their binders.

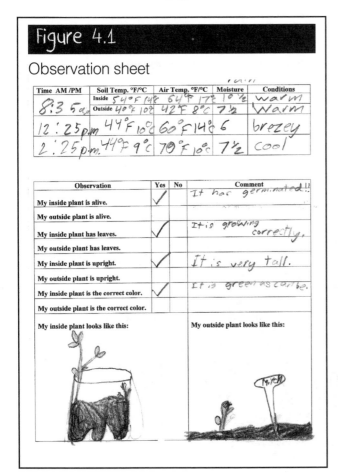

Figure 4.1

Observation sheet

Plant Pea Seeds

On the third day, we went into the garden and I modeled how to plant seeds correctly. I gathered the children around me and showed them how to use a trowel to loosen soil in an area about as large as their two hands spread out with thumbs touching. I showed them that the diameter of a pea seed is about half as long as the first joint of their index finger. I showed them how to poke a hole as deep as the first joint of their index finger in the cultivated soil for each pea. Then I showed them how to drop the seed into the hole, cover it with soil, pat the soil down firmly, and sprinkle water from the watering can to settle the soil around the seed. I then gave each botanist two pea seeds and a name label. They chose a spot, planted the seeds, and indicated the location with the marker. I then explained the function of the cloche (to trap the Sun's heat to warm the air and soil) and demonstrated how to plant the second pair of seeds, covered with the cloche, near the first pair. Safety note: Students always washed their hands after working with soil, and I reminded them that tools are to be used only for their intended purpose, and that it is important not to run on the garden pathways, especially while transporting tools.

Back in the classroom, I directed the botanists to fill their containers halfway with potting soil, plant two seeds on opposite sides of the container, add water, and place a marker. In the transparent containers, students could observe all aspects of plant growth.

During discussions about seeds and plant growth, I reminded the children that not every seed will grow. Sometimes the gardener may not have provided adequate care for the seeds, but a few seeds are not viable. We talked about why seeds may or may not be viable.

Figure 4.2

Pre- and postproject writing samples

"Gloria"
November:
My friend and I are growing lettuce. We named it Sunshine. [She] and I are naming lots of things. [She] and I are having so much fun. We love working in the garden. It's fun. We named the other one Sunny.

January:
My outside peas are very small and my inside ones are very tall. This is how I plant pea seeds. I dig a hole twice as big as the pea and put the pea inside the hole and put some soil over the pea. You have to water it. It has to have sunshine. It needs lots of air too. My inside peas have lots of tendrils. My inside pea plant has forty two leaves. My outside plant has five. My outside plant is about two-and-a-half inches long.

In November, Gloria wrote about her social interactions in the garden. She wrote her narrative in a personal voice, focusing on having fun with her friends. In January, Gloria was writing with the voice of a scientist. Her explanation of how to plant seeds was accurate and thorough: a "thick" description. Anyone following her directions would be able to plant a seed properly.

"Gabriel"
November:
Today I tried lettuce with a carrot and Ritz-bit. The Ritz-bit made the lettuce a lot slipperier. And the carrot made it a little too crunchy. The lettuce alone was just too bitter.

January:
My peas have germinated at last! I just measured my plants and my inside one is a foot tall and 30 centimeters tall. My outside one is two and a half inches tall and five centimeters tall. Right now, on 1/22/08, I can't find out anything about my outside pea plant because it is raining. I have noticed that the leaves on my inside plant have grown over the weekend. I've been trying to find a blossom lately. I'm surprised one of my peas died. My root system is so big it will probably reach to the other side of the bottle. I bet I'll need a tall trellis.

In November, Gabriel's personal narrative described a personal, physical experience and focused on irrelevant detail. In January, he used a scientific voice to provide thorough, accurate descriptions of physical characteristics and the life cycle of his plants.

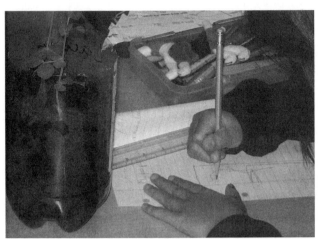
Using a plant as a model to produce accurate illustrations

Make Observations

I told students that scientists keep careful records of what they do with their subjects (in our case, plants) and how they develop. I gave them each a blank observation sheet, and I demonstrated its use, stressing the importance of accurate recordings and illustrations. The sheets included a simple list of plant characteristics to check at each reading; space for drawing; and space for information about indoor and outdoor climate conditions, temperature readings, and soil moisture levels (Figure 4.1, p. 18).

To measure air temperature, we placed one thermometer in a central location in the garden and one in the classroom near the bottle gardens. To measure soil temperature, each child placed a thermometer in the soil between the two sets of pea seeds. These thermometers remained in place throughout the project. I showed students how to read the thermometers and how to use the moisture meter, a simple device that indicates whether soil is moist. I found the moisture meter in the gardening area of the hardware store. The children loved this simple-to-use device. (To use: stick the point in the soil and read the scale to see whether soil is dry or wet.) Students also learned how to record the information on their observation sheets.

As soon as the first sprout emerged from the soil, I taught the students to use their rulers to measure the plant's height in inches and centimeters to help them gain a clearer notion of how the two systems are related. As the plants continued to grow, students counted the number of leaves, blossoms, and pods on each plant. I hoped they would use these measurements to compare the different growing conditions.

Student pea plot showing cloche, moisture meter, and thermometers

Students completed a new observation sheet each day. This took less than 15 minutes. As the project proceeded, students became more proficient in all of the skills that the observation sheets required, including the drawing and labeling.

Virtually all of the seeds the students planted were viable. Seeds planted in the bottle gardens germinated quickly and grew rapidly into tall spindly plants that required supports to remain upright. A few developed blossoms and fewer still produced pods. We found little difference between the peas grown with and without the cloches, though the results were almost certainly inaccurate due to the cloches that were repeatedly washed away by heavy rains and blown away by strong winds (lessons learned for my little scientists). Almost all peas grown outdoors turned out to be tall sturdy plants that were in danger of overwhelming their trellises. Most produced many blossoms and peas. We ended our pea project in January with a party during which each student presented his or her "Pea Project"—a book, poster, poem, song, or report.

Write About Plants

As I ended the project, I told the children that their plants would remain, but they would no longer be recording data, and that they should look back through their many pages of work to review what they had been doing and reflect on how their plants had grown and developed from those six seeds they had planted in the fall. That afternoon, I repeated November's writing prompt. ("Write about what you have been doing in your garden. You may have as much time as you need.")

The roots of the plant are visible through the clear plastic container.

My formal assessment of their writing was both quantitative and qualitative. I used four objective measures to compare the samples, tabulating numbers of (1) words, (2) focus words (from the gardening word wall), (3) illustrations, and (4) labeled illustrations. All students wrote longer pieces and used more focus words in January than in November. I analyzed their writing to determine whether they understood gardening procedures and how carefully and completely they were able to write about those procedures (Owings 2008).

It was clear that the content of the students' writing changed after their gardening experiences. Preproject writing had relied heavily on subjective narratives, but postproject writing focused more on objective presentation of scientific facts. In January, the children were writing like scientists, providing expository text meant to be informative rather than the personal narratives of earlier samples. To support their statements, students included quantitative details and technical words. Samples of pre- and postproject writing by two mid-level students show changes typical of the class (Figure 4.2, p. 19). Content learning was ongoing throughout the project. A main purpose of the writing assignment was to assess students' understanding of the relevant science concepts.

A New Understanding

I designed this project to give students opportunities to learn about plants and plant growth so they could write authentically. I was pleasantly surprised by the change from narrative to objective voice in their writing. Their explanations were more comprehensive and complex. They wrote with accuracy and enthusiasm. They showed new understandings of statistics, measurement, and problem solving.

This kind of inquiry-based learning that begins with scaffolding via modeling has been called *sheltered constructivism* and can be an effective way to teach the discourse of scientific argument (Merino and Scarcella 2005). This approach worked effectively for all students. My botanists included special needs, full inclusion, and English language learners, all of whom successfully completed the project and demonstrated growth in literacy and scientific discourse. This approach places additional responsibilities on teachers who need to know when and how to provide the kinds of scaffolding their students need. The binders and observation sheets, especially the initial modeling and ongoing monitoring, can be considered one kind of scaffolding. Other examples would include the reading and discussion that went on in the class throughout the project.

Teachers must also know when and how to remove that support so that students can develop independence. In our next project, I gave my entomologists silkworms and helped them build on their experiences to design their own experiments. In our most recent project, my students chose their own subjects and designed their own experiments!

References

Merino, B., and R. Scarcella. 2005. Teaching science to English learners. *University of California Linguistic Minority Research Institute Newsletter* 14 (4): 1–7.

Owings, S. 2008. *Gardening is the most fun time of day!* MA thesis, University of California at Davis.

NSTA Connection

NSTA sponsors free Lab Out Loud Podcasts—by science teachers, for science teachers. Listen to "Don't Be Such a Scientist" at *http://laboutloud.com/2010/05/episode-48-dont-be-such-a-scientist*.

PROCESS SKILLS

CHAPTER 5

Inquiry, Process Skills, and Thinking in Science

By Mike Padilla

Inquiry is central to science education today. But understanding its many nuances is still an issue according to research (Flick and Lederman 2004). And understanding is the first step to implementation. Here are some of the questions teachers ask frequently:

- What is inquiry?
- Does it differ from process skills, and if so, how?
- How do I know whether my students are inquiring?
- Is inquiry something students learn, is it a way for teachers to teach, or is it both?
- Do students have to be involved in hands-on activity to do inquiry, or are there ways to involve students in inquiry while using textbooks and print materials?

These are significant questions—ones that every teacher ought to be asking. So let's take them one at a time.

Inquiry and Process Skills

The National Science Education Standards define inquiry as "the diverse ways in which scientists study the natural world and propose explanations based upon evidence" (NRC 1996, p. 23). Notice the word *evidence*. This is the most crucial part of defining inquiry. Inquiry is about logic, it's about reasoning from data, and it's about applying scientific techniques and skills to real-world problems. I will say more about this later, but for now you can think of inquiry as the ways scientists think about and try to solve problems using logic.

Beginning in the 1960s, there was an attempt to break inquiry down into a set of discrete skills called process skills. Scientists observed, described, inferred, measured, and predicted. They identified variables, controlled variables, designed experiments, and hypothesized. The notion was that students could practice individual skills, and as they mastered these, they would begin to put them together to solve problems. Educators even designed a full elementary school curriculum that focused on just teaching process skills called Science—A Process Approach (see Internet Resource).

Essential Features

The process skills approach continued to be popular through the late 1980s, but it was often criticized for being atomistic and piecemeal. Although students could perform the individual skills, they could not solve problems, and they were not able to think like scientists. This led to the more holistic "inquiry approach" popularized by the National Science Education Standards. Inquiry is a central—some would argue the central—concept of the Standards. Realizing that more definition needed to be brought to the concept of inquiry, The National Research Council (2000) identified several "essential features" that describe what the learner does in inquiry. Instead of a series of skills, the features portray important broad components of inquiry, and these have become the most widely accepted conception of the process in which the learner

- engages with a scientific question,
- participates in design of procedures,
- gives priority to evidence,
- formulates explanations,
- connects explanations to scientific knowledge, and
- communicates and justifies explanations.

Notice that all of these essential features might be part of a science investigation. I personally like this definition because it allows students to focus on learning discrete parts of the process like reasoning from evidence, for example, but still keep the purpose of inquiry—problem solving—in mind.

Are Students Inquiring?

This is the million-dollar question. One way to think about it is to ask who is doing the work. If it is the teacher, then students are only observers to the process. If the students are the ones thinking, however, then it is likely that inquiry is happening. Try using the following questions when your students are doing science as a guide for judging the quality of their inquiry.

Who asks the question? That is, who asks the question that focuses the investigation (e.g., "How does soil type affect erosion rate?" or "What effect does exercise have on heart rate?" or "What variables affect flower freshness?")? Is it the student, the teacher, or the textbook? At least some of the time investigations should be driven by student questions.

Who designs the procedures? I'm speaking of procedures in an investigation, but sometimes students need to determine how observations or measurements are made. In order to gain experience with the logic underlying science, students need continuous practice with designing ways to gather information.

Who decides what data to collect? This is similar to designing procedures, but the focus is on the data itself. What data is important? Who determines that?

Who formulates explanations based on the data? Does the teacher or the text materials give the answers? Or, do questions posed during activities make students analyze and draw conclusions based on their data? The bottom line—do the questions make students think about the data they collect?

Who communicates and justifies the results? Do activities push students not only to communicate but also to justify their answers? Are activities thoughtfully designed and interesting so that students want to share their results and argue about conclusions?

Goal and Method

Inquiry is both something students learn and a method for teaching science. So far, we have considered only what students learn. But great science teachers use inquiry methods to teach. The inquiry teacher poses questions, stimulates discussion, and involves students with important scientific problems. Inquiry teachers use wait time, questions, silence, and other techniques to initiate and extend student thinking. Inquiry teaching is an approach that engages student curiosity and wonder, that inspires students to observe and reason, and that helps them to sharpen their critical-thinking and communication abilities. Without a skilled teacher guiding student learning, however, inquiry does not often take place.

Inquiry, Hands-On Learning, and Books

All this leads to the last question—do students have to be involved in a hands-on investigation to inquire? Not really. The key, often forgotten, aspect of inquiry is that it is an intellectual endeavor. Too many students have a knack for being physically but not intellectually engaged in science. So hands-on science may help many students to inquire, but skillful use of print materials can accomplish the same goal. It is what the teacher and students do with the materials—books or lab equipment—that makes the difference.

References

Flick, L. B., and N. G. Lederman. 2004. *Scientific inquiry and the nature of science: Implications for teaching, learning, and teacher education.* The Netherlands: Kluwer Academic Publishers.

National Research Council (NRC). 1996. *National science education standards.* Washington, DC. National Academies Press.

National Research Councol (NRC). 2000. *Inquiry and the national science education standards.* Washington, DC. National Academies Press.

Internet Resource

Science—A Process Approach
www.coe.ufl.edu/esh/Projects/sapa.htm

CHAPTER 6

Inference or Observation?

Tips for Teaching Students About the Importance of Quality Inferences

By Kevin D. Finson

Take a look at Figure 6.1. What comes to mind as you look at the tree? Do you begin to pick out features? Do you then ask yourself what has happened to make the tree look like that? This is a logical mental sequencing that pairs observation with inferring. One precedes the other. If you are good at it, you can quickly come up with an explanation for what you see. Would your neighbor come up with the same explanation? The explanations are inferences. So what does it mean if you derive one explanation and your neighbor a different one, when you both looked at the same thing? We see this happen in the scientific community, but many of us find that this also happens with our students. Part of the answer rests in understanding what an *observation* is, what an *inference* is, and what the differences are between them.

Beyond Definitions

There seems to be no shortage of observation- and inference-related activities in trade books or on the internet. Teachers are quick to use them with their students—and sometimes too quick to assume their students readily know the difference between

Figure 6.1

What comes to mind as you look at the tree?

these science process skills and can apply them properly. I've found my students read the definitions of these skills (and certainly hear them from me) but still sometimes stumble when applying them. So, what is it that we typically read or hear? Probably something as follows:

An *observation* is information someone gathers about an object or event using one or more of the senses, and it can be quantitative or qualitative.

An *inference* is a conclusion or explanation one makes about an object or event, and it is based on observations (Chiapetta 1997).

On the surface, such definitions are OK. But we should delve deeper into these process skills if they are to be understood and used properly by our students (and us!). Inferring is a basic process skill that is one of the keys to effective inquiry-based instruction. An inference is one's best explanation for *why* something occurred (in contrast to a prediction, which explains *what will* occur [Martin 2009]; or an observation, which is information about an object or event).

Refer back to the image of the tree in Figure 6.1 on page 27 (see NSTA Connection to download your version of the tree). Have your students write down some observations using a table (Figure 6.2). Some acceptable observations would be that it has many branches; there is a broken branch near the bottom left; branches get smaller from the center of the tree outward; the basic shape of the tree is round; and the tree has no leaves on it. Where do students trip up? They falter when they state that the tree is dead, that the tree is big, or that it is wintertime—all inferences. So, why are those latter statements not observations?

Figure 6.2

Observations vs. inferences

Observations	Inferences
The tree has a round shape.	The tree is dead.
There is a broken branch near the bottom of the tree.	It is winter.
The tree has many branches.	The tree is very large.

Keep in Mind

To answer that, let's examine more about inferences. Here are five tips to keep in mind.

Tip 1

An inference is only as good as the observations on which it is based. Typically, the more observations one has, the more accurate the inference can be. However, this presumes the observations are of relatively good quality. So, a related aspect of this tip is that the better the quality of observations used, the better the inference is likely to be. Observations that can be replicated by others are important—an important aspect of scientific literacy and the nature of science. To help students learn to make good observations, provide practice during activities that require students to make, record, and discuss observations. When possible, encourage students to replicate what some students have already observed, such as finding a particular quantity (e.g., measurement of length, number of parts). Relate the qualities observed to things with which students are already familiar.

Alternatively, one must take care to not go too far beyond what the observations warrant. Consider, for example, a student's inference that the tree died because its broken branch allowed its sap to run out. A careful look at the tree would reveal a broken branch near the bottom of the tree's canopy, and the tree is leafless—typical of trees that are dead. However, the tree picture does not show any sap or any substance running out of the broken branch. Also, trees don't lose all of their sap through a single break in a single branch. The student's conclusion that the tree died due to sap loss through the broken branch is imposing more onto the scene than is presented in the picture.

Tip 2

An inference is only one of multiple possible explanations for a set of observations. Helpful questions to use when students have difficulty with inferences include "Is there another explanation that could explain what you see?" or "Is there a good alternative to explain what you observe?" Although not always foolproof, a caveat is that the simpler the explanation, the more likely it will be the proper inference. That being said, a good inference must account for all the observations. Often, elementary students are surprised to learn their peers have other explanations for what has been observed in common (Bell 2008). For example, one student may infer that it is winter, whereas another student may infer that the tree is dead. The first student may not have considered that the tree might be dead, and the second student may not have thought about what happens to deciduous trees during the winter. It is also not uncommon for at least one student to propose an explanation that is "really out there." At these times, it is important to discuss why a simpler explanation might be more appropriate. We should also discuss why we can't pick and choose which observations to include (or exclude) in a good inference. Suppose a student observes a fan that is not operating and infers it is broken. To infer that the fan is broken may be erroneous because the student may have omitted certain observations that may have led to a different inference. The fan may not be running because it is turned off or is not plugged into an electrical outlet.

Tip 3

Inferences are not always correct. This tip derives from the previous two. If one uses incomplete or faulty data (i.e., observations), the inference made is probably going to be less accurate and less useful. When something new is encountered (an object, event), our tendency is to quickly begin inferring about it. For example, a student who is confronted with an unfamiliar green plant may quickly make the inference the plant is something that shouldn't be touched. If this is when the student's thinking stops, then he or she may decline to examine the plant more closely, and thus miss critical observations that would alleviate his or her fears. Worse yet, the student may mislead others into believing something about the plant that isn't true. The point is that students must be open to searching for more evidence in making their inferences. When other students notice differences between the plant's characteristics and what they know about plants such as poison ivy, then a healthy debate and reexamination of the evidence can take place. This is in the spirit of the scientific enterprise. This does not necessarily mean everyone will agree with the interpretation of the body of evidence gathered, but at least everyone would have the same evidence to work with in forming their inferences. In turn, this may lead to further investigation about the plant, which may yield yet more useful evidence that would guide the students in knowing how to deal with the plant. Potentially, with each additional piece of evidence, the student's initial inference might change. It would be inappropriate for someone to withhold evidence that might make such a difference, and it is similarly inappropriate for someone to exclude gathered evidence from consideration.

Tip 4

Inferences are influenced by prior knowledge and experiences (or the context in which the inference is made). In looking at the earlier statements about the tree's condition (see Figure 6.2), there could certainly be other explanations for why the tree looks as it does. Here are three cases that illustrate this. First, when I've used this tree example with elementary students in my area, a common explanation for the condition of the tree is that it is winter. Deciduous trees where we live certainly lose their leaves before winter and are bare until spring. More recently, I've had teachers share with me their students' belief that the tree is dead. Our state has been experiencing a significant invasion of emerald ash borers, which have decimated ash trees in many neighborhoods. Hence, the conclusion that the tree is dead is logical. The third case derives from some colleagues who used the tree activity in southern Florida about 15 years ago. A significant number of students stated that a storm came and stripped the leaves from the tree. This too, was logical, because Hurricane Andrew passed over south Florida in August of 1992. We would not have expected this last response from students in central Illinois. Nevertheless, the response was one that could be deemed logical and acceptable. The context in which we ask students to make inferences can be important. In each of the three cases, the students had logically drawn their conclusions based in part on what they saw in the image of the tree and in part based on their past experiences where they lived.

Tip 5

As teachers, we need to help our students examine the assumptions they use when making inferences. If the assumptions are faulty or erroneous, the assumptions that we derive from them will be, too. This is closely linked to the previous tip. A student's past experiences and what they've learned in the past will lead them to think about things in certain ways. Mentally, we become predisposed to think in specific patterns. A child who has experienced the discomfort of poison ivy may assume all similar green plants will have the same effect on skin. Assumptions may also be dependent on cultural influences. For example, there are differences between Western and Eastern thought about astronomy, so the inferences someone makes about an astronomical phenomenon will be framed in the context of the culture in which they live and function.

Advancing Science

So, back to our tree statements: the tree is dead; the tree is big; it is wintertime. Of these three, the first and the last can logically be derived from students' experiences. These might be considered relatively good inferences. The middle statement (the tree is big) is of poorer quality simply because there is nothing in the picture to which we can compare the tree to determine its size. Older students may note that as some deciduous trees become more mature, they tend to have more branches and their canopies take on a more rounded profile. Given these additional pieces of logic, the middle inference becomes more acceptable, but we might help students find information about old trees that are not large.

Learning about what inferences are, and what a good inference is, will help students become more scientifically literate and better understand the nature of science and inquiry. Students in K–4 should be able to give explanations about what they investigate (NSTA 1997) and that includes doing so through inferring. Similarly, the Standards (NRC 1996) state that elementary students should be able to "use data to construct a reasonable explanation" (p. 122), and continues in Standard C by noting that scientists "develop explanations using observations (evidence) and what they already know about the world (scientific knowledge) … based on evidence from investigations" (p. 123). Good inferences help guide scientists in deciding which avenues to investigate further as they attempt to explain things around us. Inferring is a process that helps advance science.

References

Bell, R. L. 2008. *Teaching the nature of science through process skills. Activities for grades 3–8.* Boston, MA: Pearson Education.

Chiapetta, E. L. 1997. Inquiry-based science: Strategies and technologies for encouraging inquiry in the classroom. *The Science Teacher* 64 (7): 22–26.

Martin, D. J. 2009. *Elementary science methods: A constructivist approach.* Belmont, CA: Wadsworth Cengage Learning.

National Research Council (NRC). 1996. *National science education standards.* Washington, DC: National Academies Press.

National Science Teachers Association (NSTA). 1997. *NSTA pathways to the science standards: Elementary school edition.* Arlington, VA: NSTA.

NSTA Connection
Download a tree drawing at *www.nsta.org/SC1010*.

CHAPTER 7

Nature's Palette

Budding Ecologists Practice Their Skills of Observation in This Color-Wise Investigation

By Brooke B. McBride and Carol A. Brewer

Flower petals, acorn hats, exoskeletons of beetles, and lichens are just a few of the objects students may find in a surprising array of vivid colors. These tiny examples from nature's palette can be discovered in a school yard, a park, or even along the edges of a paved sidewalk. It simply takes careful observation!

The ability to make careful observations is an important skill for budding ecologists to develop, as the skill lies at the foundation of the scientific process. The National Science Education Standards (NRC 1996) call for K–12 students to develop the disposition and skills necessary to become independent inquirers of the natural world. Engaging in keen observation is fundamental to gathering the evidence that supports scientific understanding. In addition, close observation sparks imagination and curiosity that leads to further investigation. By looking closely at the natural world and studying even the smallest details, students are inspired to begin asking ecological questions. However, just looking is not enough; most students require instruction and guidance in how to focus and observe with a purpose. Continuing in this spirit, we created an investigation based on detecting and distinguishing natural variations in color.

Our program, Ecologists, Educators, and Schools, paired graduate students in the natural sciences with local school teachers in an effort to enhance and expand existing curricula to emphasize scientific inquiry (see Internet Resource). We explored the meaning and fundamental importance of observation in depth, using the February 2008 issue of *Science and Children* on observation as one of our resources. Not only did we wish to provide students with a means of focusing their observations, but we also sought an easy and effective means of engaging students in outdoor exploration. In this investigation, conducted with many different classes of students in grades K–4, students used a set of colorful cards to help inspire and guide their exploration of the outdoors.

Teacher Preparation

To begin, pay a visit to the color display at your local hardware or paint store. These displays have a vast selection of free paint color samples, available as small cards or paint chips. Paint chips come in many colors and shades, so it can be difficult to decide which ones to select. We recommend selecting every fifth or tenth paint chip in the display; this will make the selection process quick and easy, and will ensure that you get a wide variety of colors. Be sure to get a mixture of bright and muted shades, in everything from charcoal to chartreuse. The vivid, more unlikely shades are what make this inquiry especially fun and challenging for the students!

Paint chips often come in a series of three to four shades per card, so cut them into individual colors, if necessary. Next, cut sheets of poster board in half, width-wise. We found that half-sheets of poster board provided plenty of space for students to complete this investigation and were less unwieldy to take outside than full sheets. Paste 5–10 colors on each half-sheet of poster board. Each poster board should have a different array of colors to allow for a greater diversity of results. Prepare as many poster boards as there will be research groups in your class (we found that groups

Students sort their collections according to color.

of two to four students worked well for this investigation). Pasting the colors onto a poster board rather than distributing loose paint chips will make it easier for each group member to refer to the colors as they are collecting objects. In addition, these will serve as the research posters for groups to share at the conclusion of the investigation.

Student Preparation

To get students excited about this investigation, discuss their predictions about what they will find outdoors. Ask students a few questions to help generate some predictions:

- "Which of these colors do you think will be easiest to find outside?" Students tend to shout out the more common shades of *green!* or *brown!*
- "Which of these colors do you think will be hardest to find outside?" Students tend to identify the more unusual shades—*We'll* never *find* that *color* [turquoise]*!*
- "Where do you think you might find this color (e.g., orange) in your school yard?" Students tend to identify the more obscure areas of their school yard as places they expect to find the brighter colors.
- "What object do you think you might find that contains color (e.g., hot pink)?" Some students may expect that such colors do not exist naturally—*Only plastic comes in that color!*

Hold up a poster board prepared with a variety of paint chip colors and tell students that they will be going on a hunt for *natural* objects in those colors. Explain to students that they will be collecting objects that are found in nature, *not made by people* (e.g., not bits of wrappers, crayons, plastic, string, buttons). Include on the sample poster a few of these objects and ask students to differentiate between items that are human-made and those that are not. Emphasize that students must search closely to find natural items in the given colors.

Tell students to get ready to be surprised about what they might find. Discuss with students that they will be practicing their skills of *observation*. Making an observation means to study or look at something closely. The ability to make careful observations is an important skill for scientists, especially ecologists. An *ecologist* is a type of scientist who studies nature. In particular, an ecologist studies the relation between living organisms and their environment. By looking closely at the natural world and studying even the smallest details, an ecologist can begin to ask interesting questions and make good predictions. When students are using their best skills of observation, like ecologists, they will begin to find objects in a rainbow of colors.

Divide the class into research groups of two to four students and give each group a prepared poster board. Distribute a resealable bag to each student and explain that they will be searching for and collecting natural objects that match *as closely as possible* the colors on their group's poster board. Give these additional instructions:

1.   The objects that you collect must be small enough to be glued or taped to your poster boards without falling off. After our hunt, we will be coming back inside to glue our objects onto our posters.
2.   If you find a larger object, try to collect a small piece of it rather than the whole thing; for example, collect a few petals instead of an entire flower. We will try to affect nature as little as possible.
3.   Remember, you are trying to match your colors as closely as possible. However, the whole object does not have to be the same color. If you are looking for orange and you find a feather with an orange stripe, that counts.

Safety note: Follow your school guidelines for outdoor explorations. Don't forget to explain to students the boundaries of where they are to conduct their search. Remind students of any parts of the school yard or outdoor area that they are to avoid for safety or other reasons. In particular, instruct them to avoid sharp or thorny objects and to leave living creatures. Make sure students wash their hands when they return inside. Now you are ready to head outside and begin the investigation!

Ready, Set, Search!

We found that 25 minutes allowed plenty of time for students to explore and find a diverse collection of natural objects. However, students were so engaged in this investigation that we imagine the outdoor hunt could be extended up to 40 minutes without any loss of interest. Once you arrive outside, encourage research groups to set their poster boards on the ground so that all group members can refer to the colors as they are searching for objects. Have the students add as many color-matching objects as they can to their resealable bags. Encourage students to search high and low within the designated boundaries: under, around, and in shrubs;

on the trunks of trees; and in low-hanging branches. A wooded, shrubby, or tall grassy area, though ideal, is not necessary for this investigation. Weedy patches along a fence or along the edge of a parking lot also hold many surprises. Fascinating natural objects can even be found in cracks of sidewalks, in puddles, or along the bottom edge of a building—encourage students to get down on their hands and knees and really observe! Safety note: You may need to check for ticks after students explore in tall grass.

Kindergarten and first-grade students will require the closer guidance of an adult or older student partner to help keep them on track. We found that fourth-grade students were wonderful mentors to kindergarten students for this investigation. Fourth graders led kindergarteners to the designated areas and pointed to appropriate natural objects, which the younger students then collected and placed in their bags. The older students seemed to take great care and pride in sharing their "nature expertise" with the younger students.

Assembling and Sharing Posters

Back inside (or outside, weather- and space-permitting), have the research groups gather around their poster boards and dump out their natural objects. Research groups must work quickly as teams to sort through the objects and affix them to their posters. Objects should be adhered to the poster board next to their corresponding paint chip colors. We found that glue sticks were adequate for adhering most of the students' objects, but in some cases, tape or a blob of white glue was also necessary. Although older students (second- through fourth-grade) were able to complete this task largely on their own, younger students required additional guidance and assistance. Again, we found that fourth graders proved wonderful mentors to kindergarteners; the older students helped the younger students to spread out and sort the natural objects, which the older students then glued to the posters. Give students 10–15 minutes to assemble their posters.

For the last 10 minutes of the class period, have each group come to the front of the classroom to share their poster with the class (alternately, gather students in a circle). The following questions can be used to help guide the discussion and can also form the basis of an assessment of student learning:

- "What is the most surprising color that you found outside? What color did you find the most of? What color did you find the least of?"
- "How did you find all of these beautiful objects? Which of your senses did you have to use to find them? What other senses could you use to learn more about these objects (e.g., touch, smell)?"
- "What is the most interesting object that your group found? What is interesting or unusual about it? What do you think it is? What else would you like to know about it?"

These questions helped to draw out students' descriptions of the unique and surprising objects that they found, and the ways that they were able to find them (e.g., *I had to crawl on the ground and spread apart the grass to find it!*) Students made numerous thoughtful observations and posed interesting questions about their objects:

- *I found a gray mud ball with holes in the side. I thought it was just a mud ball but the holes were really insect holes, like tunnels. Some of the holes still had mud caps on the end. I wonder what is in those holes?*
- *I think this is cool [referring to a piece of lichen]. What is it? I think it's moss.*
- *I didn't think we could find something blue. We found a fly wing that looked black and clear but if you turned it one way it was blueish. It looks fake. Why is it blue like that?*
- *We have these same things in our driveway at home [referring to flowers from ponderosa pine trees]. What are these things? They look like brown noodles.*
- *This feather is mostly brown and gray but it has an orange stripe on it. Is this from a robin? This other feather is different—it's super fuzzy. I haven't found one like this before.*

Reiterate to students that they have been excellent ecologists and practiced their skills of observation. Now that they have looked very closely at nature and studied even the smallest details, they can begin to ask interesting questions and make good predictions!

A Successful Investigation

This investigation proved to be a success with students. The number and diversity of natural objects that students were able to find in only 25 minutes of outdoor exploration was mind-boggling and far surpassed our expectations. Students were excited by the challenge posed by the array of colorful paint chips and were eager to search high and low for objects in every color. We found that using the paint chips was an effective means of encouraging students' observation of the natural world by providing a sense of direction and purpose for the investigation while still allowing for authentic exploration. Students themselves were amazed by the diversity of natural items they found in their own school yard and were pleased to share their impressive posters with the rest of the class. This investigation quickly introduced students to the potential of their school yard as an outdoor laboratory and effectively set the stage for future outdoor inquiries throughout the school year!

Reference
National Research Council (NRC). 2006. *National science education standards.* Washington, DC: National Academies Press.

Internet Resource
Ecologists Educators and Schools
www.bioed.org/ecos/inquiries

NSTA Connection
For more articles on teaching observation skills, search by the keyword "observation" in the *S&C* archives at *www.nsta.org/elementaryschool*.

CHAPTER 8

Beyond Predictions

A Variation and Expansion of the Traditional "Sink or Float" Activity

By Dennis W. Smithenry and Jenny Kim

The classic sink or float activity, in which students test predictions of the buoyancy of various objects, is a staple in K–2 classrooms (Banchi and Bell 2008; Watson 2008). Students enjoy getting their hands wet in a tub of water. Teachers appreciate having their students purposefully engaged in a hands-on activity. Yet, besides having students experience how to make and test predictions, do students learn anything about why things sink or float (e.g., opposing forces, comparative density)? Is it even possible to expect that young students could learn any aspects of such difficult concepts? I (Professor Smithenry) pondered these questions with a student (Ms. Kim) in my science methods course as she prepared to teach the sink or float lesson to her master teacher's kindergarten class.

In the end, we found that it was possible to design and enact a lesson that modified the activity to teach more than the science process skill of prediction. We will explain this science lesson and discuss how Ms. Kim's kindergarten students built a working, conceptual model that allowed them to understand how a hollow object could be made to sink by adding mass to its inside.

Professor Smithenry's Perspective

Beyond Process Skills

It is important for teachers to clearly identify what it is that they want their students to learn in any science lesson (e.g., process skills, scientific concepts). For the process skill, Ms. Kim knew that she wanted students to learn how to make predictions and then test them. As for the scientific concept, although Ms. Kim knew that density helps explain why things sink or float, she wondered whether this would be too difficult for kindergartners to understand.

To help with our own conceptual understanding, we first explored why the concept of density helps to explain why things sink or float. We did so by developing a model (Figure 8.1, p. 38) that contained a *greatly simplified* representation of three substances: liquid water,

Figure 8.1

Particulate model used to explain sinking and floating

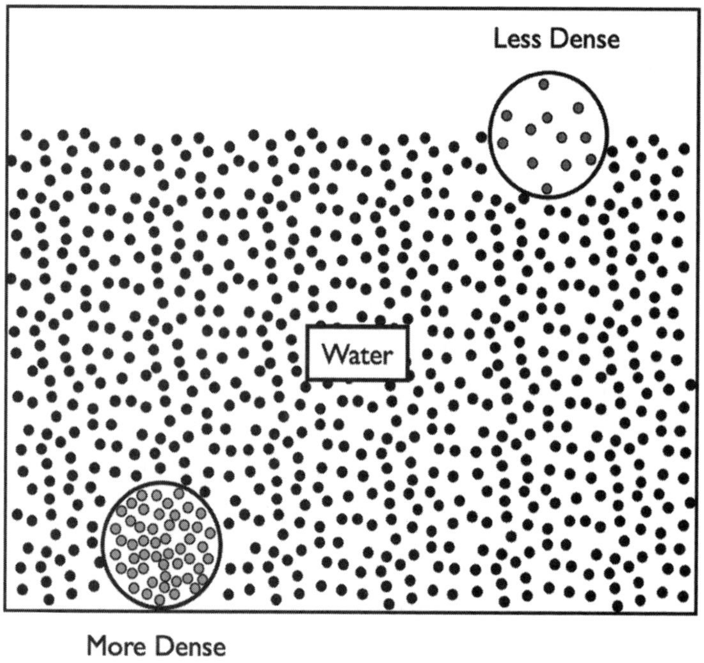

an object that floats on water, and an object that sinks in water. Each representation (a) incorporated the idea that all matter is made up of particles that are too small to be seen by the naked eye and (b) illustrated how closely the substance's particles are packed together. (Note: In the case of water [H_2O], each black dot represents one particle [or molecule] of water that, in turn, contains two hydrogen atoms bonded to a central oxygen atom.) For the object that sinks in water, the model suggests that its particles are packed more closely together in comparison to the packing of the water particles. Because of this difference in particle packing, the object is denser than water and it sinks. For the object that floats in water, the reverse is true.

Suppose the object that floats on top of the water is a piece of plastic. In this case, the plastic contains particles that may consist of millions of carbon and hydrogen atoms bonded together into long chains. In comparison to a water particle, the mass of each plastic particle is a million times greater. Yet, millions of water particles—which have a greater mass than one plastic particle—can fit into the same space that one plastic particle occupies. So, in this scenario, the net effect is that the liquid water has more mass packed in a similar volume, which is the reason why the water is denser than the plastic and causes the plastic to float.

Kindergartners cannot be expected to understand this. Research literature indicates that most young children do not view matter as being made of discrete particles that are too small to be seen by the naked eye (Driver et al. 1994; Keeley, Eberle, and Tugel 2007). Although students view matter as being continuous, the research does suggest that the earliest notion of density appears for children between the ages of 5 and 7 as they begin to refer to an object as being "heavy for [its] size" (Driver et al. 1994; Smith, Carey, and Wiser 1984). With this in mind, we tried to think of ways to use certain aspects of the particulate model that would build on the kindergartners' nascent notion of density.

Developmentally Appropriate Lesson

According to Smith, Carey, and Wiser (1984), children younger than age 5 typically ignore an object's size and focus on its "felt weight" (by picking up an object and hefting it) when predicting whether certain objects will sink or float. They commonly propose that lighter objects float and the heavier ones sink. As children grow older (between ages 5 and 7), they begin to incorporate both ideas of felt weight and size into their earliest notion of density (Smith, Carey, and Wiser 1984). This aforementioned notion has been labeled heavy for size. Thus, when children of this age are asked to predict whether an object will sink or float in water, they still have the tendency to heft the object, but also make note of its size. Interestingly, a recent study (Kloos 2008), which used a new experimental context, showed that children as young as age 3 were capable of distinguishing objects with salient differences in density. These new results suggest that children may develop an intuitive sense of density at a young age.

Knowing that kindergartners would be likely tuning into an object's mass (no matter what their current notion of density was) when asked to predict if it will sink or float in water, we refocused our attention to the concept of mass as represented in the particulate model in Figure 8.1. In doing so, we realized that, at the microscopic level, mass could be related to the number of particles (atoms) that the object contains. This realization gave us the idea that we might have students vary the mass of an object by changing the number of particles that one object contains at the macroscopic level. Why not use a hollow container that floats, and then add units of a different material until it sinks? In this way, the students would be changing the density of the container (i.e., the container's volume would stay the same while the total mass increases) by changing just one independent variable (mass).

Instead of giving students a range of common objects in which both mass and volume is varied (e.g., golf ball, penny, wood, crayon) as in the typical sink or float activity, we played with the idea of giving students one plastic egg and a pile of marbles. With these materials, the students would only be varying the mass of the system (by changing the number of marbles within the plastic egg) while keeping its total volume constant. In addition, as they added more marbles to the egg, the students would see that there was some point when the system began to sink; this point would relate directly to how many marbles (mass) they added. At least with this

scenario, if the students explained that "heavier objects sink," Ms. Kim would only need to attach the caveat "of the same volume" to make their explanations scientifically accurate. What is more, we found that this type of activity would allow Ms. Kim to introduce a powerful, easily-understood, driving question into her lesson: How many marbles must be added to make the plastic egg sink?

Ms. Kim's Perspective

The Lesson

To begin the lesson, I told my students we would be studying sinking and floating. I told them that they would

Students watch a plastic egg sink in a tub of water.

PHOTOGRAPH COURTESY OF THE AUTHORS

be scientists during the lesson who observe carefully, record what they observe, and think about what they are doing. As the anticipatory set, I asked, "Do you sink or float in the swimming pool?" I could tell that some students were uncertain of the verbs in my question, so I asked the students why children use "floaters" in the swimming pool. Several responded that they needed floaters because they could not swim on their own. I then stressed that floaters allowed children to *float* at the top of the water; without them, children might *sink* to the bottom of the pool.

Then, I introduced the plastic egg. I asked whether they thought the egg would sink or float in a tub of water. We took a blind vote, and there was a tie; nine students predicted that the egg would float, and nine predicted it would sink. When I put the egg into a tub of water and it floated, the class expressed surprise and excitement. I then showed my students how to record this result on a data chart.

Rather than asking them to explain why the egg floated, I opened up the plastic egg to show them that it only contained air and asked them to think about the following question, "How do you think that we could make this egg sink?" The students had several ideas. Frank suggested that we put rocks inside it. Blanca proposed that we should add ice cubes. Heidi wanted to add coins. Shinji recommended that we add chocolate! I acknowledged these answers, and then pulled some marbles out of my pocket, telling them that I had also thought that we should add something inside the egg. At this point, I prepared two eggs without telling the students how many marbles I had added to each. I shook the eggs to let them know that the eggs now contained marbles and proceeded to put them into the water. They observed that one floated and one sank. They were amazed!

After my students quieted down, I announced that they would work in pairs to determine how many marbles it takes to get the egg to sink. I divided the class into nine pairs and handed out a data sheet (see NSTA Connections for blank data chart and Figure 8.2 for an example of a completed data chart). I had each pair record the result for an egg with no marbles and then discussed how to test and record the results for an egg with one, two, and three marbles. Last, we reviewed how to work appropriately with the given materials. Safety note: Do not splash water or throw marbles, and do take turns.

Figure 8.2

Completed sink or float class data chart

	Sink	Float
		X
		X
		X
	X	

Once each pair had gathered their materials, I instructed them to begin by placing one marble into the egg. I circulated among them to ensure that they were placing an X in the float column of their data sheet for an egg with one marble in it. After checking in with each pair, I instructed them to finish the investigation. As I continued circulating, I heard students talking about the investigation and sharing their ideas. Some were predicting before they added the egg into the water whether it was going to sink or float. Others were debating whether an egg had really sunk if it was not fully immersed.

Figure 8.3

The calculated densities of the plastic egg with various numbers of marbles

	Observation	Mass	Volume	Density	Comparison	Float or sink?
Plastic egg		7 g	66 cm³	0.1 g/cm³	less than density of water (1.0 g/cm³)	float
Plastic egg + 1 marble		32 g	66 cm³	0.48 g/cm³	less than	float
Plastic egg + 2 marbles	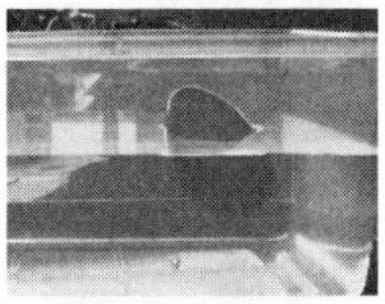	57 g	66 cm³	0.86 g/cm³	less than	float
Plastic egg + 3 marbles		82 g	66 cm³	1.2 g/cm³	greater than	sink

When most had finished their last test, I instructed each pair to clean up any water spills and then come sit on the carpet. Once everyone was seated, I revealed a big chart that I had made before the lesson. This chart was similar to the students' data tables. I asked them to report their findings and we filled in the chart (Figure 8.2). Then I asked them to think silently about the following question: Why do you think the egg finally sank with three marbles? When I let them respond, Jose said, "It was heavy." Sabina agreed with Jose, and then offered more detail, "With one marble it was a little heavy and sinking a little; with two marbles it was a little bit heavier and sinking a little more; and with three marbles, it was even heavier and sank." The students liked this answer so I recorded it on the board. I then pointed out that as we added more marbles, the egg's weight had increased, but its overall size (volume) had remained the same.

After this discussion, I had the students go back to their seats and complete a two-part assessment (see NSTA Connection for the assessment worksheet). In the first part, students were asked to (a) recall whether an egg with two marbles would sink or float and (b) predict whether an egg with five marbles would sink or float. In the second part, they were asked to draw in a specific number of marbles that one plastic egg might contain if it were floating and another if it were sinking. I ensured that they understood how to complete each part of the assessment and then allowed them to work on their own quietly.

After the lesson was over, simply out of curiosity, I tried to make further sense of the kindergartner's observations. Specifically, I wanted to confirm through measurements that the density of the plastic egg with two marbles was less than the density of water and that the density of the plastic egg with three marbles was greater. To do so, I used an electronic balance to measure the mass (grams) of the egg with the various combinations of marbles. I also estimated the volume (milliliters) of the egg by filling each half of it with water and pouring both amounts into a graduated cylinder. Note: One milliliter equals one cubic centimeter. Because the marbles were placed inside the plastic egg, its total volume remains the same regardless of the number of marbles placed within. As shown in Figure 8.3 (p. 41), my calculations confirmed that the density of the plastic egg system becomes greater than the density of water when it contains three marbles.

What Students Learned

In the first part of the assessment, 17 of 18 students marked correctly that the egg with two marbles would float. These same students also marked correctly that the egg with five marbles would sink. In the second part of the assessment, 16 students drew correctly one or two marbles into the egg that was floating. Of these same students, 10 students drew greater than three marbles (up to seven!) in the egg that had sunk, with the remaining 6 students drawing three marbles.

For several reasons, we feel that the assessment data clearly illustrates what the students took away from the lesson. Although it is likely that the students already came to this lesson with the idea that objects with more mass sink, the data suggests that the students were able to see how incremental changes in mass could make a hollow object go from a floating state to a sinking state. The results also indicate that most students had a firm understanding of the data that they had collected during the experiment. Last, the assessment data suggests that the students did not need to conduct more tests to make the connection that if more than three marbles were added to the egg, it would sink. This last finding implies that these kindergartners were able to extrapolate from their collected data and make accurate predictions about how the number of marbles affected the plastic egg's buoyancy.

Summary

By thinking about the concept of density and taking into account the research on children's ideas about this concept, we were able to unpack the typical sink or float activity and realize that it has students unscientifically making comparisons between objects by changing two independent variables (mass and volume) at one time. With this realization, we were able to modify the activity so that students were making comparisons in which they were only changing one independent variable (mass). The end result went well beyond the common "prediction" objective found in the classic sink or float activity.

Ms. Kim's students developed a working, conceptual model that allowed them to correctly answer untested questions about the plastic egg system. When the students explained that the egg was getting "heavier," they were basing this explanation on having purposefully increased the egg's overall mass (by adding marbles) while keeping its volume constant. Even though the students were unaware that they were increasing the egg's *density*, they were experimenting with the idea that putting more mass into a given space can make an object sink. And this idea will serve them well when they *are* formally introduced to the concept of density in later grades.

References

Banchi, H., and R. Bell. 2008. The many levels of inquiry. *Science and Children* 46 (2): 26–29.

Driver, R., A. Squires, P. Rushworth, and V. Wood-Robinson. 1994. *Making sense of secondary science: Research into children's ideas.* New York: Routledge.

Keeley, P., F. Eberle, and J. Tugel. 2007. *Uncovering student ideas in science: 25 more formative assessment probes,* vol. 2. Arlington, VA: NSTA Press.

Kloos, H. 2008. Will it float? How invariance affects children's understanding of object density. In *Proceedings of the 30th Annual Conference of the Cognitive Science Society,* ed. B. C. Love, K. McRae, and V. M. Sloutsky, p. 687–692. Austin, TX: Cognitive Science Society.

Smith, C., S. Carey, and M. Wiser. 1984. A case study of the development of size, weight, and density. *Cognition* 21 (3): 177–237.

Watson, S. 2008. Discovery bottles: A unique inexpensive tool for the K–2 science classroom. *Science and Children* 45 (9): 20–24.

NSTA Connection
Download a blank data chart and assessment worksheet at *www.nsta.org/SC1010.*

CHAPTER 9

A Foolproof Tool

By Linda Froschauer

Science is organized knowledge. Wisdom is organized life.

—Immanuel Kant

Science notebooks first came into the picture for me when I enrolled in biology as an undergraduate. I was impressed with their usefulness and quickly realized how important entries could be to my learning. I particularly appreciated that I could organize notes and ideas for future study. The notebook had a special place on my shelf and was always with me in class. As a new teacher, I knew that a science notebook could be valuable to my fifth-grade students, just as it had been to me.

It's difficult to think of a tool we use in science classes that provides as much for student learning as a science notebook. It supports the development of science skills, processes, and understanding as well as literacy, numeracy, and attitudes. It helps students understand the scientific endeavor through modeling the work of scientists—recording information and data while providing predictions and personal analysis of discoveries. Students find it helpful when preparing for assessments, sharing information with others, and exhibiting what they have learned. Certainly this is the ultimate tool for interdisciplinary learning. Add to that the success reported when using science notebooks to enhance science content and process skills with English language learners, and you have the perfect strategy for reaching all students.

Sounds like the perfect, foolproof tool. But I learned that the process must be structured carefully with the developmental age of my students and my goals clearly in mind. Students must be guided in creating a document that will be useful to them and the teacher. I had to determine every component prior to beginning: numbering the pages, creating a table of contents, developing a glossary, learning how to make useful entries (diagrams, tables, charts, graphs, dating), and how to personalize their notebook through creativity. Initially, I hadn't considered assessment of student work, but I soon learned that missing this important step prevented me from providing quality feedback to students and diminished my understanding of what they learned. I found that the questions "What are signs of student progress?" "How will you provide them with feedback?" and "How will you support them along the way?" are all important considerations. Think about these things before you begin. This also provides the opportunity for students to know the expectations.

And then, students must use it. One of your most important roles in the success of science notebooks is to support students in their work. Your structured lessons must bring them back to their notebooks to reflect, share, and use the information they have recorded carefully. I don't think it takes much convincing to use science notebooks. I can still describe many pages from my biology science notebook because they became an integral part of my learning.

Resource

Campbell, B., and L. Fulton. 2003. *Science notebooks: Writing about inquiry.* Portsmouth, NH: Heinemann.

CHAPTER 10

A Menu of Options

Strategies for Success With Science Notebooks in the Primary Grades

By Valerie Joyner

Many challenges face primary teachers as they consider using notebooks with young scientists. "How do I start?" "What can I expect from students this young?" "Are they really capable of writing and recording data?" "How do I assess their learning?" Armed with a few topical and organizational strategies, primary grade teachers can successfully introduce their young scientists to science notebooks. I know—I did it myself! I developed creative and meaningful science notebook experiences for my second-grade students. The following overview of notebook methods offers a menu of options. Choose and customize what works for your classroom to provide students with the background and skills necessary to inquire, observe, test, and report.

Organizational Strategies

Notebook Structure

The first step is to determine what the science notebook will look like. I prefer to use three-ring binders for flexibility because students can add and move both teacher-created materials and workbook pages as needed. I have found that using bound notebooks requires the students to glue or staple in extra pages or tear out mistakes, leading to bulky and messy results. Instead, the young scientists add each new page to the back of the binder, allowing them to create a chronology of their science experiences and rearrange pages when necessary. At the end of the year, I spiral-bind the pages for each child to keep as a record of the science they have learned.

Other important early steps are to set goals to be met through the notebook activities and plan how the results will be assessed. By first identifying instructional goals, we can develop meaningful notebook experiences tied to desired outcomes. The most important goals I set for my students involve content and organization. These two goals are closely aligned. I expect each student to include all the content required for each lesson: their name, the date, and the specifics needed for the current activity (e.g., focus question, drawing, or whatever the day's lesson demands). I also require them to keep their pages in order in the binders and put sticky notes or flags at the beginning of each activity for easy reference. When students participate in activities and record their results and conclusions in an organized fashion, it is easier to check for meaningful understanding and determine whether there is a need for a concept to be revisited. Young scientists also experience how good organization makes it easy for them to locate their data for later use. For example, when recording and comparing monthly rainfall amounts throughout the year, students can compare totals at the end of the year by creating a graph. They see firsthand how keeping their data organized makes the comparison possible. This organizational aspect is also at play when students make predictions and follow up with procedures, results, and conclusions.

Scaffolding

In the beginning, students feel more confident with a guide, so I scaffold their entries for the first few months. At this time of the year, I'm more interested in cultivating students' observation skills than in their developmental ability to write long or complex sentences. Early scaffolding helps students develop skills in recording observations. Sentence structures provided by scaffolding also help English language learners and students with special needs formulate their responses by giving them a pattern to follow.

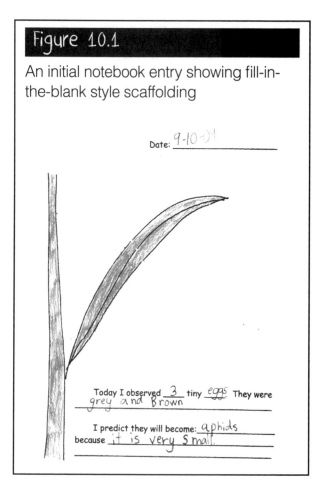

Figure 10.1

An initial notebook entry showing fill-in-the-blank style scaffolding

I often start the school year with the life cycle of a monarch butterfly using a fill-in-the-blank approach for the first few entries. For example, the worksheets I create ask the students to provide detailed observations and written descriptions and drawings. This raises their awareness of these aspects of their experiences and allows them to spend more time on observations and to communicate accurately through writing, measuring, and drawing (Figure 10.1). Over the course of a few weeks, the children are given more opportunity to describe and record their observations. After group observations and discussion, we list keywords on the board, encouraging the children to master science terms and incorporate them into their writing.

Another strategy I use is incorporating word banks (including cognates) and graphic organizers into the beginning of the lesson. As the unit and year progresses, the students write more independently about their experiences with less scaffolding. Later worksheets feature open-ended questions and direct the students to create their own drawings, graphs, and data records.

Drawing, Dating, and Labeling

Young scientists need to practice the critical skills of drawing and labeling scientific subjects. It's important to work closely with students to help them understand that science notebooks are a time

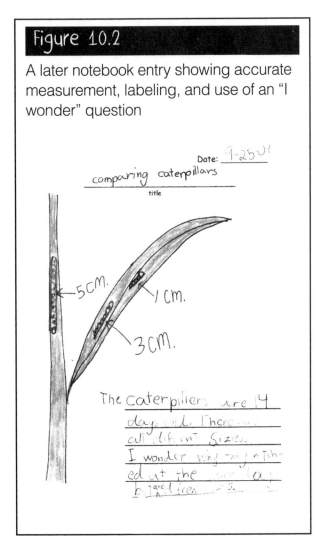

Figure 10.2

A later notebook entry showing accurate measurement, labeling, and use of an "I wonder" question

for accuracy, not inventiveness. Students must date all of their work and draw accurate pictures with labels. A larva that is 1 cm should be represented and labeled as 1 cm (Figure 10.2). Initially, I model the process with them. For example, I show them how to measure a larva, draw a larva of the correct size, draw an arrow to the larva, and record the measurement at the arrow. The students copy my model as a notebook entry. Later, they learn to draw what they observe and record important data about their observations independently. They get accustomed to adding specific dates, names, and measurements. With practice and guidance, they begin to observe, report, and strive for scientific accuracy. For students who are unable to draw accurate detailed illustrations, support can be given with precut objects or templates. In some cases, I hold the ruler for the student and let them measure and then draw their subject with my help.

Table of Contents and Glossary

It's easy to overlook the importance of organizational components, such as the table of contents and glossary, but both elements enhance cross-curricular learning and save classroom time. With regards to the table of contents, have students create it as they proceed through each assignment or save that task for later in the school year. A third option is to have students create their table of contents during a language arts period. Another path would be for teachers to create strips with activity titles and space to record the page numbers. The students in turn glue the strip into their table of contents and fill in the page numbers.

A glossary is also an important element of an active science notebook. It's essential for students to record science vocabulary as it is uncovered in lessons and refer back to the words in an organized manner. I put the key vocabulary terms on a sentence strip prior to teaching a science activity. During the activity, as the students experience these new concepts, we post the written terms on the board. Throughout the activity, we develop the meaning of the new terms in group discussions. The children then write definitions in their own words and post the glossary terms at the back of their notebooks. Composing their own definitions after the hands-on experience encourages better understanding and retention of the newly introduced vocabulary. By the end of the school year, each student should have a usable glossary in their notebooks. These standard elements of published books tend to give the students a sense that their science notebooks are important, useful, and real.

Topical Strategies

Focus Questions

Before students begin a science experience, it's important for them to focus on a question. First we talk together as a group to develop a focus question. A good focus question narrows the scientific experience into a search for a specific set of conclusions. With a tight focus, students can practice collecting and sorting data without being overwhelmed by irrelevant details. At this age, guided by their teacher, students develop a focus question such as, "What do you notice about the monarch butterfly life cycle?" Then the young scientists record the focus question in their notebooks to guide their work.

It's critical to systematically talk through the focus question in a debriefing session after all science activities. This is when I work with the class to reflect on their observations, ideas, and experiences and determine a well-thought-out response to the focus question. This vital task develops students' understanding of the focus question and ability to relate that to both the science experience and their conclusions.

The responses to focus questions can often be enhanced with accurate pictorial representations of the results. For example, one focus question I use from the Full Option Science Systems (FOSS) Balance and Motion unit is "What is the trick to balancing an object on its point?" After the hands-on activity, the students draw a model representing their actual results (Figure 10.3). They can then refer to their drawing to answer the focus question. Teaching children to focus on a question helps them succeed as they progress through the grades and are challenged to hypothesize, infer, and generate their own investigable science questions.

Making Predictions

Another essential skill for young scientists to develop is making predictions that relate to the focus questions and reveal key concepts. Predictions ask students to think about their prior knowledge and experiences and formulate in

A monarch larva crawls along a plant stem.

Figure 10.3

A focus question, answer, and detailed drawing

Focus Question: what is the trick to balancing an object on it's piont? has to be

Anser: cloths pin facing down

pencil

wire

me

cloths pin

popside stick

A monarch butterfly rests on a student's arm (above). Monarch chrysalis in the classroom (right)

their own minds what they think will happen. Often they make a quick prediction without much thought, but the students' predictions should be followed by "because …". During the monarch butterfly experience, for example, a student made the following prediction after observing the tiny eggs: *I predict the eggs will hatch into aphids because they are so small.*

When *because* is added to the science writing it forces the students to give rationale to their predictions (even when incorrect), and the predictions become more meaningful. I have my students write their predictions in their notebooks using the "because…" structure at the beginning of science lessons. This gets them thinking about their prior knowledge of the topic and develops their ability to make predictions. After the activities we go back to our notebooks as a group and discuss our predictions and how they compare to the results we observed.

I Wonder …

We have all experienced the curious minds of primary students as they ask endless questions. *How big will the caterpillar get? How many paper clips will the magnet hold? What will the seeds become?* We should capitalize on their curiosity. "I wonder …" questions allow young scientists to take ownership of their work, explore the discovery process, and develop their inquiry skills. Once they have posed their questions and recorded them, they've developed a personal investment and they want to know more.

Calendars and Graphs

As our young scientists develop their observation skills and learn to accurately record data, they become ready to work more deeply with their information. Using graphs, charts, and calendars, students plot recorded dates and use their data to answer focus questions, "I wonder …" questions, and teacher-asked questions. As an example, after the monarch butterflies hatch in my classroom, students use their science notebooks to find the dates and data they recorded about the different stages of the life cycle (Figure 10.4). They plot the data on a calendar and use their calendars to answer questions about the length of each step of the life cycle.

Another class experience is collecting and recording rainfall. We use a class rain gauge to collect data about rainfall amounts. The children use this information to create their own rainfall centimeter rulers and record the amount. They plot the rainfall amounts that occurred throughout the year on a student-made graph. When students create graphs, charts, and calendars from the data they collect in their science notebooks, it deepens their understanding of science and the process scientists routinely follow.

Start Small, Think Big

Science notebooks give vivid insight into students' learning and allow us to review firsthand their procedures, processes, results, and conclusions. At the end of each science experience,

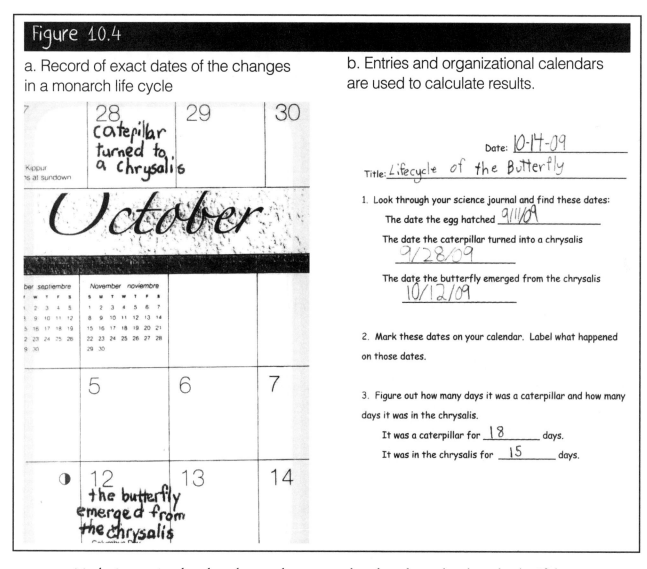

Figure 10.4

a. Record of exact dates of the changes in a monarch life cycle

b. Entries and organizational calendars are used to calculate results.

revisit the instructional goals and assess the outcome based on the students' notebooks. If the goal is accuracy in scientific drawings, one has immediate access to their pictures to measure their progress. A teacher can get a sense of their improvement in language skills from their written entries. From their writings and drawings we can shape our further instruction to ensure that student understanding is correct. The possibilities for detailed formative assessments from science notebook results are limitless.

Science notebooks are a comprehensive way to foster interest in learning, progress students in all curricular areas, and assess their multifaceted development. The question remaining is how we, as primary-grade teachers, can find the time to develop and use an active science notebook. Start small. Establish a few goals for the students and their notebooks. Look for interdisciplinary options and take a few steps forward. It's a worthy endeavor to include the use of science notebooks in any primary classroom at whatever level possible, so use and adapt these organizational strategies to customize a science adventure for your young scientists!

CHAPTER 11

Interactive Reflective Logs

Opening Up Science Notebooks to Peer and Teacher Feedback

By Cynthia Minchew Deaton, Benjamin E. Deaton, and Katina Leland

Although some students flourish during classroom discussions, other students become more reserved and withdrawn. How do we as educators ensure that all students are given the opportunity to respond? How do we engage students who are embarrassed to speak in front of others? How can students participate in a science learning community? One way to encourage students' communication with their peers and teachers is through the use of a reflective journal, which engages students in expressing their understanding of and questions about science concepts.

We created an Interactive Reflective Log (IRL) to provide teachers with an opportunity to use a journal approach to record, evaluate, and communicate student understanding of science concepts. Through a two-part design, the IRL allows (1) students to demonstrate their understanding of science concepts, and (2) teachers and other students to question or guide students' understanding. Unlike a traditional journal, the IRL incorporates prompts to encourage students to discuss their understanding of science content and science processes and to reflect on their science activities. The IRL provides a structured approach to journaling and encourages teachers and students to participate in a community of learners by sharing their IRL entries with one another. This is unlike traditional journal entries that are usually kept to oneself or only shared with the teacher. Traditional journal entries also usually result in open-ended responses that do not always show students' understanding of science content, science processes, and evidence.

Creating an IRL

Each log is broken into five sections: science content, science process, explain, questions/interests, and refine activity (see NSTA Connection for a blank IRL). These sections guide students in (1) writing about their understanding of content and procedures for investigations or inquiries, (2) developing explanations based on their evidence, (3) extending their knowledge by posing new questions, (4) listing insights they gained from their inquiry, and (5) examining and evaluating their investigation.

To aid students in completing successful writing about their science experiences, the IRL provides students with basic prompts to guide their writing about their science investigations. Although the prompts on the IRL were selected to support students in developing communication skills and explanations for a specific activity, they can be revised easily. Teachers can easily fill in the following questions to develop prompts for that section:

What did you know about_____?
What questions do you have about _____?
What did you learn about _____?

The science process section encourages students to think about what they did during an activity and uses broad prompts. These prompts can remain the same for any activity. The explain section uses prompts that encourage students to compare and contrast findings and use evidence to develop explanations. This section can also be easily revised as teachers complete the following questions:

What caused _____?
Why did it cause _____?
How do you know it caused _____?

The questions/interests section of the IRL, like the science process section, uses broad prompts and can easily remain the same from activity to activity.

Making It Reflective

Our third-grade students used an IRL to record their investigation of Earth's layers. As they participated in the "Layer-Cake Earth" activity (Tedford and Warny 2006), students responded to the IRL questions using both words and drawings. The Layer-Cake Earth activity provides a hands-on approach to learning geology concepts and investigating Earth's layers. In this activity, teachers use a layered cake to represent the sediment layers that students can take core samples from and investigate. As they responded to our prompts (Figure 11.1, pp. 56–57), the students listed the procedures they used to collect samples and what they found in each layer, and developed explanations for the location of each fossil. Most students chose to list, draw, and label their sample and fossils. They used the IRL in lieu of more traditional methods of recording their science activities. By using the IRL, students were able to record and reflect on the procedures they used and their findings. The prompts in the IRL supported students in discussing the processes they used to collect their evidence and the evidence they collected. It also encouraged them to use evidence to explain their findings.

Making It Interactive

Once students complete their IRL, the teacher selects a reflective partner. Teachers may select reflective partners based on the science group, reading and writing abilities, and previous

Figure 11.1

Sample interactive reflective log

Student	Reflective partner

1. Science Content
   a. What did you know about Earth's layers?
   There are four layers.
   They can be solid or liquid.
   b. What questions do you have about Earth's layers?
   How bright is the Earth's inner core?
   How hot is the Earth's core? Has anyone taken the temperature of the inner core? If there was not a crust, would the mantle spill out into space?
   c. What did you learn about Earth's layers?
   How to find sample. The different layers. How big they are. I didn't know there was an inner and outer core. What a trilobite was.
	P: _____
	_____
	_____
	
	T: I like your questions. It would be nice if you could research them and share what you find with the class. What could you do to find the answers to your questions?
	
	I am also glad you learned some new things. You learned how to collect samples and that there is an inner and outer core. What did you learn about the Earth's crust?

2. Science Process
   a. What happened?
   We found three shark teeth and dinosaur bones. The three shark teeth in the first layers and dinosaur bones in the second layers. Dinosaur bones in the pink layer.
   b. What did you do?
   We dug into different layers of the Earth. We got the sample from the field scientist in our group. We found three shark teeth and dinosaur bones. They were cool.
   c. What did you find?
   We found three shark teeth and dinosaur bones. We didn't find a trilobite.
   d. What safety procedures did you follow?
   We did not run in the room. We took turns getting materials. We were careful when digging. We cleaned up the floor and desk. We did not eat anything or throw anything.
	P: _____
	_____
	_____
	
	T: I'm glad you know what your group did to investigate the Earth's layers. What was your role in your group? How did you help during the investigation?
	
	I am glad that you followed the class rules and were safe during the investigation. Did you use any science tools during your investigation? How did you safely handle those tools?

Student	Reflective partner

3. Explain
  a. What caused another sample to look different?
    Shape, size, color, and layer you found them in.
  b. What caused another sample to look the same?
    Where you took your sample. Where you cored at. Layers you cored.
  c. Why do you think the sample looked different?
    Dug into different spots. Each spot was different. Some were thick. Some were thin. Each layer was a different color. Different things in each color layer.
  d. Why do you think the sample looked the same?
    Dug in same spot. Dug right next to the spot we dug the first time.
	P: _____
	  _____
	  _____
	
	T: Do you think the location of the other group's core sample made their sample look different than your group's sample? Why?

4. Questions/Interests
  a. What other questions do you have?
    What was my partner's favorite thing? Can we do this for real? Can we make two cakes and have more things?
  b. What was interesting to you?
    Finding things. To get the sample out. Core.
	P: _____
	  _____
	  _____
	
	T: What other fossils do you think we could add if we had another cake? What could we use to represent the fossils? Why did you enjoy finding things?

interactions in class. If students are asked to write about their investigations, another member of their learning community should read their comments. Our thinking was that when students know that teachers or other students will take the time to read their responses and elaborate on them, their motivation to write may increase.

When students are allowed to review their peers' work, they act as reflective peers. This role allows them to add questions and comments on their peers' IRLs. For example, they may question their peers' use of (a) scientific terminology, (b) investigation procedures, (c) data collection, and (d) explanations developed from data. It also allows group members to communicate with each other and help refine other members' ideas and explanations. Students can use their science group's or science partner's questions and comments to elaborate on or revise descriptions and explanations they developed while participating in the science investigation and completing the IRL. Their group's or partner's feedback may also enhance future use of the IRL to organize their thoughts and record their science investigation.

Many students need support in developing as a reflective partner. For students to understand how to provide feedback for their peers, they first need to understand what appropriate feedback looks like. Teachers need to model appropriate feedback and talk about their expectations for reflective partners. Teachers may also develop prompts to support students in examining their peers' IRL entries. For example, they can ask reflective peers to provide feedback on investigation procedures (e.g., do you understand the procedures they used during their investigation?), students' use of science terminology, or use of evidence when explaining their findings.

Our IRL allows both students and teachers to comment on or question students' responses to the prompts. Teachers may wish to be the only person commenting on students' IRLs, or they may like their comments to support questions or comments asked by other students. This choice provides teachers with a flexible approach for involving members of the learning community. In our case, teachers took on the role as the reflective partner. Through this role, we were able to provide students with questions and comments that valued their participation, their knowledge about Earth's layers, and the data they collected. Comments were created to encourage students to clarify and extend their responses to their IRL. Other comments were used to provide students with positive reinforcement as they reflected on their findings and responses. Although the questions and comments may have varied from student to student, they all helped students reflect on the investigation.

By participating as a reflective partner, teachers can seamlessly act as participants in the community of learners. Like reflective peers, teachers use comments and questions to guide students to further examine the content, processes, and data from their investigations. Their questions can be used as enrichment or remediation questions for certain students. Reading and responding to students' IRLs affords teachers the opportunity to assess student understanding, identify concepts they need to revisit, and challenge students to extend their understanding of a concept.

Amplified Assessment

Although the IRL itself provides teachers with a way to assess students' science understanding, the IRL rubric (see NSTA Connection) supports teachers in assessing students' science understanding and participation as reflective partners. The IRL rubric assesses both students' use of the IRL for recording their investigation and their participation as a reflective partner. By having peers and teachers respond to their IRL, students can use the comments and questions posed by their peers or teachers to refine their writing or future investigations. Teachers' feedback on the IRL and on the rubric can help students reflect on how they connect science terms and concepts, develop clear explanations, and consider the procedures and outcomes of their investigation. Depending on the students, teachers may need to revise the descriptors in the IRL rubric so that they are easily understood.

Reflective Thinkers

The IRL not only provides students with a guide for writing their investigations, it can also encourage students to reflect on their investigations and communicate with their peers. Questions and prompts from the IRL can be used to encourage future investigations and provide teachers with an understanding of students' interests and knowledge about science concepts. In addition, IRLs can enhance the classroom community as students trust one another to provide feedback on their responses about and understanding of scientific investigations.

Reference
Tedford, R., and S. Warny. 2006. Layer-cake Earth. *Science and Children* 44 (4): 40–44.

NSTA Connection
Download a sample IRL for science investigations and a sample IRL rubric at *www.nsta.org/SC1011*.

CHAPTER 12

Reuse That Notebook!

Keeping a Notebook Throughout Grade Levels as a Reference Tool

By Elizabeth Lener

How many scientists throw out their notebooks at the end of each year and start over no matter how many empty pages remain? How many of them approach a new research question or experiment without using knowledge gained from previous years? The answer to each of these questions is of course, few if any, yet we ask our students to do that every year in science.

During a graduate science methods course I taught several years ago, we recalled science notebooks we had used during our own school years. One student still had many of his science notebooks from elementary and middle school and what was most striking for him was that each of the notebooks was only a quarter full at most. The rest of the pages were blank. Each notebook was sent home at the end of the school year and each fall he would get a brand new one. Work that was done in the past was never referenced and did not inform subsequent learning.

As a writing teacher, I had students keep a notebook of their work and ideas. Because I was teaching a writer's workshop, I began to also use those notebooks as a place for students to keep a record of our writing minilessons. As notebooks filled up with tips on punctuation and writing techniques, I began to realize that students needed a way to find notes from prior classes so they could apply that knowledge to their current writing. I began setting aside the first few pages every year for a table of contents and suddenly students were using their notebooks as effective writing reference guides.

I combined the idea from the graduate class with my experience as a writing teacher, and thus, a new concept for a science notebook was born! Students would keep the same science notebook for multiple years not only as a place to make lab observations and class notes, but also as an ongoing book.

Early Considerations

As this idea began taking shape, several things became clear. There are multiple science teachers at our elementary school, so using the notebooks for more than one year meant that all of the teachers had to decide on how notebooks would be used, organized, and assessed. We had to choose a notebook design that was sturdy, contained ample pages, and was formatted for the intended age group. In our case, this was grades 3–6.

Students at our school are given laptops in fifth grade, so an electronic notebook was also considered. Because we wanted to be able to use notebooks during messy labs and the same system across all grades, however, we decided to use paper notebooks. We went with standard-ruled marble composition notebooks with 100 pages. Although older students could benefit from notebooks using grid paper, we felt strongly that they would be too difficult for young students to use. The number of pages would allow ample room for students to write on a regular basis, especially if they used both sides of the sheet. Notebooks were purchased by the school for approximately one dollar each, and because we used them for multiple years it proved to be an affordable system. Because all of the notebooks looked alike, students labeled them with their names and were allowed to personalize the cover. The notebooks remained in good condition for several years, mostly because they are stored in the classroom and students only take them home occasionally.

Once we had our notebooks, we continued the process by coming up with a list of guidelines for the notebook that every teacher could use (see Figure 12.1). These guidelines covered both the initial formatting of the notebooks and maintenance. They were discussed and modified to make sure that they would work for students across the range of ages and abilities.

The guideline sheet was attached to the inside front cover using glue sticks, and at least one day at the beginning of each year was dedicated to having students set up their science notebooks. After the first year, only third graders and new students had to set up notebooks because everyone else had one from the prior year. At the end of each year notebooks are collected by the teacher for use the following year.

Figure 12.1

Guidelines for the notebook

Welcome to your science notebook!
All scientists keep a record of the work that they do. Most scientists still use notebooks like this one even though they have computers to do much of their work. This will be *your* science notebook until each and every page is full so please take good care of it, follow the guidelines below, and DON'T LOSE IT!

Notebook guidelines
- Decorate the cover to make it your own!
- Use the front and back of every page.
- Never use markers except to decorate your cover! Pencils, ballpoint pens, crayons, and colored pencils are fine.
- Mark the date of every entry in your notebook and remember to add the title of the entry to your table of contents page.
- Write neatly and be sure to include details, drawings, and measurements in your entries.
- Return your notebook to its designated spot at the end of every class unless you have received permission from your teacher to take it with you.

Setting up your notebook
- Attach this guideline sheet to the front inside cover of your notebook following your teacher's instruction.
- Mark the top of the first six pages (front and back) of your notebook with the title, "Table of Contents." Draw lines using a ruler to make spaces for titles, dates, and page numbers as shown on the board.
- Number every page (front and back) in your notebook at the bottom outside corner.

It was important to us that each notebook was formatted in the same manner and that each student took part in this process as a way to become familiar with the idea of a notebook/reference book. We used a scanned sample table of contents page as a way to model the formatting for students with our computers and projectors, but an overhead transparency would work equally well.

Figure 12.2

Sample table of contents

date	Title	Page #
9/9/08	Hopes and dreams	7
9/11/08	Simp. mech. stations	8
10/9/08	Journal Notes	9
1/8/09	Three things I know about chemistry	10
1/8/09	Mystery Cans	11
1/9/09	Atom notes	12
1/17/09	Chemical Reaction	13
2/26/09	Chap 1 Vocabulary	16
3/8/09	Leaf and animal	18
4/28/09	Bacteria Cell	20
4/28/09	Bacteria Part	21
5/6/09	Protozoa drawings	23
5/13/09	Fungi 2.3 Lab	25
5/11/09	Sponge and cnidaria Lab	27
5/18/09	Snail Lab	29
9/6/09	6th grade hopes and dreams	31
9/1/09	What plants need + photosynthesis	32
9/17/09	Questions for farmers	33
9/22/09	Garden Observation #1	34
10/05/09	Garden Observations #2	35

1

Using Our Notebooks

Once the notebook was formatted, it was then essential for teachers at each grade level to model the practice of putting a title and date at the top of each page, and even more important, putting each entry onto the table of contents page with its corresponding page number. It proved beneficial to either write the formatted entry on the board or to write the entry onto the overhead transparency showing the blank table of contents. Teachers circulated around the room to help any students who needed additional support. Usually after a few weeks students were able to complete this process more independently. Occasional reminders and notebook checks helped ensure this process was going smoothly. Each time students are asked to take notes from a class discussion or to add a lab handout to their notebook, they add a title to the page and an entry to the table of contents (Figure 12.2).

Teachers prompt students to refer to their table of contents pages when they are trying to find past work and encourage students to check their notebooks first when they have a question about previously covered material. Teachers also help students make the connections between current topics and past lessons. For example, when we prepare fourth-grade students for their field trip to an environmental research center on the Chesapeake Bay, we can have them refer to their pH notes from the third-grade chemistry unit. The third-grade notes on pH explain what pH measures, how to measure pH, and what are examples of acids and bases. The teacher needs to give only a quick review of pH before moving on to other aspects of water-quality testing, such as dissolved oxygen and turbidity.

Student's ability to quickly find their past notes and recall the information means that the teacher can spend more time on other important aspects of the topics at hand. Because students are accessing their prior knowledge, their understanding and connection to the learning is greatly enhanced.

Summative and Formative Assessment

Notebooks are reviewed by the teacher several times each quarter. As with traditional notebooks, we look at entries to check for students' understanding, ability to follow scientific processes, and level of completion. The rubric we used as both summative and formative assessment was designed using the format suggested by Lee-Ann Flynn (2008) in her article "In Praise of Performance-Based Assessments" (Figure 12.3).

We also have students assess themselves once each quarter on how well they are using and maintaining their notebooks as useful reference guides (Figure 12.4). This formative assessment piece allows us to determine the level of guidance students need with maintenance and for effective use. If the majority of students are successfully completing entries,

Figure 12.3

Sample rubric for summative and formative assessment

Science Notebook Assessment Rubric

Name_____ Date ___4-13-10___

3=Satisfactory   2=Needs Improvement   1=Unsatisfactory

Completed investigation/activity and wrote down information accurately

3   (2)   1   *Some of your responses were incomplete-check #3 +#5.*

Provided detailed descriptions using scientific terms

(3)   2   1   *Good labeling of each organism you observed.*

Made an accurate conclusion

3   (2)   1   *Think more about how the hydra's structure affects its movement.*

Demonstrated an understanding of scientific concept(s)

(3)   2   1

Demonstrated an understanding of scientific processes

(3)   2   1   *Conducted each part of the experiment accurately.*

Total points ___13/15___

Comments:

Great detail in your drawings but pay more attention to your written responses on the next lab.

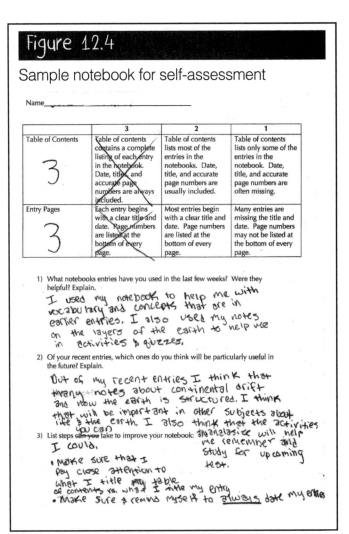

Figure 12.4

Sample notebook for self-assessment

Name_____

Table of Contents	3	2	1
Table of Contents 3	Table of contents contains a complete listing of each entry in the notebook. Date, title, and accurate page numbers are always included.	Table of contents lists most of the entries in the notebooks. Date, title, and accurate page numbers are usually included.	Table of contents lists only some of the entries in the notebook. Date, title, and accurate page numbers are often missing.
Entry Pages 3	Each entry begins with a clear title and date. Page numbers are listed at the bottom of every page.	Most entries begin with a clear title and date. Page numbers are listed at the bottom of every page.	Many entries are missing the title and date. Page numbers may not be listed at the bottom of every page.

1) What notebooks entries have you used in the last few weeks? Were they helpful? Explain.

I used my notebook to help me with vocabulary and concepts that are in earlier entries. I also used my notes on the layers of the earth to help me in activities & quizzes.

2) Of your recent entries, which ones do you think will be particularly useful in the future? Explain.

Out of my recent entries I think that many notes about continental drift and how the earth is structured. I think that will be important in other subjects about life & the earth. I also think that the activities you can will help me remember and study for upcoming test.

3) List steps can you take to improve your notebook:

I could.
- *Make sure that I pay close attention to what I title my table of contents vs. what I title my entry*
- *Make sure & remind myself to always date my entries*

then less time can be spent during class on formatting notebook entries. However, if students are having difficulty maintaining their notebooks, the teacher can decide to either work with a small group of students or conduct additional whole-class minilessons on notebook use.

Important Reference Tool

Science notebooks have long been recognized as "a tool for helping students become better questioners, observers, classifiers, and so on" (Campbell and Fulton 2003, p. 11). Our notebooks also help students become more purposeful about their learning and accountable for their prior understanding.

As students move through our science program, they become increasingly adept at taking good notes and making careful observations during labs. Having the same notebook each year tells students that work from previous years is important and that they can use their own knowledge to achieve success. Because students are asked to write in and use notebooks the same way each year, it also means that less class time is taken each year to teach students how to use this important tool.

With so much of our class work recorded in the notebooks, it has helped our teachers become more familiar with the concepts and skills that are covered at each grade level. This allows us to build on each other's work more successfully and make more efficient use of instructional time.

Finally, having students use their notebooks in this way brings them closer to real science. Scientists would never consider throwing away evidence of their hard work, nor would they fail to learn from previous experiments and research. We can provide our students with an authentic and meaningful way to make use of all their hard work by making their notebooks one of their most important reference tools.

References

Campbell, B., and L. Fulton. 2003. *Science notebooks: Writing about inquiry.* Portsmouth, NH: Heinemann.

Flynn, L. A. 2008. In praise of performance-based assessments. *Science and Children* 45 (8): 32–35.

NSTA Connection
Download a blank rubric and self-assessment at *www.nsta.org/SC1011*.

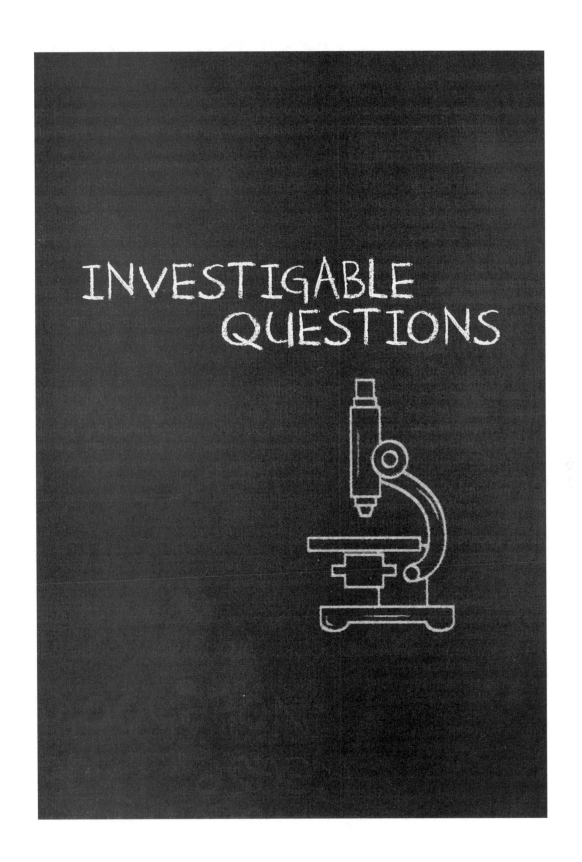

CHAPTER 13

Sparks That Ignite Inquiry

By Lawrence F. Lowery

Students ask questions all the time. They have natural curiosities about the world in which they live. *Why do trees lose their leaves in the fall? Where does the water come from on a windowpane? Why does the Moon look different tonight?* Teachers help pique this curiosity with engaging activities—making students want to know more.

Experienced teachers listen for and to students' questions to identify those that can be investigated. They know that such questions provide an opportunity for students to learn how to get answers for themselves.

Guided Inquiry

Teachers can help students ask investigable questions by modeling the way a scientist would ask them. During a lesson on the study of liquids, for example, a teacher might ask, "Do all the liquids you are studying evaporate at the same rate?" or "I think the alcohol will evaporate more quickly—how can we find out if it does?" During a study of electric circuits she might ask, "In what ways can we dim the brightness of a lit bulb?" or "I think removing a cell from the circuit will dim the bulb. How can we tell if my idea will work?" In a study of germinating different seeds, the teacher might ask, "Do the different seeds we have sprout at the same time?" or "I think the pea seeds will sprout first. How can we find out?" To recognize an investigable question, a teacher must first be able to generate such questions on their own.

The above questions are *guided inquiry* questions. The teacher formulates the question and knows the answer, but the answer is unknown to the students. They must engage in an inquiry to discover the answer. Note that the first question in each example is open-ended and the second is more hypothetical and suggests a way to design an inquiry. By modeling such questions, it will not be long before some students begin to phrase their own questions in the same way. Teachers are powerful models if they demonstrate what they ask students to do.

Open Inquiry

The teacher can make sure a question raised by students is investigable by asking, "If this were my question, could I do something to find out an answer using the resources available?" If he decides, "Yes, I could," then he can choose whether to allow students to engage in an *open inquiry* experience, one that is student-formulated and carried out through student-designed procedures. Open inquiry experiences enable students to investigate their own questions. They plan and carry out a procedure to get an answer. They gather, record, and analyze data, then formulate an interpretation of the data to answer their initial question. If the procedure does not provide an answer, they can reformulate their approach and try again. The payoff is that the students get better at collecting authentic information on their own. They gain confidence in their abilities to do this and they become better independent learners.

Teachers can increase the likelihood that students will ask investigable questions by providing hands-on experiences using provocative materials. Research-based science kits and programs provide simple materials that are developmentally appropriate for different grade levels. If a teacher does not have such a curriculum, a general guide for materials would be to engage primary level students with objects (living and nonliving) and their interactions (e.g., balance and motion, behaviors of animals, growth of plants). For upper grades, selecting materials that involve relationships and interactions in systems are of high interest to students (e.g., engineering electric circuits, modeling erosion and deposition using stream tables, putting together and separating mixtures and solutions, controlling variables).

Materials are often a novelty to students and stimulate curiosities. Watch how students touch, move, and explore objects made available to them. As they cause the materials to interact, more curiosities come to mind, and student questions begin to be asked.

Thinking for Themselves

Not all questions asked by students can or should be investigated. For these questions, teach the ways that stored knowledge can be found. For example, students can be given guidance on how the library or internet works, how knowledge can be gleaned from written materials such as articles and books, and how to determine whether the knowledge is accurate and valid. Such literature–research skills are important to learn.

It is sometimes difficult for teachers to enable students to think for themselves because a pervasive philosophy underpinning much of American education is that school experiences should pass on knowledge that has already been learned. Studies of classroom instruction reveal that teachers predominantly ask narrow questions that focus students on what is known (Flanders 1963). Narrow questions and questions that lead students to an answer are not inquiry questions. If this is the only way students are taught, educators are overlooking another goal of American education: Students should learn how to think and learn for themselves. Learning is a lifelong set of experiences—throughout most of our lives we do not have a teacher to guide us. Successful adults have confidence in their own ability to ask questions and to further their knowledge through various means of inquiry. Although investigable questions should be experienced in all fields of study (e.g., Language Arts, "What letter of the alphabet shows up more than any other in printed material?"), science instruction, because of its emphasis on inquiry, provides many opportunities and avenues for students to learn how to investigate their own curiosities.

Although there are general guidelines for enabling inquiry to take place in classrooms (provide appropriate hands-on opportunities using manipulative materials; capitalize on student curiosities and investigable questions), there is no recipe to follow to engage students in an inquiry. Personalities, styles, resources, beliefs, attitudes, and available time shape how inquiries are enabled or disabled in classrooms. What is important to remember is that to become an effective inquirer takes time. It is not accomplished with one experience. The ultimate goal is that teachers at all grade levels should provide at least several student-initiated inquiries in a school year. Direct inquiry experiences lead students toward independence, develop their self-confidence, and provide knowledge that is memorable (not knowledge that has to be memorized), because to do an investigation is personally satisfying and meaningful.

Reference

Flanders, N. A. 1963. Intent, action, and feedback: A preparation for teaching. *Journal of Teacher Education* 14: 251–260.

Resources

Christine, C. 2007. Teacher questioning in science classrooms. *Journal of Research in Science Teaching* 44: 815–843.

Koufetta-Menicou, C., and J. Scaife. 2000. Teachers' questions—Types and significance in science education. *School Science Review* 81: 29–84.

Ladd, G. T., and H. O. Anderson. 1970. Determining the level of inquiry in teachers' questions. *Journal of Research in Science Teaching* 7: 395–400.

CHAPTER 14

A Quest to Improve

Helping Students Learn How to Pose Investigable Questions

By Azza Sharkawy

If I had an hour to solve a problem and my life depended on it, I would use the first 55 minutes to formulate the right question because as soon as I have identified the right question I can solve the problem in less than five minutes.

—Albert Einstein

Questions are powerful tools that are central to scientific inquiry. Learning how to generate investigable questions—those that can be answered through empirical investigations—is identified as an important skill for all K–8 students (NRC 1996).

However, many of the questions students ask are not investigable questions that lend themselves to practical investigations (e.g., *Why does a mealworm become a beetle?*). A noninvestigable question does not lead students to collect data or firsthand evidence that will answer the question. Alternatively, students can answer an investigable question through systematic observations and interpretation of their data (e.g., *When do mealworms look like beetles? What does a mealworm look like before it begins to look like a beetle?* and *Do all worms become beetles?*).

Given the importance of investigable questions to scientific inquiry, what can teachers do to help students learn how to generate them? I explore the following possibilities in this article: (a) demonstrating to students that we value their questions, (b) providing students with opportunities to explore natural phenomena, (c) modeling asking investigable questions and providing examples of question stems, and (d) providing explicit practice identifying and refining questions.

Valuing Their Questions

Explicitly inviting students to raise questions in class and offering them positive reinforcement when they do helps create a question-asking culture in the classroom. Harlen and Qualter (2009) identified several types of questions that children ask:

1. Those that cannot be answered by science (e.g., metaphysical or philosophical questions);
2. Those that teachers do not know the answers to and are too complex for children to understand even if the answer were explained to them; and
3. Those that are simple requests for facts or definitions.

In Figure 14.1, I present Harlen and Qualter's (2009) suggestions on how to deal with children's different questions, which I have found helpful.

Because we encourage students to record ideas we consider important, providing them with multiple methods for recording their questions is another practice that demonstrates to students that we value their questions. Question boxes strategically placed in a science center provide an easy way to obtain students' questions, and because they can be anonymous, the boxes can capture a wider range of questions. A "Questions to Investigate" board that students are encouraged to contribute to provides a record of students' questions visible to all members of the classroom. Science notebooks provide students with a more private and personal record of their questions that they can refer to throughout the year and use to design independent or small-group investigations.

Natural Phenomena

Providing students with opportunities to explore a wide range of natural phenomena can stimulate their curiosity and inspire them to raise questions. For example, before a unit on plants, students can go on a nature hike, science journals in hand, and choose one or two plants to observe and record their observations. Examples of other topics commonly covered in the elementary curriculum that easily lend themselves to student exploration and observations include (a) characteristics and changes in animals, (b) everyday structures and movement, (c) properties of liquids and solids and rocks and minerals, (d) light and sound, and (e) daily and seasonal changes.

At the beginning of the year, encourage students to generate questions through a range of simple strategies:

- Invite students to make observations and then record questions that emerge from their observations. Some teachers ask students to form two columns in their science notebook; one with the heading, "Observations" and the other "Questions …" or "I notice" and "I wonder …."
- Elstgeest (2001) suggested asking attention-focusing questions such as "What do you notice about … ?" to encourage students to make qualitative observations (e.g., shape, color, behavior) and "How many/long/often…?" to invite students to make quantitative observations.
- Model for students "What happens if?" questions such as "What happens if we put the magnet under water?" Invite them to make up their own that they could investigate and answer either independently or with a partner.

Figure 14.1

Helpful suggestions from Harlen and Qualter (2009) on how to handle students' questions

Philosophical questions
(e.g., Why do we have animals?)
Validate student's question by acknowledging how interesting it is and pointing out that this is not a question that scientists can answer. This helps children begin to appreciate that science has limits; there are questions that scientists do not have the tools to answer.

Complex questions
(e.g., Why does the magnet stick to the nail?)
Turn the questions into related investigable questions by identifying variables you think may be relevant. In the above example, two variables involved include (a) the magnet and (b) the material the nail is made from. This is what Harlen and Qualter (2009) refer to as a *variable scan*.

Model turning students' "Why" question into "What would happen if" questions that involve changing one of the variables at a time. You can point out to the student that you are doing this because you want to think of things you can do to learn more.

For example, by changing the first variable (various characteristics of the magnet) one might come up with the following questions:

- What would happen if we put another object/metal close to the nail?
- What would happen if we put a small magnet close to the nail?
- What would happen if we put a magnet covered with masking tape close to the nail?

By changing the second variable (material the nail is made from) one might come up with the following questions:

- What would happen if we put a plastic nail close to the magnet?
- What would happen if we put paper next to the magnet?
- What would happen if we put a wet nail close to the magnet?

These questions model asking questions that lead to developmentally appropriate practical investigations and ones that broaden a child's understanding of factors that affect how magnets interact with different materials.

Questions requesting facts, names, etc.
(e.g., What is the name of this animal?)
Depending on the context, either encourage the student to find the answer in appropriate reference material or tell the student the answer.

Modeling and Question Stems

The questions we ask serve as models for our students. Students will develop a feel for what an investigable question sounds like when they hear a variety of investigable questions modeled for them by teachers. Krajcik, Czerniak, and Berger (1999) identified three categories of investigable questions: descriptive, relational, and cause–effect. Figure 14.2 outlines examples of each and possible question stems that can function as scaffolds for students new to posing investigable questions. Tell students that they should not feel restricted by these or other question stems because it is difficult, if not impossible, to create question stems that cover all possibilities and that are exclusive to each category.

Although modeling for students the skill of posing investigable questions can take place throughout a unit of study, I find the beginning of a unit a particularly good time to strategically model this skill. After exploring material related to the unit and recording observations and questions in their science notebooks, I invite students to share their ideas with the class. At this time, I take the opportunity to contribute some of my own questions—descriptive, relational, and cause–effect questions.

Once students have experience hearing the teacher's model turning complex questions into testable or investigable questions, they can be provided with the opportunity to practice doing the same. For primary students or those with limited experience asking investigable questions, teachers will likely need to provide more guidance or scaffolding and lead students through the process of writing good questions in small groups or with the entire class. Upper elementary students or those with more experience can be given a worksheet with a series of questions in nontestable form and in an adjacent column, one or two possible relevant variables they can use to produce a testable question. These variables can provide students with the necessary scaffolding they need until they develop the ability and confidence to independently identify variables that lead to good, testable questions. In the example below, the noninvestigable question (preferably taken from a list generated by the class or by students) is provided for students on the worksheet alongside the variables, temperature, and surface texture. Students are then encouraged to use the variables to write a question that could lead to empirical investigations. For example, for the question "Why do mealworms move so slowly?" students could be asked to consider the variables of temperature (At what temperature do mealworms move more slowly?) or surface (Do mealworms move more slowly on smooth or rough surfaces?).

Identifying and Refining Questions

Developing investigable questions is a skill that requires practice. Upper elementary students can benefit from classifying different questions written on index cards based on (a) whether they are investigable and (b) the type of investigable question. Provide students with a chance to independently and in small groups practice refining their questions or converting them into good investigable questions (e.g., the variable scan described in Figure 14.1). Challenge students to come up with two or three investigable questions related to a noninvestigable question they choose or pick out of a bag (e.g., Why does snow melt? Why do leaves fall off trees in the fall? Where do shadows come from?).

Although it may be more familiar for students to work on questions stemming from units they have already covered, students also enjoy working on questions listed on the class Questions

Figure 14.2

Three types of investigable questions

1. **Descriptive questions** produce qualitative or quantitative description of an object, material, organism, or event.

   Examples of possible question stems:
   What are the characteristics of _____?
   How many …? How often …? How much …?
   What happens when _____? (natural context implied; change not imposed)
   What happens if _____? (when you change something)

   Examples of descriptive questions:
   What kind of food do birds eat?
   Does brown sugar dissolve in water?
   What happens to leaves of maple trees when it snows?

2. **Relational questions** identify associations between the characteristics of different phenomena. These can include:
   • Identification and classification questions: identify phenomena and put them into meaningful groups;
   • Focused comparison questions: rank a group of materials based on a specific characteristic; and
   • Correlational questions: examine the extent that the presence of one variable is related to that of another variable (do not confirm cause-effect relationship).

   Examples of possible question stems:
   How are _____ similar to/different from _____?
   How can these _____be organized into groups?
   Which _____ (material/organism/etc.) is the most _____ (absorbent/strongest/best conductor/etc.)?
   How is _____ related to _____?

   Examples of relational questions:
   Is it easier to generate static electricity in a dry or humid room?
   Which material is more absorbent?
   How are these leaves similar and how are they different?
   How is the height of a plant related to the number of leaves? Do taller plants have more leaves?

3. **Cause–effect questions** determine whether one or more variables cause or affect one or more outcome variables.

   Examples of possible question stems:
   Does _____ cause/affect _____?
   How does _____ affect_____?

   Example of cause–effect questions:
   Does sunlight affect the growth of a plant?
   How does temperature affect the rate at which salt dissolves in water?

Figure 14.3

Checklist for evaluating questions

Is this question a good science classroom investigation question?

☐ **Good investigation questions are interesting.**
Am I interested in finding out the answer to this question?

☐ **Good investigation questions are those I do not already know the answers to.**
Do I already know the answer to this question?

☐ **Good investigation questions lead to a "plan of action" (a plan for what I need to do to answer the question, including the evidence I need to collect).**
Is this question written in a way that clarifies what I need to do (observe, measure, change, etc.) to answer it?

☐ **Good investigation questions are those that can be answered with available material.**
Will I be able to find the material I need to answer this question?

☐ **Good investigation questions are those that can be completed in a reasonable amount of time.**
Will I have the time I need to answer this question?

to Investigate board to which they contributed. Students can also generate, with teacher guidance, a list of good criteria that they can use to evaluate their investigable questions (Figure 14.3).

Achieving Awareness

By encouraging students to raise all kinds of questions and modeling good questioning skills in science class, we demonstrate to students how important questions are to scientific inquiry. And by asking students to refine and evaluate their questions, we promote the idea that asking good science investigation questions is a skill that requires careful thinking and editing and is a *process*—not something they should expect to accomplish instantaneously. Hopefully, this awareness will help students persist in their quest to improve their scientific-questioning skills.

References

Elstgeest, J. 2001. The right question at the right time. In W. Harlen, ed., *Primary science: Taking the plunge,* 25–47. Portsmouth, NH: Heinemann.

Harlen, W., and A. Qualter. 2009. *The teaching of science in primary school.* London: Routledge.

Krajcik, J., C. Czerniak, and C. Berger. 1999. *Teaching children science: A project-based approach.* Boston, MA: McGraw-Hill College.

National Research Council (NRC). 2006. *National science education standards.* Washington, DC: National Academies Press.

CHAPTER 15

Personalized Inquiry

Help Your Students Classify, Generate, and Answer Questions Based on Their Own Interests or Common Materials

By Patricia Simpson

Having taught K–12 students and preservice teachers for almost 20 years, I know the problems that arise when students are asked to generate an investigation of their own design. Like many of you, I have seen student presentations on the effects of music on plant growth, and I know how popular science fair idea books become each spring as science fair season begins.

But in the last few years, I used some different lessons that significantly increased the diversity and quality of the investigations students generated. These lessons helped students learn the variety of questions that scientists might use and strategies to generate research questions based on their own interests or materials that are commonly available to them.

What follows is a description of three lessons that I introduced to my preservice teachers as they attempted to generate personal full-inquiry projects and later successfully tried with students in grades 4–5.

Begin With Observations

The first day of class begins with an introduction to observations, with insects as our subject. I begin class by asking my students whether they have seen an ant, which of course they all have. So I ask them to each draw an ant with as much detail as possible. I visit each table of students to review their pictures and ask specific students to replicate their drawings on the board. I look for drawings that represent the greatest diversity. The pictures I see vary most in terms of the number and type of legs, body segments, and facial features. This activity not only generates interest in the ant's appearance but also creates an awareness that we don't always observe carefully.

Ants are not always available for observation in class, but because we study mealworm life cycles, I always have darkling beetles. I supply each group of four students with a large covered petri dish containing 8–10 darkling beetles. Safety note: Remind students to wash their hands after handling insects and to be careful not to injure the insects. I do a general introduction on criteria for effective observation, and armed with a plastic spoon and hand lens, the students write at least 10 observations of the darkling beetles. Focused observation of a real object or organism before generating questions is important. After sharing and critiquing the observations, I ask each student to write at least five questions about darkling beetles. I explain that each student will be asked to share at least one question with the class and that there will be no duplication of questions while sharing. I have found that asking students to write an assigned number of questions or observations keeps them focused. Knowing that the class will have to generate at least 24 questions, one per student, also helps stimulate their efforts. It also ensures that I will have lots of volunteers to share their questions because no one wants to have to come up with the 24th question.

Lesson 1: Classifying Questions

I list the questions on the board, and then as a group we try to classify the questions into categories based on how each one might be answered by a scientist. First is what we call *observational studies,* those that require a well-structured protocol for observation but can be answered with observation of the beetles. These are questions such as "how long do the beetles live?" The second category we identify as *experimental questions,* those that ask about the effect of some factor on darkling beetles. For example, "Does surface make a difference in the speed at which beetles move?" The third category is *literature-based research questions,* those that can be answered through research into what has already been discovered and reported by others—in this case, about darkling beetles. A typical question of this type might be, "What is the natural habitat of the darkling beetle?" These questions are answered by contacting beetle experts or reviewing the published literature. You could look at literature-based questions as a last resort or in some cases, a first step. All researchers do a survey of the literature to see what is already known and to build on that information. So, before we test whether mealworms can live on Cheerios, we might want to know if they eat grains or nectars. Still, I only use this category for questions that we cannot personally answer in a classroom setting, such as, "Where are they found in the world? What is their scientific name? Do they cause disease?" We also discover that some questions cannot be answered in science—largely those that ask why something wants to behave as it does. Figure 15.1 provides a sample of questions (with their classification) that a recent class generated about darkling beetles.

This activity is important because it helps students recognize that scientists may use a variety of strategies to gather data depending on the type of question they want to answer. Many of my students think all scientific research requires experiments. The National Science Education Standards (NRC 1996) point out the diversity of research strategies used by each science discipline and also provide examples of how an investigation of a single phenomenon may involve the use of various questions and their associated research strategies to fully investigate a topic. The lesson also helps students recognize that there are many questions that they can answer for themselves without having to be told or sent to find the answer online or in a book.

Lesson 2: Generating Questions

The next step for my students is to pose a researchable question for an experiment. For this step, I use another series of questions that Cothron, Giese, and Rezba (2006) developed. The idea is to take any topic, X, and then generate as many questions about that topic as possible. This process is designed to generate a variety of research questions on a single topic. The ques-

Figure 15.1

Examples of darkling beetle questions

Question	Type of question
How many legs do darkling beetles have?	O
What is the effect of temperature on the activity level of darkling beetles?	E
How many types of darkling beetles are there?	L
Do darkling beetles live in Minnesota?	L
How do darkling beetles reproduce?	O/L
What do they eat?	L/O
Do they lay eggs?	L/O
Can you use them for fish bait?	L
Do the beetles cooperate with each other?	O/L
Why do beetles flip over on their backs?	N

E = experimental question; L = literature-based question; N = question not answered in science; and O = observational question

tions are (1) What materials are readily available for conducting experiments on X? (2) How does X act? (3) How can you change the set of materials to affect the action of X? and (4) How can you measure or describe the response of X to the change?

I start this lesson by reminding students of the coleus plants (*Solenestemon* spp.) we grew from cuttings. We answer the four questions as a class by using the knowledge we gained from keeping journals on the coleus over a period of weeks.

In response to question 1, in our classroom some of the materials we have available include types of soil, different sizes and types of cups, light sources, water, and fertilizers. Our response to question 2 is that coleus plants grow roots, stems, leaves, flowers, and buds of various types. For question 3, we discuss changing the types and relative amounts of soils; sizes of cups and depth of planting in cups; the type, amount, method, and scheduling of water; and various concentrations of fertilizers.

We answer question 4 by discussing our ability to measure changes in growth of plant leaves by measuring the size of a leaf, the average size of all plant leaves, or the number of leaves. We list the length of roots, concentrations of root hairs, and the number of days it takes for roots to appear on a cutting. Stem growth might be measured by overall stem length, stem width, or increased length of internodes. Then we use the information on the board to form questions. Sample questions include:

- What is the effect of varying periods of light on the color of coleus leaves?
- What is the effect of water temperature on the number of days before roots appear on coleus cuttings?

- Does phase of the Moon have an effect on the number of days it takes before coleus cuttings sprout roots?
- Does percentage of sand in soil have an effect on the growth of coleus stems?
- Does type of watering, above soil or through soil, have an effect on the number of leaves a coleus plant produces?

It's one thing to do this as a whole class, but I find that when students have to transfer this process to a new subject it can become more difficult for them, so our final step is to work through a series of stations.

Lesson 3: Series of Stations

The goal for the stations is to continue assisting students in learning how to create their own research questions. I select four topics, objects, or phenomena with which I think most students are familiar, and we practice within these new areas. Teachers can decide on the area that relates to their topic of study, using the Standards as a guide. I establish a station for each topic at a table. It includes the object or phenomena along with a list of materials that I tell students we have available in the classroom. Each list includes 5–10 items along with an opportunity for students to ask for any other two materials. I call these their *wild card* choices. We assume that the classroom also contains any measurement tools they might commonly find in a science classroom.

As a group of three or four, students spend 30 minutes at the first station and must answer all four questions in regard to the station and then write five researchable questions with their answers to the four questions. The remaining stations take less time to complete as the students improve in writing questions, so I allow about 20 minutes at each of the remaining three stations. By the last station they are very comfortable with the process and seem to be able to transfer their skills at generating questions to a topic from home. See Figure 15.2 for a list of station ideas, material lists, and student responses to questions.

Assessment

When we first begin using the questions, I assess students' work by their ability to answer each question and then use that information to generate questions in an appropriate format (one that demonstrates the effect of one variable on another). But eventually, I ask them to use a checklist to evaluate the questions based on the following criteria:

- Does the question ask *what* happens, not *why?*
- Does the question study something observable?
- Are the materials needed to investigate the question available?
- Is the scope of the investigation sufficiently limited?
- Are all but one variable being controlled?
- Is there a behavior to measure?
- Do tools (mechanisms) exist for measurement?
- Is there sufficient time for the investigation?
- Does the researcher have necessary skills?
- Is the topic of interest to the researcher?

Figure 15.2

Sample stations

Station 1. Corn-based foam packing peanuts

What materials are available?
Books, water of various temperatures, plastic bags, hard-boiled eggs, hammers, wild cards
How do the peanuts act?
Dissolve, cushion, float, compress
How can you change the materials?
Change the temperature or water, smash peanuts
How can you measure the response of peanuts to the change?
Measure ability to cushion eggs, observe time to dissolve
Sample questions
What is the effect of peanut compression on the ability of the peanuts to cushion an egg?
What is the effect of water temperature on the rate at which peanuts dissolve?

Station 2. Gobstoppers

What materials are available?
Salt, water of various temperatures, spoons, cups, wild cards
How do Gobstoppers act?
Dissolve, change color, float
How can you change the materials?
Change density of water with salt, change temperature of water
How can you measure the response of Gobstoppers to the change?
Measure speed of color change, observe floating
Sample questions
What is the effect of salt concentration on a Gobstopper's ability to float?
What is the effect of water temperature on the speed at which Gobstoppers dissolve?

Safety note: Do not allow students to mix Gobstoppers with any acids (even weak ones like vinegar) or eat in the lab.

Station 3. Paper plates

What materials are available?
Scissors, wax, tape, dirt, mustard, wild cards
How do paper plates act?
Roll, fly, stain, decompose, hold food
How can you change the materials?
Reshape the plate, cover plate with wax, cut it into smaller pieces, cover it with mustard
How can you measure the response of the plate?
Measure distance it flies, measure mass it can hold, measure rate of decomposition, measure rate for staining
Sample questions
What effect does size of paper plate pieces have on the rate of decomposition?
What effect does depth of wax covering on the plate have on time it takes to stain the plate?
What effect does shape of the plate have on the distance it can fly?

Station 4. Mealworms

What materials are available?
Petri dishes, paper towels, light sources, food sources
How do mealworms act?
Molt, move, grow, reproduce
How can you change the materials?
Change surface, change temperatures, change foods
How can you measure the response of the mealworms?
Count the number of worms, size of worms, and days between changes in stages
Sample questions
What effect does the type of food have on the number of mealworms produced?
What effect does the temperature of culture have on the days between stages?
What effect does the surface have on the speed of mealworms?

Investigating the Familiar

I have used some variation of these questions with almost every one of the classes I teach and with teacher workshops. It seems to work equally well with students of all abilities as long as the students are initially familiar with the object or phenomenon they are working with. Familiarity with the topic is key. Some teachers suggest that students will generate more questions if they are working with an unfamiliar object or novel phenomenon, but in my experience, students spend more time being surprised or amused by what they see rather than framing questions.

The more practice students have with this process, the less they seem to need it. Over the course of the semester, I find that students become more aware of the possibilities for research that exist with each topic we examine. And their questions extend beyond the classroom—my nephew started to ask his father about the relationship between the size and shape of logs being cut for firewood and its effect on burning time after he had learned this strategy for questioning. A student who was making Christmas cookies began to ask about the relationship between the type and temperature of the shortening used in the recipe and the crispiness of the cookies—how's that for personalized inquiry!

References

Cothron, J. H., R. N. Giese, and R. J. Rezba. 2006. *Students and research: Practical strategies for science classrooms and competitions.* 4th ed. Dubuque, IA: Kendall/Hunt Publishing Company.

National Research Council (NRC). 1996. *National science education standards.* Washington, DC: National Academies Press.

CHAPTER 16

Picture This!

*First Graders Explore School Grounds
With Cameras in Search of
Science and Wind Up Learning About
How Objects Rust*

By Leslie Bradbury, Lisa Gross, Jeff Goodman, and William Straits

Early in the school year, we took first-grade students on a walk around the school grounds and asked them to take pictures of familiar objects that represent science. Students were enthusiastic as they realized that so many common objects relate to science in some way—from the cracks in the pavement and ants marching at the base of a tree, to the balanced seesaws and flags fluttering in the wind. In addition to sparking student interest and curiosity, this walk served to assess students' knowledge about their surroundings and to use these foundational experiences for instructional planning.

We found the school yard to be a rich source for authentic science questions. Along our walk, a small group of students came across a pumpkin with one side completely caved in, exposing the seeds within. These students not only wanted to share what they thought had happened but also had comments and questions about the smell. In the point and click of a digital camera, the moment had been captured, and the images saved as a spark for further investigation!

Preparing for Exploration

Children today become technologically savvy quickly; our first graders were surprisingly familiar with digital cameras from home. However, students were reminded that in this situation our cameras were important tools for scientific investigation. The cameras that we used were funded by our college of education; they are available to classroom teachers for student use. Before we started, we reviewed the basics of framing, focusing, and shooting pictures with our students, and reinforced that the cameras needed to be treated with care. We then provided small groups of three to four students with a camera and instructed them to take pictures of science-related images that they noticed on the walk. Safety note: Follow your school guidelines for outdoor explorations and safety considerations.

A photographic survey of "Science in the Schoolyard," such as this rusty nail, led to a class investigation.

Revisiting Bloom's Taxonomy

In our attempt to develop higher-order thinking skills through questioning, we have found Bloom's taxonomy to be a valuable tool to prompt our own reflection and to guide us as we help students to generate investigable questions. Anderson and Krathwohl (2001) presented a revised version of this framework that we have found especially useful. In it, the six cognitive dimensions are now actively described by verbs. Both teachers and students can develop a range of questions about the digital images collected using the categories of the taxonomy. Figure 16.1 provides an overview of this revised taxonomy including a brief description of the types of questioning words used.

Although teachers do not need to memorize specific taxonomic classifications of questions, it is important that students generate questions beyond the Understanding or Remembering level (Figure 16.1). By reviewing the class's questions as recorded in the PowerPoint presentation and considering them in light of the revised Bloom's taxonomy, teachers can push themselves and their students toward more complex thinking. Teachers might decide to record all of the questions that students ask within a lesson and then identify the types of questions most frequently asked. Share that information with students and then focus on trying to generate more questions that are higher-level. With encouragement and modeling, students will begin to naturally ask questions that promote higher-order thinking. Another benefit of the revised taxonomy with its emphasis on active verbs is that the transition from asking questions to conducting investigations is easy to facilitate.

At the outset we provided some gentle guidance to help students look for science images in a wide range of places, as in our experience some students initially focused only on human-made objects, such as cars or computers. Throughout the process we kept in mind that our goal was to broaden students' perceptions of what science is and at the same time empower them to explore what interested them.

Generating Questions

Back in the classroom, each group of students reviewed their photographs and chose images they found most interesting to learn more about. While still in their groups, students spent time brainstorming about their images; they shared what they knew and generated a list of questions. The selections were downloaded and imported into a PowerPoint presentation in which teachers typed some of the students' questions on the images. In this way, we not only helped students to use images to develop good questions but also leveraged the power of the visual to support language development.

The next day, each group's images were projected onto the screen for the whole class to see and group members briefly introduced the selection and questions for the class to consider. We then opened the floor for additional questions or curiosities of the group. As the class discussed the images, we recorded their ideas in the notes section of the PowerPoint presentation. Because our primary objective was the development of student questioning skills, we noted the types of questions asked to document student growth. Our initial goal was to steer students away from basic *What is this?* queries and to direct them to ask *why?* and *how?* (see Revisiting Bloom's Taxonomy for more about developing students' questioning skills.) We also facilitated discussions to help students construct some questions

Figure 16.1

Revised taxonomy and questions

Bloom's category	Questions that ask the learner to	Student questions about digital photos
Creating	Generate, plan, produce	• Develop a plan to grow the biggest pumpkin and keep it for Halloween. • Design a metal support structure that does not rust when exposed to natural forces over time.
Evaluating	Check, critique	• What would be the best way to keep a pumpkin from rotting? • Steel, iron, or tin? Which metal is the best material for an outdoor patio set?
Analyzing	Differentiate, organize, deconstruct	• What factors make a pumpkin rot? • Why do some metals not rust?
Applying	Execute, implement	• When do you plant pumpkin seeds to have pumpkins at Halloween? • Why does it take some things longer to rust than others?
Understanding	Interpret, classify summarize, infer, compare, or explain ideas or concepts	• How does rotting help a pumpkin plant? • Why do materials rust?
Remembering	Recognize, recall	• What are the parts of a pumpkin plant? • What color is rust?

that could be explored directly. With help, they learned to change a broad question such as, *Why do dandelions have fuzzy heads?* into a more readily testable form, *How far can the wind carry different kinds of seeds?*

Because science is truly all around us, every picture has the potential for students to build on existing knowledge, share personal connections, and explore interpretations of a particular image. Questions lead to investigating. For example, in our walk around the school grounds, we noticed that many students had taken pictures of objects that were rusting and during discussion had formed some ideas about how and why objects rust. Group members asked, *What causes an object to rust? Do only metal objects rust? Do all metal objects rust?* Realizing that this topic fit into curricular content related to properties of objects and materials, we encouraged the students to pursue their interests.

Investigating Rust

Working with small groups, we spent one day developing questions and designing plans for the inquiries to follow. On the next day, students set up their investigations. One group of students put washers made of different materials in small cups of water and observed what happened to them over several weeks. They were surprised to discover that the stainless steel and zinc washers showed no rust, thus challenging their thinking that all metals rust. Another group questioned whether water was the only liquid that had the potential to cause rust; for their inquiry, they put drywall screws into cups of water, Sprite, and orange juice and observed changes over time.

As students made observations, they were encouraged to use the digital cameras once again, but this time to collect data about their investigations. After putting the pictures in their science journals, they wrote words or short sentences to describe what they saw. Once the students had completed their initial hands-on investigations, we followed up by finding additional information from books and websites. In this process, we have two goals: (1) to help young students see how they can extend their thinking through research and (2) to help students recognize that not all information is equally useful or trustworthy. However, given the overwhelming amount of information available online and in the library, it is important for teachers to preselect some related websites and books that are at an appropriate level for their students (see Print and Internet Resources). Using this manageable collection of resources, the teacher then can model the process of gathering and assessing information. Results from the first round of work prompted further questions, and students were able to follow up by developing additional tests. For example, students wondered whether conditions such as light and dark might affect rusting and set up new investigations. In this way, the students' own observations and photographs led to several investigable questions that served as a basis for ongoing scientific inquiries.

As groups reported their findings, we discussed what was learned in the process. We engaged in a discussion about how the group's questions led to different actions and outcomes. The students who explored the rusting of washers were able to talk through the steps taken and, with guidance, explain what was meant by a fair test. The class concluded that some questions could be answered through hands-on investigations, whereas others required seeking additional information from class textbooks, trade books, or online resources.

A Personal Connection

Digital photography energizes students and focuses their attention on their environment. The personal connection to science helps students develop a habit of mind in which everything they see inside or outside of school can prompt them to wonder and investigate.

This tool provides students with means for observing virtually any science topic—weather, living things, ecosystems, matter, forces and motion—and investigating questions about it. Creating questions promotes higher-level thinking and is an engaging way for students to develop vocabulary that is descriptive and specific.

Working in this way reinvigorates students' and teachers' sense of wonder and ongoing engagement with science. Picture this—a classroom full of scientists noticing the world around them and seeking answers to their own questions!

Acknowledgment

The authors thank Reich College of Education at Appalachian State University for support through a Successful Applications of Learning Technologies grant.

Reference

Anderson, L. W., and D. R. Krathwohl. 2001. *A taxonomy for learning, teaching, and assessing: A revision of Bloom's taxonomy of educational objectives.* New York: Longman.

Resources

Stille, D. R. 2006. *Chemical change: From fireworks to rust.* Minneapolis, MN: Compass Points Books.

Zoehfeld, K. 1998. *What is the world made of? All about solids, liquids, and gases.* New York: HarperCollins.

Internet Resource

How does rust work?
http://science.howstuffworks.com/question445.htm

DATA
COLLECTION and
REPRESENTATION

CHAPTER 17

Helping Young Learners Make Sense of Data: A 21st-Century Capability

By Joseph Krajcik

Knowing how to read, interpret, and see trends in graphs is a critical 21st-century capability; it is a skill that all learners use throughout their lives because it helps judge whether a claim is supported by evidence. A major aspect of doing science (in and out of the classroom) is asking questions about how the world works and then designing investigations to collect and analyze data that will provide solutions to those questions (Duschl, Schweingruber, and Shouse 2007; McNeill and Krajcik 2011; NRC 1996, 2000). But once your students collect data, how can you help them make sense of that data?

Young students are capable of asking questions—like *How many different types of birds come to my bird feeder?*—designing and carrying out investigations, and then analyzing data to use as evidence to support claims that respond to their questions (Duschl, Schweingruber, and Shouse 2007; Metz 1995; NRC 1996, 2000). *Data organization and analysis* is the process of making observations, taking measurements, and sorting out the information in ways that facilitate sensemaking, allowing possible patterns to become apparent.

The ability to analyze data is an essential aspect of scientific literacy and will be critical for young children as they grow in a world that is filled with information. To make sense of data, scientists transform it into various representations. By creating tables, graphs, diagrams, or other visualizations, children can transform data into different forms that will allow them, just as it allows scientists, to see patterns and trends. Helping young children see the value in creating these different representations will build important stepping stones to develop tools they can use throughout their lives. When learners grapple with data to support claims, their understanding of the science content changes, and their image of what science *is* also changes.

An Example

Young children often collect tallies or counts of data to answer questions. For example, children in a third-grade classroom might explore what types of birds visit their school bird feeder. The children might make a record of the type and number of birds that visit their bird feeder.

A simple list of information might be difficult for children to see a pattern. Children can create a table to more easily see the pattern. The table helps children see the type of bird and how frequently each type visits their feeder. The transformation helps learners see trends in data. For example, sparrows are the most common bird that visit the feeder.

Once students have constructed their tables, they should write summaries describing what their tables mean. In this case, a child might write, *Sparrows visited our bird feeder more than other birds.* Such summaries are another way to transform data. Students could also construct tables for qualitative data that provide descriptive rather than numeric (quantitative) accounts (e.g., students could add a column to their table that describes the type of chirping the bird makes).

Children could even create graphs of data to make a visual representation. Graphs show how one variable (dependent) changes or relates to another variable (the independent). Transforming data into graphs will help students see trends in quantitative data. To continue with our bird example, rather than a count of the type of birds, students could create a bar graph. A bar graph of the number versus types of birds is much easier for students to "read" because it more effectively illustrates patterns. In elementary classrooms, students can transform their data into pie charts, bar graphs, histograms, and line graphs (NCTM 2000).

Supporting Students

Making and interpreting tables and graphs are cognitively challenging tasks for children (Duschl, Schweingruber, and Shouse 2007); however, with the support of teachers, it is within the intellectual capability of all learners. You can support children in this important scientific practice by modeling, giving feedback, and allowing them to critique one another's graphs and interpretations (Krajcik and Czerniak 2007).

Another way to support students is to have them come up with statements that describe what the graph means. Have them look for a pattern or a trend in the shape of the graph. Once students have written their own interpretation, members of the group can compare the statements. If your students are too young to write, you can have them say what they see. You can further support them in this process by using sentence starters, such as the following:

The bird that we saw at the bird feeder most often was a _____. We saw the _____ at the bird feeder _____ times.

Although such prompts are helpful to start students learning how to interpret charts and graphs, you do not want to use this type of support too often, otherwise students could see science as filling in the blanks.

Conclusion

Providing opportunities for students to ask questions about scientific phenomena that they encounter in their world is a critical aspect of students learning science. Asking questions leads to students designing ways to collect data to support their claims with evidence. Transforming data into graphs and charts can help students better see trends in the data. Crafting such learning opportunities will support all students in developing critical scientific practices and developing 21st-century capabilities that they will use throughout their lives as lifelong learners.

References

Duschl, R. A., H. A. Schweingruber, and A. Shouse. 2007. *Taking science to school: Learning and teaching science in grades K–8.* Washington, DC: National Academies Press.

Krajcik, J. S., and C. Czerniak. 2007. *Teaching science in elementary and middle school classrooms: A project-based approach,* third ed. London, England: Taylor and Francis.

McNeill, K. L., and J. Krajcik. 2011. *Supporting grade 5–8 students in constructing explanations in science: The claim, evidence and reasoning framework for talk and writing.* New York: Pearson Allyn & Bacon.

Metz, K. E. 1995. Reassessment of developmental constraints on children's science instruction. *Review of Educational Research* 65: 93–128.

National Council of Teachers of Mathematics (NCTM). 2000. *Principles and standards for school mathematics.* Reston, VA: NCTM.

National Research Council (NRC). 1996. *National science education standards.* Washington, DC: National Academies Press.

National Research Council (NRC). 2000. *Inquiry and the national science education standards: A guide for teaching and learning.* Washington, DC: National Academies Press.

CHAPTER 18

Early Primary Invasion Scientists

First Graders Engage in Real Research to Help Battle Invasive Plants

By Katie V. Spellman and Christine P. Villano

"We really need to get the government involved," said one student, holding his graph up to USDA scientist Steve Seefeldt. Dr. Steve studies methods to control *invasive* plants, plants that have been introduced to an area by humans and have potential to spread rapidly and negatively affect ecosystems. The first grader and his classmates had become invasive plant scientists themselves during a yearlong inquiry of invasive plants in Alaska. In this meeting, the students had called on a colleague for advice about their findings. They had discovered something no older scientist had yet uncovered. The invasive plant commonly known as bird vetch (*Vicia cracca*) could threaten nearby areas that had been burned by recent wildfires. It was time to communicate their science to fellow experts and act.

Up until about 10 years ago, few land managers, educators, or scientists had paid much attention to invasive plants in the far North. However, the rate of invasive plant-spread has rapidly accelerated (Carlson and Shephard 2007) and is likely influenced by changing climate and increasing human disturbances. Little is known about how invasive plants will act in arctic and subarctic ecosystems around the globe, and research is sorely needed. Who would have thought that early primary students could be capable of rising to help meet this need? We did! Our mother-daughter team—a first-grade teacher and plant ecologist—knew that these students could offer real research to aid in Alaska's battle against invasive plants. We believed that given the right opportunity to observe the ecosystems around them, to interact with scientists, and to use cooperative-learning techniques to accomplish challenging scientific tasks, these young learners could significantly contribute to the knowledge gap on this issue.

Noticing a Problem

On a field trip to a local wildlife refuge, Mrs. Villano and fellow Denali Elementary teacher Deana Martin-Muth's first-grade classes noticed a beautiful purple flower growing all over

PHOTOGRAPH COURTESY OF THE AUTHORS

Students visit a nearby forest fire site with ecologists at the Bonanza Creek Long Term Ecological Research Program's Caribou-Poker Creeks Research Watershed.

the fields. Mrs. Villano's daughter, who the children called "Scientist Katie," had come along on the trip as a chaperone.

Scientist Katie told the story of what the refuge was like when she was a little girl. The fields had native wild irises and many types of grasses and wildflowers. There were only a few individual plants of that pretty purple flower, invasive bird vetch, which now covers the fields. What had caused the bird vetch to spread so rapidly? Was the bird vetch the reason there are few wild irises left in the fields? Katie told the kids how science could be used to answer these questions.

Immediately, the kids began collecting seeds in plastic bags (making sure no seeds escaped!) to do their own investigations back in the classroom. As they collected their seeds, they noticed that portions of the field had been burned. To help create optimal wildlife habitat for migrating birds, the refuge often burned portions of the fields. "What if the vetch likes the burned fields?" one student asked. What if…?

Field Data Collection

Fueled by the observations the students made at the wildlife refuge, we began to investigate both invasive plants and fire. We took the 50 first graders to a nearby burn area in the Bonanza Creek Long Term Ecological Research (LTER) Station's Caribou-Poker Creeks Research Watershed. The students worked with Katie and her fellow LTER ecologists to collect data just as the scientists do. The scientists showed them a real study site in the burn where they had planted different types of trees to see how the forest would regenerate, counted seeds that fell into the burn, and looked at how the permafrost (soil that is frozen all year) changed after the fire.

After the scientists modeled how to collect data and how to make good observations, the first graders made their own observations of burned and unburned forest sites. We made simple data sheets on which students were asked to make detailed drawings and observe the soil, light, and groundcover in each site. Was the soil in the old forest and the burn moist or dry? Were plants on the ground getting full light or were there shadows? What was covering the ground: moss, lichen, bare soil, rocks, or charcoal? The students then conducted a simplified vegetation transect just as the LTER scientists did. Scientists use vegetation transects, or lines of a known length through a plant community, to help reduce the amount of counting they have to do to understand how many plants are in their study area. The transect is randomly placed in the plant community to help remove bias from the data. We counted the number of trees at each site by counting the tree trunks we could touch with our arms outstretched as we walked along a 30 m measuring tape. We then did a group count of tree seedlings in three 25 cm × 25 cm quadrats along each transect. Normally, a scientist would collect information from many transects in their study area and count the number of seedlings in more than three quadrats. However, these simplified field sampling techniques allowed early primary students to successfully participate in the collection of valid field data. In addition, the variety of observation approaches (drawing, counting, moving, and thinking) allowed a diversity of learners to successfully complete field data collection.

Finally, each student collected soil cores from the burned and unburned sites for experiments back in the classroom. Soil cores were collected by drilling vertically into the soil with a bulb planter and removing a plug of soil. To transport the cores back to the school, the intact soil core was then placed in plant pots of the same diameter and depth as the bulb planter.

Safety note: Follow your school guidelines for field trips and outdoor explorations. Be aware of hazards on site, such as dangerous terrain or harmful plants or animals. Make sure students wash their hands after touching soil and plants. When working in an area infested with invasive plants, be sure students have brushed any seeds, plant parts, or soil clumps off of shoes and clothing before leaving the site.

Figure 18.1

Experimental setup for a study comparing invasive plant growth in soil cores to burned and unburned forest sites

Classroom Data Collection

Armed with their observations from the wildlife refuge and the wildfire sites, students were ready to start their investigation. Several questions emerged from our field experiences, such as *Can a bird vetch plant grow under a spruce tree? Can a bird vetch plant tangle and kill an animal?* We kept coming back to the big "what if" question that emerged from our trip to the wildlife refuge: "What if bird vetch likes the burned fields?" We focused our study on a topic that we could address in our classroom during the cold Alaskan winter, and a question that would allow us to use science to help our community. We chose one major question: Would invasive bird vetch grow better in soil from a burned forest or an unburned forest? Students took seeds from bird vetch that they had collected on their refuge field trip and grew them in the soil cores they had taken from the burned and unburned field sites (Figure 18.1). Seeds were sown on the top of the soil core to mimic wild dispersal patterns. The students diligently observed and measured their plants for three months. Observation with science notebooks helped build science process skills, incorporate math and literacy, and encourage learning for a purpose. We modeled how to make good scientific drawings using concepts to which early primary students can readily connect such as shape, size, and color. When a student began to draw daisies in her journal, we used questioning to help refine her observations. Did you really see a daisy? What shape was the leaf? What color was the flower? This questioning process allowed the students to engage in more meaningful thinking and review their own work. This teacher review and self-reflection process with their science notebooks allowed formative evaluation throughout the project.

Ensuring accurate data collection in early primary student experiments is often challenging. For example, can you be sure all students are using their rulers correctly? We relied heavily on cooperative learning within small groups to ensure data quality. "Everyone check your shoulder partner," Mrs. Villano would say before a measuring session. "Is the ruler in the right direction? Is your partner using centimeters and not inches?" Upon corrections or consent, the vetch measuring could proceed.

At the end of an investigation with invasive plants, be sure to carefully dispose of plant material and soils. To do this, double bag all materials in durable plastic bags and dispose in a landfill or incinerator.

Age-Appropriate Data Analysis

For students to fully experience doing what real scientists do, they need to participate in data analysis. This presents a major hurdle for most early primary classrooms in which essential mathematic concepts involved in analyzing data, like averages, are not developmentally appropriate. By using teacher modeling and a peer–partner approach to compiling student data, the first graders were able to succeed at a high level. In partners, one student read aloud her invasive plant height measurement for the burned and unburned soil cores for each date, and the partner recorded the numbers in a table. Student partners then transferred these numbers into an Excel spreadsheet on the computer. Using a computer projector, we were able to guide the young students in how to click on a cell and type in a number. One partner would read the numbers from their table aloud, while the second partner would highlight the cell and hunt for the numbers on the keyboard. Teacher modeling and supervision played an important role in making sure all student pairs were typing in the correct spreadsheet cell and pushing the correct button to create a graph. Using this approach, every student was able to produce a computer line graph of the changes in plant height over time (Figure 18.2). When we printed the graphs, students were incredibly proud and felt like bona fide scientists.

To summarize the data from all first graders who conducted this experiment, we had to deal with the problem of averages. This was the most difficult concept for the students throughout the whole study. To introduce the idea of an average, we lined the students

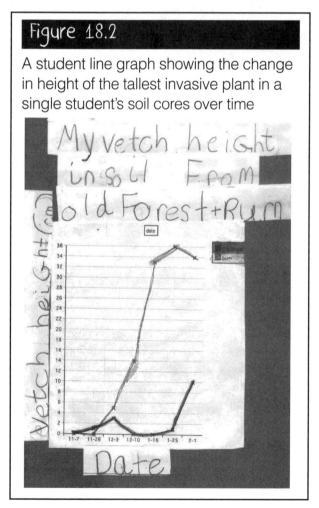

Figure 18.2

A student line graph showing the change in height of the tallest invasive plant in a single student's soil cores over time

up by height and grouped them into tall, medium, and short categories. If we only looked at one student, and said all first graders were that height, would that be true? Were more students in the tall, medium, or short category? Can plant heights be compared to first-grader heights? Through this visual and kinetic demonstration, we were able to give students a rudimentary understanding of how scientists use averages to summarize their findings. The students then took the average plant heights and made bar graphs of the final results (Figure 18.3). Using plenty of teacher modeling and guidance, we read the plant heights aloud as student pairs added the numbers on calculators and divided by the number of students. Bird vetch had, on average, grown taller in soil cores from the burned forest than in cores from the unburned forest.

The first graders used the observations of their soil cores

A close-up view of bird vetch

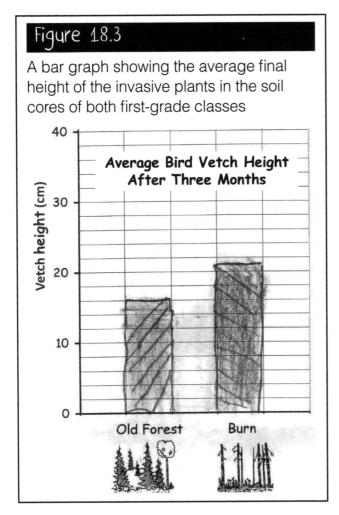

Figure 18.3

A bar graph showing the average final height of the invasive plants in the soil cores of both first-grade classes

to make conclusions and explain their results. *The soil from the old forest had lots of moss, but the soil from the burn has tiny moss. I think the moss was like a helmet, protecting the old forest from the invader's seeds*, Marley wrote in her science notebook. Drawing from knowledge gained from their field observations, students were able to use inference skills to forecast which habitat the bird vetch would grow best in the field. Jack wrote in his science notebook, *If Alaska keeps getting warmer and drier, there will be more fires. I think vetch will keep spreading in the burns.* We used the students' completed science notebooks as the summative evaluation for the project. We assessed the observation skills of students, age-appropriate mastery of science process skills, and ability to extend their data into meaningful conclusions. After making conclusions about their investigation, these young learners were able to extend their new knowledge to ask new questions and to address the big "what if" question that began the project during their wildlife refuge trip. Perhaps burning the fields at the refuge really was helping the bird vetch grow out of control.

Putting the Data Into Action

The search for answers to the student's new questions provided an avenue to further knowledge and to communicate their results with scientists. No researcher had ever looked at how bird vetch might act in burned areas in boreal forests, and scientists were interested in the first graders' results. They presented their journals to scientists at real conferences with LTER and invasive plant ecologists.

The kids felt completely empowered by their knowledge and felt ownership over their scientific contribution to the state. The first graders designed "first-grade vetch scientist" t-shirts and went to community fairs armed with pamphlets on invasive plants. By the first week of school the next year, the students went back to the wildlife refuge to conduct a gigantic invasive plant pull. In a matter of two hours, the students had pulled over a half-ton of bird vetch. As a result of this action, the refuge began actively managing the fields for invasive plants. The first graders' data convinced the land managers to shift the timing of their controlled burn to before the vetch was going to seed. Meaningful science and an impassioned group of six- and seven-year-olds had an incredible effect on our community.

To extend the vision of this activity, we were able to create *Weed Wackers! A K–6 Educator's Guide to Invasive Plants of Alaska* (see Internet Resources). With this curriculum guide, and teacher workshops around the state, we are taking action ourselves. We want more students thinking like scientists, engaging in relevant ecological study, and making a difference.

Reference

Carlson, M. L., and M. Shephard. 2007. Is the spread of non-native plants in Alaska accelerating? In *Meeting the Challenge: Invasive Plants in Pacific Northwestern Ecosystems,* PNW-GTR-694, eds. T. B. Harrington and S. H. Reichard, 111–127. Portland, OR: USDA Forest Service, PNW Research Station.

Resources

Batten, M. 2003. *Aliens from Earth: When animals and plants invade other ecosystems.* Atlanta, GA: Peachtree Publishers.
Souza, D. M. 2003. *Plant invaders.* New York: Watts Library.

Internet Resources

For lessons and ideas on planning a similar study with your students:
Center for Invasive Plant Management
    www.weedcenter.org/education/k-12.html
National Invasive Species Information Center
    www.invasivespeciesinfo.gov/resources/educk12.shtml
Weed Wackers!
    http://weedwackers.wikispaces.com

CHAPTER 19

Measure Lines

Students in Grades 3–5 Explore Weight and the Nature of Matter Using Investigations From the Inquiry Project

By Sally Crissman

Data are at the heart of science. Within data lies evidence that can be used to support a claim; anchor a discussion or debate; and ultimately, answer scientific investigation questions. A challenge for educators is finding ways to help young children make sense of data in the science classroom.

Children typically begin working with data during math activities. They learn to collect, organize, and represent information. They are introduced to some conventional representations used in science, such as Venn diagrams, bar graphs, and line plots. Despite this prior experience working with data, students often need plenty of time to review data literacy concepts and skills when they are asked to apply them in the context of a science investigation. Science "ups the ante" as data are essential for finding answers to questions—The evidence is in the data!

One tool for enhancing students' work with data in the science classroom is the measure line. As a coteacher and curriculum developer for The Inquiry Project, I have seen how measure lines—a number line in which the numbers refer to units of measure—help students not only represent data but also analyze it in ways that generate scientific questions and greater understanding of key science concepts. The Inquiry Project, led by TERC, an education research organization in Cambridge, Massachusetts, and Tufts University, engages children in grades 3–5 in science inquiry about the nature of matter. To illustrate how measure lines are used in the project, let's first visit a third-grade classroom as the students begin to investigate how good their hands are at sensing weight.

Using Measure Lines

Children are gathered in groups around sets of eight cubes. The cubes all have the same volume, but are made of different materials. One student picks up an aluminum cube in one hand and an acrylic cube in the other, moving them up and down in her hands as she tries to feel and compare the weights.

Each group in the class tries to order the cubes by "felt weight." Later they use a pan balance to check their order. The results yield some surprising results and a discussion ensues on the reliability of felt weight. The discussion leads to questions about how much each cube weighs and the students begin to see the need for establishing a unit of weight measurement.

Students first weigh the cubes using nonstandard counterweights (paper clips, washers, counting bears) and then use grams. They record their data in a table.

A strip of adding machine tape marked in increments from 0–200 and labeled *grams* is rolled out on the floor to use as a measure line. Students represent the same data by placing each kind of cube the measured distance from zero grams on the gram weight line (Figure 19.1). With the cubes in place, students find that the weight line shows vividly and graphically the differences in weight of same-size samples of some woods, plastics, and metals in a way that the same data represented in a table does not.

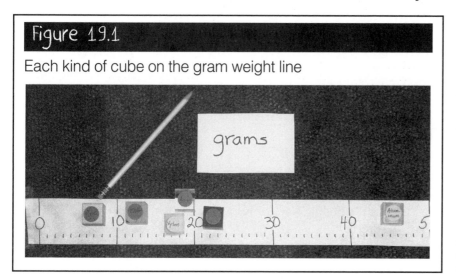

Figure 19.1

Each kind of cube on the gram weight line

With their data displayed on a weight line, students look for evidence to make claims about how much heavier a same-size cube of one material is than another. We prompted students with "We've seen the same data in a table. What more can we learn when we display the materials cubes on a weight line?" Let's review some of their ideas:

> *Cubes that weigh almost the same are very close together on the line—like pine and oak, or PVC and acrylic. The copper cube is much heavier than pine, so there's lots of space between these cubes.* (Joshua)

> *I can see that the aluminum cube is about twice as heavy as the plastics and about 4 times as heavy as the wood. Copper is really heavy! About three times heavier than aluminum.* (José)

> *The data table has lots of detailed information but I like the weight line because you can put the real thing next to the number that's its weight and the spaces between things help you compare.* (Sal)

What Do the Data Say?

In a fourth-grade Inquiry Project class, students continue to study matter and they investigate the question: When the volumes are the same, are the weights the same? They use the now-familiar measure line to display the weights of same-size samples of four kinds of earth materials: water, mineral oil, sand, and soil. Seated around the weight line with the actual materials located on the appropriate numbers, students refer to their data to discuss the property they call *heavy for size* (that is, the weight of a material for its size—e.g., Styrofoam is light for its size whereas a rock of the same size is heavy). Their experience with weights and volumes of different materials foreshadows the important concept of density that will be addressed in middle school.

Once again, the measure line proves to be an effective tool for highlighting how the data provide supporting evidence for some important ideas in the study of matter. The visual display of the data along the measure line provides students with immediate information about the weights of each object and how they relate to each other. It contains the ingredients for evidence-based claims and insights into patterns and relationships in a way that is much more accessible than a table of numbers.

As students examine the data to make claims about which materials are heavy for their size and which are not, their observations also raise questions. Students begin to wonder about the nature of materials and seek explanations: Why are 40 cc of gravel and sand so close together on the weight line and, therefore, so similar in weight? Why does 40 cc of oil weigh less than 40 cc of water even though oil looks so "thick?"

As students continue their investigations of matter, these and similar questions will continue to be raised. More experience

Figure 19.2

Written critiques of four different weight lines

Dear Darwin

Tell Darwin what you think is good or not-so-good about each line using pictures and words.

Dear Darwin,
I'm going to tell you what I think is good or not-so-good about each character's number line. You'll see a star* by the one I think is best to use.

Leila's line was O.K in distance, but the pattern was Instable.

Tomas's line was WAY out of order and the distance was not equal.

*Fern's line was good, because It didn't change pattern and the distance was equal.

Deneb's line was like Fern's line EXCEPT there was no zero at the beginning of the weight line.

Heavy for Size 2: *Comparing weights: What does the weight line show us?*

Students used a pan balance to compare weights.

with materials and time to test their ideas enable students to construct their own explanations.

Developing Criteria

In addition to being able to use and read data displayed on measure lines, students should be able to critique measure lines and describe their advantages and disadvantages. The Inquiry Project uses a concept cartoon (a cartoon-style drawing; see NSTA Connection) to engage students in developing a set of criteria for effective weight lines. Students write critiques of four different weight lines; three of them flawed in some way (e.g., one line is missing a zero). In addition to engaging students in developing criteria for effective weight lines, these written responses provide the teacher with formative assessment data (Figure 19.2, p. 99).

Armed with these criteria and their earlier experiences, students are now ready to construct their own weight lines and use them to compare equal volumes of four different samples of earth materials. Observing students at work and listening to their conversations is another formative assessment opportunity.

Do Very Tiny Things Have Weight?

Children initially think of weight in terms of felt weight, or how light or heavy something feels. The following assumption is that if you can't feel it, an object doesn't have weight. The student who believes that an eraser shaving or piece of thread or a grain of salt doesn't have weight will surely have difficulty with the idea that matter is made of particles too small to see and each of those particles weighs something.

The weight line plays a critical role in helping students wrestle with the idea of smaller and smaller pieces of matter weighing less and less, their weights getting closer and closer to zero grams (but never quite weighing nothing!). A discussion of these ideas can be anchored by a firsthand experience.

Students investigate the question: Do very tiny things have weight? They are given an 8 g piece of Plasti-

Figure 19.3

Ordering Plasticine on a weight line

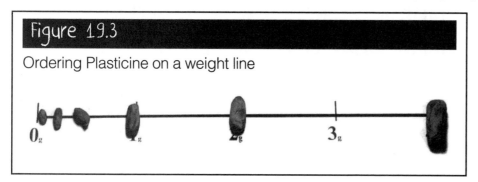

PHOTOGRAPHS COURTESY OF THE AUTHOR

cine (a type of modeling clay) and a desktop weight line labeled from 0 to 4 g. They begin by dividing their piece of Plasticine into two equal pieces and place one of the pieces on the 4 g mark on the weight line. They divide the other 4 g piece into two equal pieces and place one of these on the 2 g mark on the weight line. The other 2 g piece is halved, one piece placed on the 1 g mark.

Now the fun begins! The remaining 1 gram piece is divided in half and students must grapple with where to place the half-gram piece on the weight line (Figure 19.3). Where does half of the half-gram piece go? And half of the one-quarter-gram piece?

As fine motor skills limit the size of the pieces, students can continue to subdivide, a thought experiment is posed: Imagine you had microscopic hands and tiny little scissors and could keep cutting the pieces of Plasticine in half as many times as you want. In their discussion, students debate questions such as:

- Would you ever run out of Plasticine?
- As the pieces of Plasticine get smaller and smaller, will you ever get to zero on the weight line?
- Can you ever have a piece of Plasticine—no matter how tiny—on the other side of zero on the weight line?
- Do you think objects have weight even if we can't feel the weight?

Anticipating the Coordinate Graph

Data tables and measure lines are two of a set of representations that elementary students can use to represent data in science. Students also learn to use Venn diagrams, bar graphs, line plots, box and T-charts, and of course, coordinate graphs. Coordinate graphs are challenging. However, students who are experienced with representing data on measure lines are poised to understand that the *x*-axis and the *y*-axis are both measure lines that start at zero.

Children compare magnitudes all the time (e.g., this plant is shorter, copper is much heavier for size than plastic). In science, we encourage students to be more specific as we ask them *how much* shorter or heavier? After choosing appropriate units of measure and a reliable method for measuring, students can represent data on measure lines and see a clear view of the data. When the same-size materials are placed on a weight line, no matter what the volume, woods cluster closer to zero grams than plastics, and steel and copper will be more than 10 times as heavy as the woods. Using a weight line, we can see that as long as the volumes are the same, oil will always weigh a little less than water and much less than sand or gravel. In students' science investigations, the simple, versatile measure line helps students use the data they collect to gain more insight into their world.

Internet Resource
The Inquiry Project
 http://inquiryproject.terc.edu

NSTA Connection
For more information about concept cartoons, visit *www.nsta.org/SC1101*.

CHAPTER 20

No Duck Left Behind

Fourth-Grade Students' Data Analysis Supports Scientists' Theory of Declining Duck Populations

By Sandi Cooper, Julie Thomas, and Tammy Motley

Recently, a group of fourth graders joined Pintail Partners—a yearlong collaborative research effort of scientists, students, classroom teachers, preservice teachers, museum educators, and university professors. Students and teachers followed satellite tracking data marking the pintail ducks' spring migration and interacted with scientists via the internet. Looking to the quality of wildlife support in their own community, students gathered data regarding local weather patterns, food source availability, wetland disturbances, and geographic diversity. We hoped students would ask and answer questions about pintails right along with biologists—and be able to make applications in their own nearby wetlands.

Rationale

Dr. Dave, a research biologist, wanted to more fully understand pintail population dynamics to determine the limiting factors on population recovery (research results would guide useful wildlife management remedies). As he explained in a classroom visit, the annual pintail population continues to fall below the objective level established by the North American Waterfowl Management Plan (see Internet Resources). The professors wanted elementary students and teachers to shadow the biologist's research work with the help of hands-on learning and internet resources. This real-world application of scientific research with elementary students would help strengthen students' desire to apply scientific knowledge to their everyday lives as well as help build the relationships between the educational setting and professional scientists. The use of the STS model (Science, Technology, and Society) was the driving force for the format of this research. In developing this model, teachers would create and follow integrated curricula (science and mathematics) in an effort to help resolve this real-world problem.

Beginning Our Research

The Pintail Partners project was designed to follow female, satellite-fitted pintail ducks across fall, winter, and spring seasons to learn about the declining pintail duck population. Dr. Dave provided knowledge from a population management perspective and led fieldwork experiences. He and his biology research partners shared their ongoing data collection via the Discovery for Recovery website. (Although the study no longer collects data from students, the accumulated data is available from Sound Waves. See Internet Resources.) University education professors organized wetland field trips, curricula development, and overall project support. The elementary teachers designed and implemented the supplementary curricula needed to guide students' inquiry. These lessons consisted of technology application of the PinSat satellite tracking program, geography lessons, and science lessons to enhance understanding of adaptations, migrations, and suitable habitats.

Students observed pintail ducks being tagged and then followed their progress online.

PHOTOGRAPHS COURTESY OF THE AUTHORS

As we began, my fourth graders immersed themselves in the life patterns (habitat, nesting habits, and migration patterns) of a sample of pintail ducks for one spring semester. We read fiction and nonfiction literature about many different types of ducks and their adaptations, researched information on the internet, and e-mailed and telephoned questions to Dr. Dave when we needed a "professional opinion." With PinSat satellite technology and the guidance of Dr. Dave, we followed our ducks' migratory route from our region in west Texas (where Dr. Dave had fitted the satellites during winter) to their spring nesting grounds in southern Canada. Every three days, the students would log on to the PinSat website and, using the duck's unique ID number, locate its latitude and longitude reading. Students would then map their duck's new location on their personal map and on the classroom map. Routes for each duck on the classroom map were traced by different colors of yarn, which helped the students see the cumulative data. Daily predictions were made in the students' science notebooks.

By the end of the semester, my fourth graders would generate a reasonable hypothesis about why the pintail duck population is declining and submit ideas to the Discovery for Recovery biologists. We had frequent brainstorming sessions about the reason for the decline in population. As the students proposed a new hypothesis, it was recorded on a class chart where it could be researched by any other group in the class. This helped the students guide their own investigations, because it gave them a direction in which to research. For example, one group hypothesized that the mallard ducks flew faster than pintails, which allowed them to get to the nesting areas first. Students reasoned that this allowed the mallard ducks to get the "better" nesting spots. After some additional research about flight speeds, students concluded that this was not a viable hypothesis and started brainstorming new ideas. Another student suggested that the mallard duck was a less desirable duck for hunters so pintails were hunted more (and this led to their decline). Students also researched the time of year that the mallards and the pintails began their migration journey. Because many of the pintails regressed on their

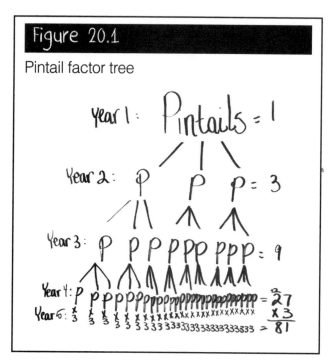

Figure 20.1

Pintail factor tree

journey north when they ran into extreme cold weather, the students hypothesized that the pintails were migrating too early and thereby using up their fat storage, which caused them to lack the energy to get to their nesting areas.

What About the Eggs?

Having learned about the effects of competition for environmental resources (such as food, water, and shelter), my students wondered about pintail ducks' annual egg production. The students mentioned that they thought mallards might be "bully" ducks and that they ate up the pintails' food when they land in the same resting areas. So, I used two lessons from the Project Wild Curriculum (*Oh Deer!* and *How Many Frogs Can Live in This Pond?*) to teach about competition for resources. (See Internet Resources.)

Dr. Dave explained that pintails lay an average of 6 to 12 eggs per year. To show the effect egg-laying differences could have on ducks' competition for natural resources, my students created a factor tree, similar to what we were using to study prime and composite numbers in math, displaying the differences between a pintail duck laying 6 eggs and a mallard duck laying 25 eggs (Figure 20.1). Students saw how quickly the exponential figures grew. To simplify the analysis, we decided to see how quickly the difference in populations would become evident when a mallard duck laid just one more egg than a pintail duck.

They found that in just five years, the number of mallards could outnumber the pintails by three to one (due to renesting). They concluded that these larger populations of mallards could "edge out" the pintails when competing for food, water, shelter, and nesting areas. Now my fourth graders were ready to share their insights with research scientists via a website that was used for the scientists' organization of data during the project time. This website provided real-time data, background information, photos, and links to communicate with the scientists. No other external reward (grade or sticker) could have provided the accomplishment we felt when the scientist-moderator verified my students' problem-solving analysis—scientists were actually collecting data to calculate the same population factors (Figure 20.2).

Integrating Mathematics

Reflecting on this experience, I wondered how this scientifically centered project could end in such a mathematically defined conclusion. I realized there were many opportunities to explore these relationships and that students frequently applied previously learned mathematical concepts to complete other project tasks.

Julian Dates. Students faced their first mathematical challenges when we visited the PinSat website to collect our birds' migratory data. The satellite transmissions from the ducks' transmitters were reported in Julian dates (JD). To follow our ducks via satellite transmission, students needed to understand how to calculate JDs. Julian dates are a continuous count of days starting on January 1st where January 1st =1, January 2nd = 2, and December 31st = 365. To practice calculating these dates, students first calculated their birthday in JD. Cooperative problem-solving techniques began immediately when students shared patterns and ideas with each other. Armed with a current annual calendar, most students decided to simply count the days until they reached their birthday. It wasn't long before some students, with birthdays near the middle and end of the year, discovered that counting the individual days was not the most efficient way to find the answer. Students began grouping months into those with 28 days, 30 days, and 31 days. Adding these month-groups reduced the redundancy of counting individual days. Students with birthdays late in the year discovered that it was easier to start with JD365 and subtract the months until they reached their special day.

Dr. Dave's Involvement. Dr. Dave met with us to show how the transmitters are attached to the ducks and how to use the satellite transmitting technology on the PinSat website. He explained that the transmitters, attached to the ducks' backs using a harness of Teflon ribbon, were programmed to transmit signals for six hours every third day. These signals were picked up by polar-orbiting weather satellites and transmitted back to researchers in California. Those researchers would then plot the information on the website. The students plotted on nonelectronic maps and class maps to help integrate geography and mathematical concepts.

Plotting the Course. The students were paired with a duck, and then they checked the PinSat website for satellite transmissions every three days and plotted the duck's path in their science journals. To share the project with the rest of the school, the ducks' paths were also plotted in our hallway on a large map. My fourth graders used pushpins to mark the location of their duck's transmission and connected it via yarn to the previous transmission. The JD was added to the pin and the number of miles that the duck flew was calculated using the mileage gauge on the map.

Figure 20.2

Electronic communication with scientists

4th grade, group #2
Monday June 10, 2002, at 9:48 a.m.
We found out that Pintail ducks, on average, lay fewer eggs than other ducks so we did a mathematical comparison. To make a simple model, we did our comparison showing each pintail having three babies and each mallard having four babies. Our data showed: Year 1—P=1, M=1; Year 2—P=3, M=4; Year 3—P=9, M=16; Year 4—P=27, M=64; Year 5—P=81, M=256. Our conclusion is that in just a short time, having an average of just one more baby can make a big difference in whole populations. We believe that mallards and other kinds of ducks that lay more eggs are "edging out" the pintail population. If ducks are like humans, they gain power in numbers. The larger, more aggressive groups of ducks will naturally dominate a habitat, overtaking food, water, shelter, and space.

Moderator's response: You young scientists may be on to something! Every hunting season, a few chosen duck hunters collect a wing from each duck they bag and send them to the U.S. Fish and Wildlife Service. Once the hunting season is over, biologists look at the wings and determine how many are from young and adult ducks. This gives an "age ratio" of young to adult, and the higher the ratio, the more young ducks that were in the population. Biologists have learned that mallards generally produce more ducklings per adult than pintails do, for some of the reasons you mentioned. But pintails have been very abundant in the past, and the trick is to learn what conditions have changed that now limits their populations.

Finding More Real-World Learning

I have learned that collaborative projects like Pintail Partners benefit both university faculty and classroom teachers and students. For others, getting involved in a similar experience might be as easy as contacting a local university or finding a local scientist who is willing. Some might find real-world, data-collecting opportunities in a local museum or aquarium.

Similar real-world teaching and learning opportunities are also available via the internet. A suite of studies, available from *Journey North for Kids* (see Internet Resources), encourages students to gather local data (on tulips, robins, and monarch butterflies, for example) and upload their observations to a regularly updated map display. Through these investigations, students discover the effect of sunlight on all living systems. The website offers engaging stories, photos, videos, and slide shows as well as student/teacher guides. Additional features (such as ask-the-expert, news updates, and challenge questions) enable real-time interactivity, inspire scientific thinking, and create fertile ground for classroom discussions and theory-building.

Visiting the Wetland. The students employed their mathematical skills when we took a field trip to the playa wetland on the university campus. Playa wetlands and other wetlands along the central migratory flyway are invaluable resting places for ducks during their seasonal journeys. We looked forward to gathering data to learn how this wetland provided food and habitat for ducks. Students were organized into botanist, hydrologist, soil scientist, entomologist, and wildlife biologist expert groups. A research scientist, teacher, or professor guided each group and supervised the collections to help students with questions. Safety note: General field-safety guidelines reminded students to stay together as a group, wear gloves when collecting specimens, and wash their hands when they returned to the classroom. Equipped with field observation logs, cameras, compasses, rulers, field guides, hand lenses, and gloves, students set out to gather data.

The botanists collected and measured plant specimens—comparing each plant's size to other plants and flowers in the area. These data helped students identify and research playa plants; field guides helped students know which of their plants provided food or shelter for wetland inhabitants.

The hydrologists gathered 50 ml water samples at different points on the playa. Each water sample was analyzed for levels of pH, nitrates, pesticides, and dissolved oxygen. Graphed sample results showed the differences in water samples around the wetland—and were later compared to nearby pond water samples. Soil scientists collected soil samples from different parts of the wetland—the upland, the edges, and the basin. They shook equal amounts of soil and water in test tubes to observe differences in how the soils separated. Students in this group later organized different soil samples in plant pots and applied consistently varied amounts of water for several weeks. Students' results showed that different amounts of water promoted unique plants in each set of pots. Fourth graders understood why native plants can vary from year to year depending on the amount of rainfall, with greater amounts of food and cover being available in wetter years.

The entomologists collected insect samples and later estimated overall wetland insect populations. Working first with 1 ft. × 1 ft. sections, students took a census of the insects that could be found at several places around the playa. Using measuring wheels, the students estimated the area of the playa and calculated the playa insect populations. Wildlife biologists measured and recorded the dimensions of animal tracks they found around the playa.

Once students' data were analyzed, each group created a display board. Parents and other students were invited to view these displays and learn about how and why migratory birds depend on healthy playas. This display day provided real-world assessment of students' growing expertise with data analysis and scientific understanding. The students presented their information to the class and discussed the cause-and-effect relationships managing the resources of the playa (many summers with minimal rainfall or excessive rainfall for many years in a row). The necessity for a balance to maintain a healthy playa was discussed as well as a need for humans to take an interest in these special wetlands to support the migratory birds that frequent them.

Fieldwork included soil analysis as well as plant, insect, and water studies.

PHOTOGRAPHS COURTESY OF THE AUTHORS

Assessing My Own Learning

This Pintail Partners project proved to be one of the most profound learning experiences in my teaching career. In this experience, students realized how scientists actually collect and analyze mathematical data to generate new scientific ideas. Interactions between my fourth graders and the research scientists made my students feel like they were a part of something bigger than just our classroom. The guidance and support from the project professors and scientists made integrated instruction manageable. My students maintained semester-long enthusiasm about better understanding their duck data. The project exemplified how involving students in real-world learning makes them want to take responsibility for their future, whether engaging in t-shirt sales to save acres of rain forest in Mexico, or considering careers in environmental science.

Acknowledgment

This project was supported by a U.S. Department of Education grant under the program, *Preparing Teachers to Teach with Technology* (PT3), Grant #P342A990098, 1999–2002.

Internet Resources

Journey North
   www.learner.org/jnorth
North American Waterfowl Management Plan
   http://migratorybirds.fws.gov
Project Wild!
   www.projectwild.org/index.htm
Sound Waves
   www. soundwaves.usgs.gov/2002/11/fieldwork.html

SELECTING an INQUIRY EXPERIENCE

CHAPTER 21

Pathways to Inquiry

By Lynn Rankin

We keep a "Calvin and Hobbes" comic strip by Bill Watterson posted in the Institute for Inquiry office. In the first panel, the boy and his tiger are looking at something on the ground, and Calvin exults, "Look! A trickle of water running through some dirt!" In the second panel, the two are hunkered down next to the trickle as Calvin says, "I'd say our afternoon just got booked up solid."

Although Calvin and Hobbes are merely cartoon characters, this comic strip deftly portrays the heart of inquiry, the innate urge to explore and understand how the world works. What fuels this afternoon-long investigation of water flowing through the dirt is the simple, powerful phenomenon of human curiosity. It's the same curiosity that drives inquiries which scientists carry out at a more sophisticated level in their laboratories or in the field. This curiosity, when shaped by an effective pedagogical structure, can also fuel and sustain students' science learning in the classroom.

We know it is a challenge to provide inquiry experiences in the classroom. There can be issues of time, of topics best suited to inquiry, and of ways to best facilitate to develop all students' thinking. When supporting teachers to provide inquiry experiences, we have found that one of the most important considerations is how to structure the experience so it is meaningful in a doable amount of time. Although humans are born inquirers, students don't come to the classroom with the natural ability to carry out productive investigations that lead to a greater understanding of scientific concepts. Doing inquiry in the classroom requires laying a foundation for students to take more responsibility for their learning. The learner must become adept at using the process skills of science (observing, questioning, predicting, hypothesizing) to make decisions about what questions to raise, which to follow in depth, what materials and science tools to use for various tasks, how to organize data, communicate findings, and participate in discourse.

Full Inquiries

In the end, there's no substitute for giving students—at every grade level—the opportunity to experience full inquiries, or scientific investigations where they have the opportunity to use all the process skills and have some ownership of the process of investigation. Full inquiries give students the opportunity to experience science as a process of building theories from evidence, much akin to how scientists operate in the real world. This does not mean that students must work from their own questions or pursue independent investigations. Productive investigations can result from a class working on the same question, or small groups of children working on different questions. Moreover, investigations can proceed through different stages over time, starting with an initial exploration to develop curiosity and questions, followed by more focused experimentation, and ending with sharing discoveries to support understanding of scientific ideas. The different stages can take place over several hours (within a day or over several days) or unfold over extended periods of time.

One of the most frequently discussed topics by teachers in our workshops is the question of balance between structure and freedom, or the amount of responsibility given to the learner compared with the amount of teacher direction. We have found that there is no prescription for this balance; it needs to be decided on an individual basis, according to a teacher's goals for an activity or topic and the students' ability to use the process skills. But no matter how much responsibility students are given, a teacher must still play an active role in guiding the learning experience to help students develop their abilities to investigate in ways that add to their understanding of science concepts and the scientific endeavor.

One way to move science teaching in the direction of inquiry is for a teacher to make subtle shifts—strategic changes in pedagogy or modifications to existing activities that gradually give students more responsibility for using process skills. Often it is the teacher or the instructional materials (including kits and hands-on science activities) that make the decisions for the student about how they will use the process skills. Activities can be analyzed, and shifted, in terms of who is making the decisions (ownership of the investigation questions, procedures to follow, how to collect data, and how to communicate the findings). For example, once students have developed the skill of recording data, they can begin to experiment with creating their own data templates, rather than using ones that are provided for them. Research has shown (NRC 2007) that students of all ages are capable of using all the process skills—even the youngest students are capable of predicting, interpreting, and hypothesizing—and that each of the skills can be practiced at simple and increasingly complex levels. Nurturing the growth of all the process skills throughout the school years is essential if we want students to learn to reason scientifically, develop claims backed by evidence, and explain their findings.

A Powerful Approach

Although we are big proponents of inquiry-based science, we recognize that inquiry is not the only way to teach science; it is not an either/or proposition. As stated in *How People Learn: Brain, Mind, Experience, and School,* "Asking which teaching technique is best is analogous to asking which tool is best—a hammer, a screwdriver, a knife, or pliers. In teaching, as in carpentry the selection of tools depends on the task at hand and the materials one is working with" (NRC 2000).

However, we know that inquiry-based science can be a powerful approach to learning scientific concepts and keeping wonder and curiosity alive in the classroom. As stated by Hubert Dyasi, professor emeritus, City College New York, "Inquiry aligns with children's natural impulses to learn. It is an affirmation of a person's capacity to learn, an essential ingredient in every child's wholesome intellectual and cultural development."

The challenge for us as educators, even amidst pressures to teach for accountability, is to find ways to continually create the pathways that nurture this development. We can afford to do no less to prepare our students to take their place as citizens of an increasingly complex world.

References

National Research Council (NRC). 2000. *How people learn: Brain, mind, experience, and school, expanded edition.* J. Bransford et al., ed. Washington, DC: National Academies Press.

National Research Council (NRC). 2007. *Taking science to school: Learning and teaching science in grades K–8.* R. A. Duschl, H. A. Schweingruber, and A. W. Shouse, ed. Washington, DC: National Academies Press.

Internet Resources

Institute for Inquiry
   www.exploratorium.edu/ifi
Foundations
   www.nsf.gov/pubs/2000/nsf99148/start.htm

CHAPTER 22

Inquiry Into the Heart of a Comet

Third- Through Fifth-Grade Students Model Science in Action

By Whitney Cobb, Maura Rountree-Brown, Lucy McFadden, and Elizabeth Warner

On July 4, 2005, NASA's *Deep Impact* science team witnessed a spectacular event. The team had sent a copper impactor spacecraft on an intentional collision course with a comet, hoping to create a crater that would allow them to look beneath the crust of the comet's nucleus. What they got was a brilliant display of scattered light, beyond anything the scientists had imagined.

Scientists and engineers were stunned. What did it all mean? This suggested that the comet's composition differed in key ways from what they had predicted—it was made of far fluffier, finer, even microscopic, stuff. The team needed to talk about what just happened. They needed to prioritize what should be investigated first. They had so many questions, and not so many answers. Not yet.

Real science means wrangling with peers over real ideas. The *Deep Impact* science team was passionate about sharing ideas and challenging those ideas with new queries. It wasn't quarrelling—They were developing and transforming each other's thinking. Further, it was, and is, an element of inquiry crucial to absolutely every step of every NASA mission.

Wouldn't it be thrilling to emulate that real-life model of science in action in classrooms? How? By starting with a great, hands-on activity modeling an object in space, which introduces both key vocabulary and science concepts with visuals to support retention and learning; encouraging collaboration to enrich student engagement with those concepts as students develop their models; and capping the experience by scaffolding an opportunity for students to engage in scientific argumentation as they discuss the strengths and limitations of their models and brainstorm ways to improve them. Read on to find out how we did all of that and more with the activity *Comet on a Stick!*

The Details

Through *Comet on a Stick*, your students can experience the authentic process of NASA mission engineers and scientists. Student teams examine concepts of comet science by designing and

Students used common materials to construct comet models.

building a comet model using common classroom art supplies. Created through a collaboration of NASA scientists and science educators, and field-tested in classrooms by teachers, the activity, as well as a gamut of supportive resources, are free and downloadable (see Internet Resources). *Comet on a Stick* is aligned with the National Science Education Standards, specifically Science as Inquiry and Earth and Space Science as well as AAAS Benchmarks for grades 3–5. The goal is to have children replicate the inquiry processes of observing, modeling, forming an explanation, making new observations, and revising. Your students' models will parallel scientists' physical models, and the conversations children have as they explain both the limits of their model and what they learned from it will mirror the dynamic discussions of NASA mission teams.

Collaboration and Modeling

To uncover background knowledge and preconceptions, begin *Comet on a Stick* with a discussion of what students believe might be true about comets recording and categorizing elements in a large KWL chart on the board or butcher paper. From there, choose from a range of resources located on NASA comet mission education pages for children to deepen background knowledge: a slide show of images, short video clips illustrating comet behavior, engaging articles and fact sheets that can be read aloud as a class or within teams, as well as information included in the student activity guide. To conclude the introduction to *Comet on a Stick*, the class revisits the KWL chart to revise understandings and add questions.

From there, students break into small groups to design and build their own comet model. This is a ripe opportunity for students to review what it means to be collaborative. *Comet on a Stick* includes guidance for this process, a T-chart to remind children what collaboration sounds like and looks like. Each team works together, deciding which characteristics they wish to incorporate into their comet, sharing in the building process. Along the way, children discuss what is true and what is not true about their model:

Grace: *We knew from the start we wanted to do a cross-section of the comet, to show the parts you usually can't see.*

Aiden: *So we used this big Styrofoam ball for the coma.*

Grace: *It's solid, but all the air in it makes sort of like the floating dust in the coma.*

Aiden: *And we can use a little ball inside—we're going to use this one. It's too big, so I'm carving it to make it smaller.*

Mike: *Thomas is making the ion tail, blue with beads.*

Thomas: *Beads on a wire so I can make it straight because the ion tail shoots straight away from the Sun.*

In this process, children emulate aspects of the experience of discovery that make science so exciting.

Scientific Discourse

Once comets are built, groups share their models with the class without offering explanation. Peers take turns discussing what characteristics they believe their colleagues' comet is illustrating. Because there are many effective ways to model the differing concepts, it is in the discourse that understanding is deepened. As teams evaluate their peers' models, they appreciate one another's ideas and flesh out their own.

Picture a wide circle of students sitting in clumps around their respective models. They hold them high for peers to see, hands clamped over their mouths to let others speak without interruption. Here's a clip from one discussion:

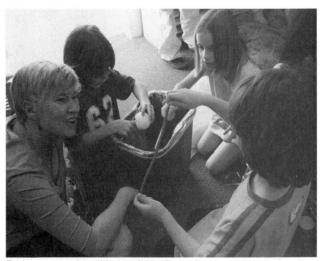

Each group explained its model to the teacher.

Children: *Well, the ribbons act like the dust tail I think, but it isn't connected to the nucleus like that for real. Right?*
The tail comes from the nucleus, but it's not connected to the nucleus. It's glowing dust being carried by the Sun's wind.
But it's not glowing, really. I mean, the ion tail really glows, not the dust tail.
Right, well, ok, but it does catch the sunlight—it looks like it glows from Earth.

Teacher: So what's the difference? What does "glow" mean when we're talking about comets?

Children: *Well, like light being given off.*
Like a lightbulb glows, like the Sun glows.
The ion tail gives off that glowing light.

Teacher: A fancy word for that is *emit*—light is emitted by the lightbulb, the Sun, the ion tail. How is the dust tail different?

Children: *Light's reflected off it! It bounces off!*

Aha!

Children should have "opportunities … to become aware of the tentative status of some aspects of scientific knowledge so that they are better able to cope with uncertainty when having to make choices and decisions" (Maloney and Simon 2006, p. 1818). After a chance to explain their cometary vision to the class, each team regroups to reflect on and write about how they might improve their

Comets

The nucleus of ices and rocky dust left over from the earliest epochs in our solar system are usually small compared to many solar system bodies—1 to 50 kilometers in diameter. Dark and bitterly cold while in the outer reaches of the solar system, comets grow spectacularly as they rocket toward the inner solar system in their elliptical orbits, their ices sublimating in the radiant heat of the Sun. The resulting gas and dust jettisoned from the nucleus' surface create a coma tens of thousands of kilometers wide. Solar winds, energetic particles ejected from the Sun's surface, blow gas from the coma into a glowing blue ion tail that always points directly away from the Sun. The dustier debris is left behind the comet like a trail of crumbs reflecting the light of the Sun. Smaller dust particles can also be blown by the solar wind; the dust tail can be very broad. Comet tails can be millions of kilometers long!

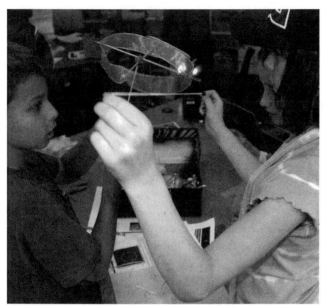

Comparing tail materials

own model and what they have learned in the process. Just like scientists, they wrangle with where their physical models are able to represent authentic phenomenon and where they were limited as they make plans for next steps. For example, one student discussed how his bead ion tail was accurate with its blue color and the way it shot straight away from the Sun, but he was frustrated because his model was solid whereas a real ion tail is gas. Another team created a coma with wire-rimmed ribbon but realized that it didn't fully show how jets spray in three dimensions to create the coma, nor did it merge with the tail, as a real comet's coma does.

Use this opportunity to affirm a thoughtful analysis of the comet models as well as remind students that even scientists' models never simulate real phenomenon completely. It is from knowledge gained by exploring the pros and cons of a model that mission scientists and engineers form questions, make predictions, and then test them—inquiry in action.

Evaluation

In a national field test, students noted overwhelmingly that they had fun building the model and working in teams. Further, they enjoyed learning about new science concepts: the structure of a comet and how the Sun's energy affects it, and how to design, build, evaluate, and revise a model. Teachers emphasized that it helped their students understand how scientists make observations and models as well as relate to scientists conducting science. Teachers were also enthused by their students' level of engagement and ability to absorb new concepts: "I asked my students to respond to the learning portion of the KWL chart in their science logs. They were able to express their ideas with unusual fluency and incorporate new vocabulary, such as *ellipse* and the parts of a comet, with accuracy. Even my struggling writers concentrated to communicate their findings."

The Story Keeps Unfolding

The year 2011 was an exciting time for comets, asteroids, and our solar system. During NASA's *Year of the Solar System*, several missions encountered comets. *Stardust-NExT* had a flyby of comet Tempel 1 on February 14, 2011, to continue the story of *Deep Impact,* and *EPOXI* captured brilliant images of comet Hartley 2 in November 2010, adding an entire new dimension to our understanding about the nature of comets. *Dawn* arrived at asteroid Vesta in the main asteroid belt in the summer of 2011. Each mission had an Education and Public Outreach team charged with bringing compelling mission science and engineering to children, their adults (teachers, out-of-school-time leaders, parents), and the general public. Through a connection between activities like *Comet on a Stick*, your students experience the thrill of inquiry in action and emulate mission scientists. As one teacher noted, "Tie science lessons to real actions from real missions and kids are hooked."

One student offered a suggestion to improve *Comet on a Stick*: *If they taught me how [a comet] is made!* If we only knew! We do know that it is time for children to believe that many of the impressive tools of inquiry in the hands of scientists—a thoughtful scientific process informed by modeling and collaboration and empowered by dynamic discourse—are powerful in their hands as well.

Reference

Maloney, J., and S. Simon. 2006. Mapping children's discussions of evidence in science to assess collaboration and argumentation. *International Journal of Science Education 28* (15): 1817–1841.

Internet Resources

Comet Interactive Video
> *http://stardustnext.jpl.nasa.gov/multimedia/comet_inter active/index.html*

Comet on a Stick
> *http://epoxi.umd.edu/4education/mod_cometstick/ Modeling_Comets_EG.pdf*

EPOXI Education
> *http://epoxi.umd.edu/4education/index.shtml*

Stardust-NExT Education: handouts, fact sheets and slide shows
> *http://stardustnext.jpl.nasa.gov/education/index.html*

NASA's Year of the Solar System Education Page
> *http://solarsystem.nasa.gov/yss/index.cfm*

CHAPTER 23

Thinking Inside the Box

Using Discovery Boxes and Learning Centers to Promote Inquiry and Teach Healthy Food Choices at the Preschool Level

By Carolyn Jeffries

Sandra was interested in infusing inquiry into her packed preschool curriculum while teaching children about healthy food choices. Her parent aide, whom I had previously worked with, asked me to share some early childhood activity options. Having developed early elementary discovery boxes for the California Science Center, I recommended testing discovery boxes as a viable preschool activity because they are child-centered and require little space, supervision, maintenance, or time. Meeting once a week for six weeks, we designed a box that would stimulate preschoolers' natural inquiry processes, develop fine-motor skills, and provide knowledge of healthy food choices. Below we describe our experiences developing and setting up a discovery box learning activity center for children ages four and five.

Designing the Box

Discovery boxes differ from boxes of similar materials (e.g., sets of blocks) and from science kits, which typically include recipes and materials for clearly directed tasks. Discovery boxes house durable science materials, tools, and media that are carefully selected to stimulate problem solving, exploration, creativity, literacy, and inquiry. Box media typically consist of a challenge question card, pictures, and books.

We began by writing objectives and brainstorming ideas. Our list of potential science challenges included the following: weigh and find the heaviest food, measure and determine the longest and shortest foods, identify food smells, sort food by color, assemble a healthy meal puzzle, measure an appropriate volume of cereal, identify healthy foods, look over food books and pictures, and put together a healthy meal. We also compiled lists of required materials and tools (e.g., scales, rulers, measuring cups), food-related fiction and nonfiction books, posters, and puzzles.

We refined our goals and objectives based on early learning guidelines and the National Science Education Standards for grades K–4 (NRC 1996) and crafted objectives related to both inquiry and nutrition. Our inquiry-related objectives were that preschoolers would engage in at least one of the following behaviors during box use: make observations; pose questions; examine materials and media; and use tools to predict, test, and gather information based on their questions and ideas. In addition, they would share explanations about food with other children and the teacher. Our content objectives were that the children would be able to accomplish at least one of the following: identify a major characteristic of foods (parts, colors, shapes, odors, textures, or sizes); use the property of color to sort foods; state the main message from Eat Healthy, Feel Great (Sears, Sears, and Kelly 2002), which is to eat a variety of different-color foods; practice fine-motor skills by measuring food volume, length, or weight; identify and select healthy foods to create nutritional meals; and identify less healthy foods.

Challenges and Considerations

The goal when creating a discovery box is to select and create materials and media that address scientific, pedagogical, and implementation criteria that at the same time offer a fun and stimulating experience. At first glance, developing a discovery box appears simple: obtain theme-related media, objects, and games, and then place them in a box. When we tried this, we found that we had to modify store-bought products or create our own to fulfill our objectives, prompt engagement and inquiry, and address the preschoolers' developmental abilities. The challenge was to create a totally learner-centered experience in which the children would be free to choose when and how they would interact with the materials found in the box, as opposed to being directed. I knew we could promote box exploration and at the same time prompt for learning and inquiry by including

1. challenge question cards that share information about the content area (e.g., *Rocks are everywhere, underfoot, inside walls, even in jewelry. In fact, the Earth is made of rocks. Rocks can be big or small, round or angular, shiny or dull, smooth or rough. Rocks can be identified by their hardness, their color, and their materials. The oldest rocks come from outer space. New rocks are being made all the time under the ocean, inside the Earth, and*

Figure 23.1	Figure 23.2
Text of chant	Food puzzle

The Chew Chomp Chant
By Diana Barker Price

Go get 'em green,
I'm an eating machine!

Slow down yellow,
not so much, be mellow.

Stop and think red,
pick and choose with my head.

Always feel great,
healthy food on my plate!

even shooting out from volcanoes!). Cards list a number of activity suggestions that ask the children to come up with ways to solve a science problem and test their ideas using the box components (e.g., *Use the tools in the container with the red top to see what you can discover about the nine big rocks in the clear container. What could you do to see rocks close-up? What would happen if you brought a magnet close to a rock? How could you tell which rocks are heavy? Which rocks make a mark on the small white tile? Real gold makes a gold mark so why do you think the gold-colored rock makes a black mark?*);

2. pictures that illustrate some possible solutions to the problem or challenge (e.g., colored pictures of rocks); and

3. pieces of a potential activity linked together with a metal ring and housed in separate smaller boxes and bags. Or all the pieces could be painted the same color, so the children can see easily which components typically go together or are used for a similar purpose (e.g., linking all the match-the-rock-name-with-its-picture game cards together with a metal ring).

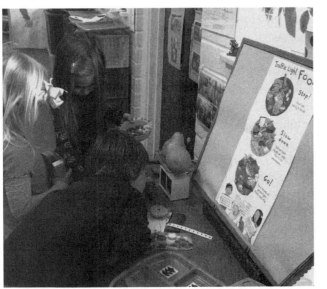

Students weigh oranges and pears during learning center time.

Overall, we found the easiest way to design the box was to brainstorm potential activity ideas, place the required materials in a box, and then review. Our first challenge was addressing that most preschoolers can't read a challenge question card. Our solution was to read aloud, record, or make visual (with pictures and drawings) any information that would typically be placed on a challenge card. During box development, we found or photographed and laminated pictures of other children using the discovery box tools and materials in proper scientific manner and then attached the pictures to the relevant objects. To add an auditory component to the box, we asked a local poet to write a food chant related to information in *Eat Healthy, Feel Great* (Sears, Sears, and Kelly 2002). The teacher had a friend put the chant to music (Figure 23.1, p. 119) and recorded it on a CD, which was introduced during music time.

The second challenge was making sure we didn't inadvertently include materials and media that could lead to misconceptions. Because children were free to engage with the discovery box materials in any manner during learning activity center time, we considered possible scenarios and decided to reject several food puzzles and posters because they included illustrations of foods with high levels of sugar, fat, and salt. Instead, we created our own healthy food puzzles by gluing pictures to blank puzzle pieces and magnets. We reviewed a variety of books—reference, recipe, science, and fiction—as potential resources and rejected several popular fiction books with food themes because they presented ideas that could lead to misconceptions.

The third challenge was that most of the children had never studied nutrition or worked with discovery boxes. Our solution was to change the box contents each Monday. The first week we would present the box with materials that introduced general categories of foods, some healthy meal choices, and basic characteristics of foods (parts, colors, shapes, odors, textures, and sizes). It prompted the children to look at pictures of healthy foods in *We Are What We Eat!* (Smallwood 2008); put together a puzzle of foods that made up a healthy meal (Figure 23.2, p. 119); smell a variety of foods pictured in a scratch-and-sniff book; sort fruit and vegetable magnets by color on a rainbow food puzzle; and measure the length of foods using a measuring tape, three plastic foods of various lengths, and a picture of hands measuring the length of a piece of fruit.

The second week, we switched out the contents with materials that prompted more advanced engagement and nutrition concepts. This second box built on the concept of identifying and making healthy food choices by asking the children to create a healthy meal on a cafeteria food tray—marked with red, yellow, and green traffic lights to illustrate the food choice theme from *Eat Healthy, Feel Great* (Sears, Sears, and Kelly 2002)—a variety of plastic foods in a grocery bag, a chef hat, pictures of healthy meals, and the book. It also built on the children's skills in measuring foods by prompting them to (a) weigh a large orange and a pear using the included simple scale and pictures of a variety of scales and people weighing foods, and (b) measure a volume of cereal using a measuring cup, cereal bowl, spoon, cereal box with biodegradable craft noodles, and a picture of cereal in a measuring cup. This change from week one to week two would also reinforce that there was a new discovery each time the box was available. See Figure 23.3, page 122, for a list of all components.

Implementation and Student Engagement

We were limited to five days over a two-week span to make the discovery box available, due to scheduling and curricular requirements. During learning activity center time, the box was placed on a table with two chairs. Safety note: The children were given free access after safety reminders about not placing any of the materials in their mouths. Teacher intervention only occurred when there were squabbles or safety concerns. After each use, the condition and number of components were checked and the box was moved to a storage area.

The discovery box was the topic of just one of a dozen unrelated learning center activities, all of which were available to the students during its five-day implementation. We documented all discovery box activity and found that 14 of the 16 preschoolers interacted with the box components an average of three times each in five days. All of the anticipated activity behaviors were observed at least once. The children's behaviors were both investigatory and sociodramatic.

For these 14 children, our objective that preschoolers would engage in at least one inquiry-related behavior during box use was met. All of the children closely investigated the food items, pictures, cereal noodles, and tools. All made statements and posed questions either aloud to themselves or to another child at the box. Typical questions included: *How much does it weigh? What color is it? What should we do with the [orange/pear/cereal/food] now? Can you smell this? What is it?* Common statements included: *the orange weighs more; the ice cream is a red-light food; the banana is longer; they all weigh something; and the cereal fills this cup.* Half of the box visits involved measuring cereal volume. One-third involved weighing items, observing how the scale needle moved when additional items were added, and comparing their weights. Several children took the tray off the scale and tested how that affected the process.

Figure 23.3

Discovery box components

Week 1
- Healthy foods puzzle
- *We Are What We Eat!* (Smallwood 2008)
- Short measuring tape
- Picture of a child's hands measuring the diameter of a fruit
- One plastic banana, stick of butter, and french fry
- *Scratch & Sniff: Food* (Dorling Kindersley 1999)
- *Catch a Rainbow Every Day!* poster
- Food rainbow magnetic puzzle

Week 2
- Chef hat
- Food chant
- Measuring cup
- Cereal bowl
- Spoon
- Small cereal box filled with biodegradable craft noodles
- Photograph of measuring cup with cereal
- Plastic foods in small grocery bag
- Plastic food tray with traffic light pictures glued onto specific tray sections
- *Eat Healthy, Feel Great* (Sears, Sears, and Kelly 2002)
- Four healthy meal pictures on a metal ring
- Simple scale
- Photographs of scales and a person using the simple scale

Safety note: Check for allergies before bringing any food items into the classroom.

Evaluation of Box Effectiveness

We used observation checklists and a pre–post interview to evaluate the effectiveness of the discovery box in prompting scientific inquiry and promoting the learning of basic nutrition in relation to the Standards. We focused on the basics in each category. First, the teacher conducted informal individual interviews with each preschooler to determine whether he or she could (1) share some basic information about food and identify a physical characteristic of food, (2) explain how the body uses foods and how foods contribute to health, and (3) give an example of a healthy and a not-so-healthy food item. The preschoolers' knowledge was assessed the day before and one day after the five-day discovery box implementation. The teacher asked each child the following questions (sample post activity answers are in parentheses):

1. What can you tell me about food? (*There are healthy and unhealthy foods; Food tastes good sometimes; Candies are bad for you; Some food is good and healthy like peppers, broccoli, and strawberries*)
2. Which foods are good for you? Can you tell me why? What happens when you eat healthy food? (*We eat healthy food to make us big and strong; Food is for keeping you healthy and giving you energy; Food is good for you because they have vitamins; Good foods make you stronger and healthy*)
3. Which foods are not so good for you? Can you tell me why? What happens if you eat too much unhealthy food? (*Unhealthy foods don't have vitamins; Unhealthy foods are bad because they make you grow fat instead of taller; Too much sugar is not good for you because it makes you run out of energy, makes you weaker*)
4. What foods do you like? Not like? (*I like meat, fish, rice, tofu, and kim chi; I don't like avocado; I like sweet bananas, cucumber; I don't like bananas, eggs, and onions; My favorite food is turkey, pasta, and bacon; I don't like stew because it looks like mud and has carrots*)

Differences between the preschoolers' pre- and post-interview answers showed an overall increase in their understanding about nutrition and food. They shared new, better explanations for why some foods are healthy and what happens when you eat healthy foods (e.g., makes you strong, gives you energy, helps you grow, contains vitamins) and for why some foods are less healthy and what happens when you eat less healthy food (e.g., makes you overweight, makes you weak, contains too much sugar). All children added something new about why healthy food is good for you.

Capitalize on Curiosity

Overall, our test to determine whether we could incorporate a discovery box into a preschool setting was successful. It stimulated preschoolers' natural inquiry processes while promoting understanding of healthy foods and allowing for practice of fine-motor skills. It was easily incorporated into

A preschooler inspects the contents of the discovery box.

the curriculum and classroom space. Future plans include decorating the box with pictures of healthy food and children engaged in a scientific activity, placing it on a designated floor area, and adding some visual and skill-based items to the pre- and postassessment tasks.

Preschoolers are naturally curious and employ trial-and-error techniques to learn about the world around them. Encountering the contents of the discovery box for the first time, they tried to determine and predict how the tools and components worked. They inspected the materials and used the tools to measure, analyze, and create mental models. They constructed their own explanations. Sometimes they checked and rechecked what they thought would happen and compared the results to what they already knew, changing their ideas based on what they had learned. Because discovery boxes are made up of nonconsumable materials and require little space, supervision, maintenance, or time, this preschool now has a discovery box that can be used again with future students!

Acknowledgment

The author thanks preschool teacher Sandra Wernstrum who supplied her class and expertise, and parent Livian Perez, who shared her knowledge of early childhood and instructional design.

Reference

National Research Council (NRC). 1996. *National science education standards*. Washington, DC: National Academies Press.

Resources

Dorling Kindersley. 1999. *Scratch & sniff: Food*. New York: DK Publishing, Inc.

Learning ZoneXpress. 2004. *Catch a rainbow every day!* Poster. Owatonna, MN: Learning ZoneXpress.

Sears, W., M. Sears, and C. Watts Kelly. 2002. *Eat healthy, feel great*. Singapore: Little, Brown Books for Young Readers.

Smallwood, S. 2008. *We are what we eat!* London, England: Zero to Ten Limited.

CHAPTER 24

Concept-Based Learning

Sixth Graders Ask Questions to Find Answers in a Problem-Based Pond Activity

By Bethany Schill and Linda Howell

Did you learn to swim by jumping in and doing it? Or did you take lessons and practice? I am a jump-in-and-do-it type person, whereas the enrichment specialist at my school is a take-lessons-and-practice type person. So when a new approach to teaching comes along, I enjoy working with her because she balances my splashes. This year we collaborated on an ecology unit with sixth graders that incorporated concept-based instruction into a problem-based activity. Students used their scientific skills of observing and inferring to explore and address an aerator problem in a pond ecosystem.

Developing a Concept-Based Unit

A major part of developing concept-based instruction is the use of an overarching idea to provide a conceptual lens through which students view the content of a particular subject. By using a conceptual lens to focus learning, students think at a much deeper level about the content and its facts (Erickson 2007). Using a conceptual lens also frames the learning in such a way that students are being asked to think and use language as a practitioner would in that discipline (Tomlinson et al. 2002). We used several steps in the process of developing our concept-based unit:

- Choose a topic of study. We chose to develop a concept-based unit around the topic of ecology with potential expansion into other units and topics taught at the sixth-grade level in science.
- Decide on a concept. We next decided on the conceptual lens of "change." In looking over the various lists on macroconcepts that can be found in the literature, we felt that change fit best (Erickson 2007). We then used a planning web to gauge how change would fit into other science units for possible future concept unit development (Figure 24.1).
- Develop essential understandings and questions for the unit. The next step in our unit planning was the creation of essential understandings based on New

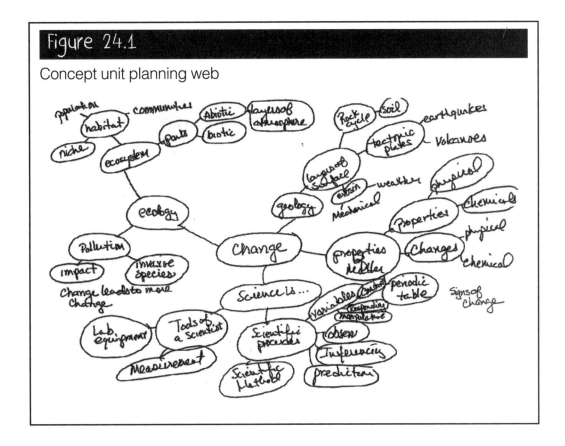

Figure 24.1

Concept unit planning web

York Science Standards, National Science Education Standards, and our district's
standards-based curriculum. These essential understandings provided the focus for
student learning in a unit of study while the essential questions acted as a means to
lead students to uncover these understandings (Figure 24.2, p. 126).

- Develop a problem-based learning activity as the focus of the unit. The problem-
  based activity served as the framework for the conceptual focus on change and its
  relationship to ecology as well as fostering scientific thinking. The problem dealt
  with a change that had occurred with the pond located on the school campus—a
  pond aeration system had been added. The question we posed was, "Is this a good
  thing for the pond ecosystem?" This set the stage for students to use their scientific thinking to investigate the problem, ask questions, and find answers. The end
  product was the writing of a letter of recommendation to the District Pond Committee from the point of view of an ecologist using scientific evidence to support
  their recommendation on the pond aeration issue.
- Use inquiry-based investigations to explore the pond environment. The students
  used the same type of procedures and kits that scientists would use in the field. We
  used the procedures developed by the GLOBE program (see Internet Resources).
  By taking the time to thoroughly plan our unit, we felt ready to tackle concept-
  based learning.

Figure 24.2

Understandings and essential questions

Understandings	Essential questions
• Organisms adapt to a changing environment in order to survive. • Plants and animals are interdependent upon each other and their environment. • A change in any of the components in an ecosystem results in other components changing. • The Sun is the main source of energy for ecosystems and organisms. • Matter undergoes changes in the form of cycles as it is transformed through the environment. • Photosynthesis is the process by which solar energy is changed into food energy.	**Overarching:** • Are there consequences if change doesn't happen? **Topical:** • Why do scientists call it an *ecosystem*? • Is it necessary that living and nonliving things interact in an ecosystem? • Is change important in an ecosystem? • How do different factors affect an ecosystem? • Is it possible to progress as a nation and not change our environment? • How do human activities affect Earth's resources? • Is it important that matter changes as a cycle in ecosystems? Why? Why are natural cycles important to ecosystems? • How does energy change as it flows through an ecosystem?

Introducing the Concept of Change

To introduce the concept of change to our students, we had them form small groups and brainstorm 30 examples of the concept of change. Students came up with ideas such as leaves, time, seasons, and money (i.e., change you receive from making a purchase). Next, the students needed to brainstorm 30 nonexamples. They then created four categories and sorted the examples into one of each of the categories. All of the examples had to fit a category and students soon realized that some examples could fit into more than one. This then required either modifications or consolidations of categories. Students came up with such categories as physical change, economy, outdoors, history, and humans. We then explained the idea of a generalization and asked the students to develop three to five generalizations using the information they had created, analyzed, and evaluated to form categories. The students in each group had many thoughts and ideas. They struggled with forming generalizations. It was a process that lent itself well to deep thinking. Some examples of student-generated generalizations were (1) *everything grows at a different pace*; (2) *time is constantly changing so that affects things*; and (3) *change may be caused by people or nature*. Student generalizations were placed on a word wall that was made up of the word *change* and our teacher-selected generalizations. These generalizations were (a) change leads to more change; (b) change can have positive or negative consequences; (c) change is inevitable; and (d) change may happen naturally or may be caused by people. We chose these four generalizations as they aligned best with the unit's essential understandings. Student generalizations were then grouped under one of the related generalizations. For example, the student generalization, *Everything changes in nature* would be placed under the generalization, "Change is inevitable." The word wall became a teaching tool and was referred to whenever we made connections back to the four generalizations throughout the teaching of the unit.

The Ecology Unit
Problem-Based Learning

Once the introduction of concept of change and its generalizations were completed, students were ready to begin the ecology unit. To help frame the learning and to promote scientific thinking, a problem-based learning activity based on a real problem was introduced to the students. The problem was designed to bring in all of the topics and skills that were embedded in the ecology unit. Students were prompted to think scientifically through the use of a modified KWL chart.

Purposeful questioning techniques were used to guide students to come to the conclusion that one of their main questions was, *What is an ecosystem?* Students tended to focus on the minor points such as *What is an aerator?* or *How does an aerator work?* Although these questions are important, they are not the overarching question. To help students uncover this question, prompts such as the following were used: "What do you know or need to know about the pond to find out whether the aerator is a good thing? What can you tell me about the organisms found in the pond? How do organisms rely on their habitat for survival?" The point of this line of questioning was to encourage students to start thinking about the interdependence that exists between organisms and the abiotic and biotic factors found in an ecosystem.

Once students understood the overarching question, "What is an ecosystem?" became the basis for introducing the key topics and ideas related to ecology. Periodically during the course of the unit, we revisited our pond aerator problem to see what additional questions the students still had.

Five Stations

As part of the investigation into the pond ecosystem, we used the hydrology protocols from GLOBE (see Internet Resources) to create five stations (Figure 24.3, p. 128). Students were assigned to a station based on their readiness level to handle the complexity of the testing protocol. Students were responsible for learning the protocols of their station only. This allowed them to become experts in that station and to share that information later with others. The necessary materials for each station were placed in 10-gallon plastic buckets to make it easy for the students to transport the materials to the pond. Also included in each bucket was a laminated copy of the GLOBE protocol for that station, water-sampling kit procedures, and data collection sheets. Materials can be obtained from any science supply company and some are at local drug stores. They do not need to be the materials that are specifically used by the GLOBE program.

Safety note: It was important to follow school outdoor safety procedures during the water sample collection and testing. We made sure both were conducted under the direct supervision

Figure 24.3

The five stations

Station	What you need	What to do
Alkalinity testing	Alkalinity test kit [we used LaMotte] Distilled water Timer Data sheet Map of pond GLOBE protocol and kit instruction sheet Clipboard Pencils	This station tests for the ability of a body of water to maintain its neutrality. This is especially important to those areas exposed to acid rain.
Nitrogen testing	Nitrogen test kit [we used Hach model NI-14] Distilled water Data sheet Map of pond GLOBE protocol and kit instruction sheet Clipboard Pencils	This station tests for the amount of nitrogen found in water. Too high levels of nitrogen can result in algae bloom.
Dissolved oxygen testing	Water test kit [we used LaMotte] Timer Distilled water Data sheet Map of pond GLOBE protocol and kit instruction sheet Clipboard Pencils	This station tests for the amount of dissolved oxygen in water. This is an important indicator of a healthy water ecosystem.
Water characteristics	Secchi discs GPS Camera Measuring tape Bucket with string to collect water Long-handle net Sampling pans	This station looks at the physical characteristics of the pond site—turbidity, type of pond bed, location of pond, weather at that time, types of plants and animals found, population count, and so on.
Water temperature and pH	pH meter and calibration solutions Thermometer Map of pond Data sheet GLOBE protocol and kit instruction sheet Clipboard Pencils	This station tests different locations of the pond for temperature and pH level of the water.

of an adult that was assigned to that station: the classroom teacher, the enrichment specialist, or a student observer from a local university. Children were reminded of the importance of keeping within sight of an adult when near the water. We practiced and used a buddy system, as well as practiced using a whistle (provided to each child) to use only in an emergency situation. A ring buoy with throw line was located at the pond. A cell phone with preprogrammed principal and school nurse numbers was also carried by the teachers. A first aid kit was also on site. Other necessary safety requirements included disposable gloves, safety goggles, a waste bucket, and a reminder to children to dress appropriately for the outdoor weather, including enclosed footwear. To make the most of our experience at the pond, we had each group collect its bucket of materials, read the procedures, and practice in a dry run. This allowed us to monitor students' use of the materials and to ask and answer questions about the testing materials, procedures, and potential results. Students were required to bring in permission slips. Under adult supervision, students made pond observations, collected water samples, conducted testing, and recorded their results. This was accomplished in 50 minutes.

Sharing Data

The next class period was devoted to sharing the different stations' data with the whole group. Students were to look at the significance of the collected data and what it meant for the health of the pond ecosystem. Students were given a teacher-developed resource that summarized the particular component their station was measuring. The resource included a definition of the component, its significance to the pond ecosystem, and the range of normal testing values (see Print and Internet Resources). Part of the students' research focused on discovering the acceptable limits for the different sets of data collected. For example, students discovered that dissolved oxygen levels more that 4 mg/L were sufficient to support most aquatic organisms.

The collected data was compared to data that had been gathered over the years by various elementary groups as part of their fifth-grade pond unit. The students used this to look at changes that have occurred over time to the pond and to develop a baseline picture of the pond ecosystem. The students were then able to use their data and observations to investigate changes that may have occurred to the pond as a result of the new addition of a pond aerator system. This is much like the work ecologists do when they conduct environmental impact studies.

Results and Assessment

Students were excited to write letters to the pond committee about the aerator. Studying and investigating a real-life problem that existed in their own backyard allowed students a rare opportunity to share their knowledge on a problem that they had become passionate about. We were pleasantly surprised by the students' use of content vocabulary and their application of science skills and processes in their letters (for a sample letter and a rubric, see NSTA Connection), for example:

- *The aeration system breaks down the algae that some organisms need to survive.*
- *It clears duckweed into different parts of the pond, and it even puts more oxygen in the pond for fish and aquatic life. The aerator makes the pond healthier.*
- *We found that there is 12 mg per liter dissolved oxygen. In addition we found more organisms have come to live in the pond.*
- *The pond is healthier now for producers, consumers, and decomposers.*

The concept of change was reinforced and reflected on throughout the unit. Students were consistently asked to reflect on what changes were taking place, categorize the changes, and place the changes into the context of the unit concept web. The idea that scientists use quantitative and qualitative data as a basis for their decisions throughout the process of an investigation was likewise an important part of the unit. In addition, formative and summative assessments were used throughout the unit to maintain focus on the content of ecology and the process of being a scientist and to document student mastery of identified learning objectives. Figure 24.4 is a warm up in which students were asked to compare and contrast a food web with a food chain. This ongoing assessment was created to check student understanding on three concepts: food web, energy pyramid, and the connection between the two. Figure 24.5 shows the large group debriefing of this warm up. By using this assessment, we were able to identify students who had a sound understanding of this concept, those who understood bits and pieces, and those who were still confused and had misconceptions. We were then able to use this information to adjust our instruction for the next class.

Reflection

As teachers, this was our first attempt at building and using a concept-based learning unit to teach scientific learning. Our personal reflection is that we learned as much as our students, maybe even more. There are parts of the unit that we would definitely keep and parts that we would do a little differently. This is change at its finest! The ability to bounce ideas off of another person, ask questions, and reflect with someone

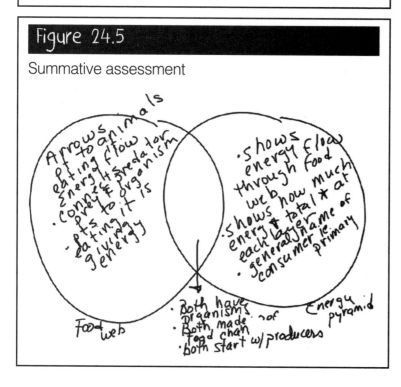

Figure 24.4

Formative assessment

Warm up 11/18/09

- Compare and contrast food web with energy pyramid. How are they alike? How are they different?

Figure 24.5

Summative assessment

cannot be underestimated. Throughout the unit both of us continued using our own approach to lesson planning and science. My desire to jump in and do the science often needed to be counteracted with the enrichment specialist's desire to step back and think out the steps. At times, this made it easier for the students to know what had to be done and to do it safely. Alternatively, students were able to gain enthusiasm for the practice of science by my show of passion for the science. By combining our two different teaching styles, our students benefited. We both feel that our first attempt at planning a concept-based unit was a success.

References

Erickson, L. 2007. *Concept-based curriculum and instruction for the thinking classroom.* Thousand Oaks, CA: Corwin Press.

Tomlinson, C., S. Kaplan, J. Renzulli, J. Purcell, J. Leppien, and D. Burns. 2002. The curriculum of parallel practice. In *The parallel curriculum: A design to develop high potential and challenge high-ability learners,* 163–207. Thousand Oaks, CA: Corwin Press.

Resources

Avery, L., and C. Little. 2003. Chapter 5: Concept development and learning. In *Content-Based Curriculum for High-Ability Learners,* ed. J. VanTassel and C. Little,101–124. Washington, DC: The National Association for Gifted Children.

Erickson, L. 2002. *Concept-based curriculum and instructions: Teaching beyond the facts.* Thousand Oaks, CA: Corwin Press.

Internet Resources

Pond and Lake Management
   www.otterbine.com/assets/base/resources/PondAndLakeManual.pdf
The GLOBE Program
   www.globe.gov
What Is Problem-Based Learning?
   www.udel.edu/pbl/cte/jan95-what.html

NSTA Connection
For a sample student letter to the pond
committee and an assessment rubric, visit *www.nsta.org/SC1102.*

CHAPTER 25

Inquiry Is Essential

By Rodger W. Bybee

Teaching children science as inquiry can present challenges to elementary teachers. One specific challenge is incorporating full inquiries as part of the school science program. With the process described here, elementary teachers can complement their use of hands-on lessons with full inquiries.

The Essential Features of Inquiry

First, it is important that you understand the learning outcomes associated with the essential features of inquiry in elementary classrooms. The following descriptions are based on *Inquiry and the National Science Education Standards* (NRC 2000) and adapted for teachers of science in elementary school.

Children engage in scientifically oriented questions. Children ask many questions and some may be about objects, organisms, and events in the natural world. Your job is to help them ask or restate questions that lend themselves to empirical investigation and gathering and using data to answer their questions. In the lower grades, the important learning outcome is helping students ask questions that can be answered through observations and simple investigations.

Children give priority to observations (evidence) that will help them answer their questions about the natural world. This essential feature of inquiry centers on observations and their role as data and evidence. Help the students understand the importance of accurate observations, and that measurement increases their accuracy. Depending on the grade, you may make the connection between observations and the evidence.

Children use their observations (evidence) to formulate answers to their scientific questions. The ability to use evidence as the basis for an explanation is one vital to science and one that will be helpful to all children as they develop as citizens.

Children evaluate their answers in light of alternative answers. Scientific explanations must be held as tentative. As new evidence becomes available, explanations may be revised and in some cases discarded. Children can learn this valuable lesson of science through group discussions that center on alternative answers to the same scientific questions and the role of more, better, and different observations (evidence) used to form their answers.

Children communicate and support their answers using evidence. Scientists make their evidence and explanations public in professional meetings and published articles. Children can complete their investigations by stating a clearly focused question, the procedures they used to gather data, the formal presentation of evidence, a statement of their answer to the question, and a review of any alternative answers or explanations.

Elementary teachers can introduce these essential features of classroom inquiry in individual lessons. For example, one can imagine a lesson on scientific questions, another in which students are given observations (evidence) and asked to form an explanation, and a group activity in which they learn to listen to other students present alternative results. All of these are worthy means to help students develop the abilities and understandings of scientific inquiry.

Elementary teachers also can use the essential features of inquiry as a means of helping students develop more self-direction as they pursue full inquiries. Figure 25.1 restates the essential features of inquiry and provides a continuum of more to less direction from the teacher and less to more self-direction by the learner.

Figure 25.1

Essential features of classroom inquiry and their variations (NRC 2000, p. 29)

More.............Learner Self-Direction.............Less
Less......Direction From Teacher or Material.....More

1. Learner engages in scientifically oriented questions.	Learner poses a question.	Learner selects among questions, poses new questions.	Learner sharpens or clarifies question provided by teacher, materials, or other source.	Learner engages in question provided by teacher, materials, or other source.
2. Learner gives priority to evidence in responding to questions.	Learner determines what constitutes evidence and collects it.	Learner is directed to collect certain data.	Learner is given data and asked to analyze.	Learner is given data and told how to analyze.
3. Learner formulates explanations from evidence.	Learner formulates explanation after summarizing evidence.	Learner is guided in process of formulating explanations from evidence.	Learner is given possible ways to use evidence to formulate explanation.	Learner is provided with evidence.
4. Learner connects explanations to scientific knowledge.	Learner independently examines other resources and forms the links to explanations.	Learner is directed toward areas and sources of scientific knowledge.	Learner is given possible connections.	Learner is provided explicit connection to scientific knowledge.
5. Learner communicates and justifies explanations.	Learner forms reasonable and logical argument to communicate explanations.	Learner coached in development of communication.	Learner provided broad guidelines to use sharper communication.	Learner given steps and procedures for communication.

Engaging Children in Full Inquiries

With the essential features in mind, the teacher can engage students in full inquiries. Of course the scope of the inquiry should be appropriate to the children's age, grade, and developmental levels. The following discussion incorporates the essential features in the context of full inquiries.

First, the activities of a full inquiry should engage children in identifying and shaping an understanding of the question under inquiry. Children should be aware of what the question is about, what background knowledge is being used to frame the question, and what they will have to observe to answer the question. The students' questions should, as much a possible, be authentic questions for them. To help focus investigations, students should consider questions such as "What do we want to find out about...?" "How can we make the most accurate observations?" and "Is this the best way to answer our questions?"

Second, the activities of a full inquiry should involve students in establishing and refining the methods, materials, and data they will collect. As students conduct investigations and make observations, their groups should consider questions such as "What observations (data) will help answer the question?" and "What are the best observations to make or measurements to take?" Children should be encouraged to repeat data-collection procedures and to share data among groups. In upper elementary grades, students recognize the relationship between the evidence they collect and the explanations they propose, that scientific knowledge guides the design of investigations, and that observations and the interpretations of data can vary. In turn, the observations and investigations students conduct become experiences that then shape and modify their scientific knowledge.

Third, a full inquiry has students produce an oral or written report based on the results of their inquiry. Such reports and discussions should occur once or twice a year in school science programs during the early years. To help them focus their thinking, the students' discussions should center on questions such as "How should we organize the data to present the clearest answer to our question?" or "How should we organize the evidence to present the strongest explanation?" Out of the discussions about the range of ideas, the background knowledge claims, and the data comes the opportunity for learners to shape their experiences about the practice of science and the rules of scientific thinking and knowing. An important element of doing full inquiries is developing the language, mathematics, and practices of science.

Inquiry is essential to science and should be basic to the science education of children in elementary school. To state this in the clearest and strongest terms, science as inquiry, including full inquiries, should be basic in the design of school science programs, selection of instructional materials, and implementation of teaching strategies. Students should learn science in the context of full and partial inquiry-oriented activities.

Reference

National Research Council (NRC). 2000. *Inquiry and the national science education standards: A guide for teaching and learning.* Washington, DC: National Academies Press.

CHAPTER 26

Five Strategies to Support All Teachers

Suggestions to Get off the Slippery Slope of "Cookbook" Science Teaching

By Paula A. Magee and Ryan Flessner

Many teachers shudder at the thought of implementing an inquiry curriculum. Perhaps they envision a rowdy classroom with little learning. Maybe they wonder, "How will this connect to all the standards?" Fortunately, these legitimate concerns can be addressed, and all students can engage in thoughtfully constructed inquiry science experiences. In this article, we outline five strategies that we have used with elementary school teachers as they moved from a "cookbook" approach in science to an approach that is inquiry-based. Having presented these five strategies in a linear format, we know that on the surface this may seem close to the slippery slope of cookbook science teaching, but we also know that thoughtful practitioners working in classrooms across the country will see these strategies as interactive, overlapping, and nonsequential.

What Is Inquiry?

As teacher educators who consistently work with preservice and inservice elementary teachers, we have found that it helps to clarify inquiry before looking more closely at specific cases of inquiry-based teaching. Because inquiry has been defined in many different ways (e.g., Banchi and Bell 2008; Martin-Hansen 2002; Settlage 2007), teachers can quickly become overwhelmed and frustrated. We use the National Science Education Standards as a guide (NRC 1996). The Standards describes inquiry "as a step beyond the process skills," (p. 105) in which content, process, and reasoning are synthesized as a way for students to learn. Although this definition can be helpful, it does not offer concrete suggestions for how to engage students in these kinds of experiences—let alone how to make the jump to open inquiry.

Because of this, we align ourselves closely with those who write about an inquiry continuum (e.g., Ansberry and Morgan 2007; Banchi and Bell 2008). An inquiry continuum assists teachers in envisioning the many types of experiences they can provide for their students. Typically, the continuum consists of three levels of inquiry: structured inquiry, guided inquiry, and open inquiry. Structured inquiry consists of teacher-generated questions that students explore through predefined procedures. This type of inquiry is typically used as a transition for teachers and students as they begin to move away from more traditional forms of teaching and learning in the science classroom. As they become more comfortable with inquiry-based teaching and learning, teachers and students engage in more collaborative inquiry processes. Guided inquiry provides teachers and students with opportunities to work together to define questions for study and the procedures for exploring those questions. In open inquiry situations, the learners typically formulate their own questions, develop the procedures for collecting evidence, and define the ways in which the data will be analyzed to answer the questions under study. We have seen each type of inquiry in the classrooms we have visited, and we believe that teachers all over the country are effectively using each type of inquiry in their classrooms (see Figure 25.1 on page 135).

To investigate quality teaching practices, we started by asking some general questions: What kinds of activities encourage reasoning and synthesizing? How do we include process skills and content? In our work with elementary teachers, we have tried to answer these questions by identifying strategies that support learning while considering student choice and decision making, each a central tenet of inquiry-based teaching. For us, inquiry experiences allow students to develop rich questions, to take lead roles in decision making, and offer opportunities for physical and mental messing around (Hawkins 1965), all as a way of making sense of the natural world.

Strategy 1: Use "Thinking Starters"

In some cases, it is feasible for teachers to solicit topics for investigations from students at the beginning of a unit of study. However, in most cases, teachers are asked to teach certain standards as part of their required curriculum. This requirement need not force a teacher to abandon an inquiry approach. As described, a structured inquiry approach is often a feasible starting point for many teachers and their students. The first strategy we recommend encourages students to ask questions, work with physical materials, and become devoted to an investigation in order to collect evidence that will allow them to reason through the possible answers to the questions they are pursuing. Although a more traditional activity may carefully list steps to follow, a thinking starter activity should be intentionally open-ended and encourage students to generate questions about the topic under study. In this way, even if the teacher has preselected the topic, then students are given an opportunity to share ideas, generate questions, and develop ownership in the investigations to come.

Strategy 2: Listen to Children's Ideas

To facilitate inquiry, it is critical to identify children's thinking and encourage them to share their ideas. When a teacher better understands her students' thinking and ideas, she is better able to develop experiences that will resonate with the children. We suggest two highly successful ways for teachers to hear children's ideas. One is through listening in on small-group discussions. The other is by recording whole-class discussions in which students share ideas from the work in which they have been engaged. Although it may take time for children to get the hang of a whole-class discussion, it has been our experience that once they become comfortable, they relish the opportunity to share. Obviously, it will take time to build this culture of sharing, but teachers with whom we have worked have shown great persistence. In doing so, they have been able to dismantle some of the children's beliefs about "how we do school." When possible, a circular sitting arrangement—with the teacher as part of the circle—works well.

A first-grade teacher whom we worked with routinely used the science circle to listen to her students discuss their ideas. During one robust discussion the class was wondering how the pond behind its school was formed. Students had already made many observations at the pond. They had generated topics of interest based on these observations and researched to find out more information. As a result of these investigations, the question *Where did the pond come from?* emerged. The children brainstormed ideas to find out. These ideas included: researching text sources, making more observations, and asking experts. Ultimately, the children asked the principal (an "expert" whom the children viewed as knowing the history of the school well) to share his expertise about the history of the pond. By listening to her students' questions and thoughts, and by providing a space for those discussions to occur, the teacher was able to successfully support her children.

Strategy 3: Use Standards as a Guide

Teachers, often under intense pressure to cover the standards, can get trapped in a mentality of squeezing in content. This can result in step-by-step activities that often lack student input and leave little space for student reasoning and questioning. We have found that children's ideas often connect to big ideas that are part of most state standards.

For example, an inquiry investigation using worms as a thinking starter encouraged students to generate many complex questions (see Thinking Starters on page 140) that connected with the state standard of interdependence. Keeping an expert ear open to the questions that students were developing, the teacher was able to connect strongly to the standards without sacrificing student input or reasoning. Supported by the strategies, students developed questions such as, *How does the anatomy of a worm affect soil?* and *How are other animals living in the soil impacted by the worms?*

Strategy 4: Develop Complex Questions

In one classroom that we visited, students were asked to examine Pop Rocks candy and to document things that they noticed that were interesting to them. At first the questions that the students developed were pretty basic, such as Who invented them? and What year did they come out? But after mixing the Pop Rocks with water, students began to notice additional things and generated questions such as: *Why do they pop? Do they pop in other liquids?* and *Why do they sound like Rice Krispies?* These questions prompted the teacher to focus on the popping component of the candy, and the students began an inquiry that helped them make sense of the carbon dioxide in the candy (by investigating the packaging in more detail and generating even more questions) and the pressure necessary to create the candy in the first place. If the teacher had stopped the children after the first round of questions were developed, the inquiry would not have become as complex. Instead the teacher continued to supply materials for further investigation (water, oil, Rice Krispies), and the students were able to develop questions around the chemistry of the candy.

Thinking Starters

In one fourth-grade classroom the teacher wanted to start an inquiry unit on composting. As a way to generate questions, she developed a thinking starter that asked the children to make observations while looking at a small teacher-created compost bin. The children generated many questions and were able to develop a two-month-long study that far exceeded the teacher's expectations. In this case, thinking starters were further supported by supplying the children with written or oral prompts that always included statements such as What do you wonder about? What would you like to understand better about this? What would you do next if you could choose?

Strategy 5: Document and Reflect

When teachers want to engage students in thinking beyond the facts, they often struggle. It is all too easy to fall back on predetermined lessons that ask students to fill in the blank. Even when thinking starters are used, teachers and students can get stuck determining how to make sense of all the different ideas that students might have. Teachers may wonder, "How do these seemingly disconnected ideas come together to help a child understand?" We have found that documentation (using science notebooks or specific prompts) and reflection (through writing, talking, and drawing) are critical. Most important, documentation honors the ideas that children have and allows them to return to these ideas over again. Strong documentation skills teach children to listen carefully and to find multiple ways to capture ideas that they and others put forth. Reflection further supports learning as teachers revisit students' ideas and ask them to think deeply about them as they work to identify connections that make sense.

In another classroom we visited, the teacher engaged his fifth graders in a unit on oceans— a state standard he was expected to cover as a fifth-grade science teacher. Because no oceans were readily available for the students to explore, the teacher encouraged the children to examine the school's pond. The class devised a tool to measure the depth of the pond. The classroom teacher collected the measurement data for the students using the student-designed tool. Using this data, students created 2-D and 3-D representations of the pond. Intrigued by their documentation, the teacher in charge of maintaining the school's outdoor lab (where the pond was located) alerted the class that they had "rescued the fish." The winter months were approaching. Based on the children's measurements, the water was not deep enough to sustain life underneath the sheet of ice. Because of their documentation, students and teachers were able to reflect on the situation, devise a solution, and continue the inquiry cycle.

Conclusion

It is our hope that teachers will see these five strategies not as a recipe to be followed, but rather, as suggestions to explore, discuss with colleagues, and inspire experimentation. This flexibility requires teachers to know their students, to understand the broader ideas within the field of science, and to constantly assess the teaching and learning taking place in the classroom.

Teachers who engage their students in successful inquiry projects are deliberate in their planning, in their listening and questioning, and in the pursuit of resources that will support their children's inquiry projects. We look forward to the day when the cookbooks are replaced by the ideas, questions, and inquiries of the creative individuals in classrooms across the country.

References

Ansberry, K. R., and E. R. Morgan. 2007. *More picture-perfect science lessons: Using children's books to guide inquiry,* grades K–4. Arlington, VA: National Science Teachers Association.

Banchi, H., and R. Bell. 2008. The many levels of inquiry. *Science and Children* 46 (2): 26–29.

Hawkins, D. 1965. Messing about in science. *Science and Children* 2 (5): 5–9.

Martin-Hansen, L. 2002. Defining inquiry. *The Science Teacher* 69 (2): 34–37.

National Research Council (NRC). 1996. *National science education standards.* Washington, DC: National Academies Press.

Settlage, J. 2007. Demythologizing science teacher education: Conquering the false idea of open inquiry. *Journal of Science Teacher Education* 18 (4): 461–468.

Internet Resource

Learning Science Through Inquiry
www.learner.org/resources/series129.html

CHAPTER 27

Fire Up the Inquiry

Lose the Routine, Tweak Your "Cookbook Lab," and Reach a Level of Open Inquiry With These Strategies Used During a Unit on Heat

By Kimberly Lott

Does the level of inquiry in your classroom need a boost? Highly structured "cookbook labs" are common in elementary classrooms because they are driven by step-by-step procedures. They are easy for teachers to set up and easy for to students to perform. However, they require minimal intellectual involvement for either the teacher or the student (see Internet Resource). With cookbook labs, students are not learning basic inquiry skills they will need to advance to more guided and open inquiry on their own; therefore, teachers get stuck in a lower-level inquiry routine. By following the basic steps outlined here, teachers can create activities to engage their students in higher forms of inquiry. To illustrate how a typical cookbook lab can be shifted to structured, then guided, and finally to open inquiry, I will describe a simple investigation third graders did on how insulators are used to reduce heat transfer. The heat activities I used were adapted from the heat unit found in *Science in Elementary Education: Methods, Concepts and Inquiries* (Peters and Stout 2011).

Scientific inquiry *can* occur on varying levels (Figure 27.1), but to reach the level of open inquiry, students must be able to master certain scientific process skills, including formulating questions, planning investigations, using tools and techniques of data collecting, and making evidence-based conclusions (NRC 1996). Every advance in inquiry levels allows students to develop and master more of these skills.

How do teachers break out of the cookbook routine? The obvious answer is to do more guided and open inquiry activities. To many teachers this sounds like an impossible task because they have the misconception that this would involve creating all new activities—but that is simply not true! The process of moving to full inquiry often requires only subtle changes to the existing cookbook labs teachers are currently using. Obviously, not all labs are appropriate for full inquiry, but most can be shifted to at least structured inquiry, and many can be shifted to open inquiry.

Figure 27.1

Levels of inquiry

Inquiry level	Question	Procedure	Solution
Confirmation Inquiry: Students are confirming previously learned material.	✓	✓	✓
Structured Inquiry: Students are given the question and procedures, but make their own conclusions based on their collected data.	✓	✓	
Guided Inquiry: Students are given the question, but they plan the investigation, collect and organize their own data, and make evidence-based conclusions.	✓		
Open Inquiry: Students generate their own questions, plan their investigation, collect and organize their data, and make evidence-based conclusions.			

ADAPTED FROM BANCHI AND BELL (2008)

Step 1: From Confirmatory to Structured Inquiry

Confirmatory inquiry activities are the typical "cookbook labs." Students are simply confirming what they already know. The teacher has usually introduced a topic and given the students background information on the objective of the activity. Next, the students are given a question for investigation and the procedures to follow to answer the question. Because the students have been given background information, they already know the correct outcome of the investigation. In a structured inquiry activity, students are given the question and procedures, but the solution is still a mystery to them. Shifting from confirmatory to structured inquiry allows students to practice the science process skill of using the tools and techniques of collecting data to form evidence-based conclusions. This step toward full inquiry is easiest for teachers to make because it requires the fewest changes to an existing activity. First, change the title of the activity to a question (if it is not already). Because the students did not generate the question, it needs to be engaging to spark their curiosity. Next, remove any objectives from student handouts that would clue the students to the "answer." In addition, make sure questions for students are unbiased and require them to make conclusions based solely on their collected data (Sherwood and Zavoral 2007). Some additional tips include modifying questions so that they (a) require students to make general summary statements from their data instead of specific objective answers and (b) lead students to ultimately discover the intended learning objective.

The final and most crucial step toward structured inquiry is to perform the investigation *before* instruction or text reading. Start the inquiry with an engaging book or demonstration to introduce the topic, but then let the students explore the concept through the investigation. After the exploration, teachers can then introduce the specifics about the concept (i.e., scientific explanations for results and vocabulary).

Figure 27.2

Confirmatory inquiry activity

Keep in the Heat

Background information:
Most houses have an inside and outside wall. Packed between the double walls of many houses is insulation. Insulators are used to reduce heat transfers; therefore, keeping the heat inside.

Objective:
Students will be able to explain that insulators are better at keeping temperatures constant (either hot or cold) because less heat is transferred.

Materials:
2 baby food jars, hot water, two airtight plastic containers, quilt batting, thermometers

Procedures:
1. Take two small baby food jars and fill them with hot water. Place the lid on each jar.
2. Wrap one jar with quilt batting. Place in the container and cap it. Place the other jar in another container and cap it.
3. After 20 minutes, remove the jars from the containers. Open the lids. Use a thermometer to take the temperature of each jar of water.

Data table:

Jar	Temperature
Jar without insulation	
Jar with insulation	

Questions for discussion:
Which jar of water felt warmer after 20 minutes? Explain why the jar with insulation was warmer.

Figure 27.3

Structured inquiry activity

Why do we have insulation in our houses?

Materials:
2 baby food jars, hot water, two airtight plastic containers, quilt batting, thermometers

Procedures:
1. Take two small baby food jars and fill them with hot water. Place the lid on each jar.
2. Wrap one jar with quilt batting. Place in the container and cap it. Place the other jar in another container and cap it.
3. After 20 minutes, remove the jars from the containers. Open the lids. Use a thermometer to take the temperature of each jar of water.

Data table:

Jar	Temperature
Jar without insulation	
Jar with insulation	

Question for discussion
Were there any differences in the temperatures after 20 minutes? What do you think is happening?

Why Do We Have Insulation in Our Houses?

I started with a typical confirmatory investigation of heat and insulators in which background information is given to students, so they simply confirm the information with the investigation (Figure 27.2). With a few subtle changes, the heat and insulator activity was easily transformed into a structured inquiry lesson (Figure 27.3). The activity title was changed into a more engaging open-ended question that would not lead students toward the "right" answer. The objective was removed from the activity. The questions provided after the activity led the students to confirm the previously learned concept that insulators reduce heat transfer, so they were replaced by a single question that allows students to make possible conclusions based on their data. Using the modified activity, the students can investigate the effects of insulation on the temperature of water and discover for themselves that insulators reduce heat transfer.

Step 2: From Structured to Guided Inquiry

Guided inquiry occurs when students practice not only collecting data to make evidence-based conclusions but also plan the investigation. The shift from structured to guided inquiry is not as easy as moving from confirmatory to structured inquiry because not every activity is appropriate for this shift. The questions a teacher needs to ask when considering this shift are

- Do students have the background knowledge to develop the procedures to investigate this question? and
- Are there multiple methods of investigating this question?

If the answer to either of these questions is "no," then guided inquiry is not an option for this investigation; however, these types of inquiries can be made less structured. The teacher can demonstrate the procedures, but allow the students to plan the data collection and organization. Remove any data tables or graphs from the student handouts to allow students to make decisions about how data should be organized and to choose the most appropriate graph for their data (Sherwood and Zavoral 2011).

If the answer to both these questions is "yes," then guided inquiry is an option for this investigation. The teacher can simply remove the procedures, data tables, and graphs from the student handouts. Give the student the question and offer a list of possible materials. Guide the students to think about which variables are relevant and how they can measure them (Sherwood and Zavoral 2011).

Allow students time in class to develop their procedures. As they are working, monitor their progress and offer guidance. Ask questions to spark ideas and reduce frustration levels. Some example questions might be

- "What are you doing?"
- "What are you thinking?"
- "What do you think would happen if … ?"

When students answer a question, the teacher must be objective as to not lead them toward the "right" answer (Sherwood and Zavoral 2011). Safety note: Even though students will be developing their own procedures, their procedures must still fit within classroom safety parameters (Sherwood and Zavoral 2011). Teachers need to discuss safety concerns with their students while they are making their investigation plans and make sure to "sign-off" on their procedures before they begin. Students need to understand that just because their investigation passed the safety approval does not mean that it is the correct way to solve the problem (Sherwood and Zavoral 2011).

Which Material Makes the Best Insulator to Keep Heat in?

Because I wanted to have my students do a more guided inquiry, I set up the structured activity before school (Figure 27.3). Using that activity as engagement, I then challenged the students to see whether we could determine which material makes the best insulator. My students were now performing guided inquiry (Figure 27.4, p. 146). Instead of simply investigating the effect

Figure 27.4

Guided inquiry activity

Which material makes the best insulator to keep heat in?

How will you know which is the best insulator?

What materials will you need?

What steps will you take to investigate different insulators?

Question for discussion
Which materials were the best insulators? Why?

of insulators, students were now highly engaged in a competition to find the "best" insulator. Working in cooperative learning groups, students listed the materials they might need. I had several different insulators on hand (cotton, wool, sawdust, torn paper, hay), but I encouraged the students to think of other materials that might be used. Students then planned their procedures to test their material. Many of the student groups used the same procedures as I had demonstrated in the structured inquiry activity. However, other groups felt that a thicker layer of insulating material was needed, so they changed the container that held the insulating material to accommodate more insulation. Safety note: Because hot water from the tap will be used for this experiment, I advised my students on the proper procedure for obtaining the hot water (out of the hot water tap), carefully transporting it back to their desk (with a Styrofoam cup), and then making sure it was immediately placed in a sealed container to reduce the risk of spilling and accidental scalding of group members. After they were cleared for safety, students tested their material and class results were shared to determine which group had the "best" insulator. A class discussion followed about why certain materials (or combinations of materials) were better insulators.

Step 3: From Guided to Open Inquiry

To have open inquiry, students must be able to generate their own testable questions. Many times student questions come from observations they make during structured or guided investigations. Observation skills are found at all levels of inquiry, but they are especially crucial for open inquiry. Even if they have participated in lower levels of inquiry, students may need to practice their observation skills before beginning an open inquiry investigation (Anderson, Martin, and Faszewski 2006).

Along with observation skills, students often need teacher modeling on how to turn their observations into questions. A strategy called think-aloud can help students make the transition between their abstract observations to testable questions (Martin-Hansen and Johnson 2006). Teachers talk aloud with their students as they make observations and discuss questions that emerge. By modeling this behavior for the students, they will be able to start generating their own questions from their observations.

Once students start to generate questions, they must be able to distinguish which questions are appropriate for inquiry investigations (Martin-Hansen and Johnson 2006). Sometimes questions that arise can be answered by making careful observations. For example, a student might ask, *Do certain butterflies have a favorite flower?* This type of question would have to be answered by careful observation because creating a butterfly garden in the classroom is not a feasible option. If a student asks, *What poisonous snakes live in our area?* The answer to this question can be found through books or internet resources.

Another technique for helping students develop questions for investigation is the Four Question Strategy (see Internet Resource). This strategy can be used during a whole-class discussion or could be used with smaller student groups. The teacher starts by asking the students the first question, "What materials are available for studying _____?" (Fill in the blank with the topic of interest.) Students then make a list of everything they might need. The teacher then asks the second question, "How do (does) _____ act?" The students make a list of observable changes in the object/organism/material being studied. The teacher then asks the third question, "How could you change the materials to affect the action?" The students review the list of materials from the first question and list ways they could change them. Last, the teacher asks the fourth question, "How can you measure or describe the response of _____ to the change?" Students review their list of actions from the second question and list possible methods of recording the actions.

After working through the four questions, students are then ready to form a question for investigation by simply stating *What would happen to _____* (insert action from the second list) *if I were to change _____* (insert material from the first list)*? From their list from the third question, they can identify the material they will change (independent variables) and all the other materials that have to stay the same (controlling variables). Their list from question 4 will help them identify the response to the change (dependent variable) and the most accurate methods of data collection to record the change.

Many times open inquiry questions emerge from guided or structured inquiry activities. The question a teacher should ask when considering whether an activity is appropriate for this shift is, "Can this activity be extended to another area of student interest?" If the answer is "yes," then open inquiry is a logical, easy step for students to make.

During our discussion about the best insulators, a student asked, *Are insulators good at keeping heat out? What if we had started with ice water?* And just like that, we were about to embark on open inquiry! Students used the same procedures they developed for the guided inquiry activity, but this time they were investigating their own question about insulators.

Subtle Shifts, Deeper Engagement

Advancing the levels of inquiry from confirmatory and structured inquiry to more guided and open inquiry should be a slow and deliberate process to alleviate stress on both the students and the teacher. With every step, students are given more control of the scientific process. Most students are not prepared initially to take on this control. This can be an especially frustrating endeavor for students who have grown accustomed to being told what to do (i.e., through cookbook labs). Students must have time to practice their inquiry skills at lower levels of inquiry before moving up to the higher levels. To determine when the students are ready to move up the inquiry level, I developed a set of criteria for assessing inquiry skills (see NSTA Connection for a complete list). The assessment is designed for individual students but could also be used for small student groups or a whole class if appropriate.

Just as students need more practice taking on more control of the scientific process, teachers need practice at giving up that control. When students start to design their own procedures, teachers need practice guiding students through this process and should avoid the tendency to just tell them what to do. Teaching higher levels of inquiry requires additional research and planning, because this is an exercise that requires a deeper intellectual engagement into the topic and not just a superficial understanding to explain the step-by-step procedures. However, just like the students, the teachers practice these skills at lower levels before moving up to the next level. Learning to make those subtle shifts from cookbook to full inquiry provides a mechanism for teachers to slowly wade into the pool of full inquiry instead of feeling they have to jump in to either sink or swim.

References

Anderson K. L., D. M. Martin, and E. E. Faszewski. 2006. Unlocking the power of observations: Activities to teach early learners the fundamentals of an important inquiry skill. *Science and Children* 44 (1): 32–35.

Banchi, H., and R. Bell. 2008. The many levels of inquiry. *Science and Children* 46 (2): 26–29.

Bass, J. E., T. L. Contant, and A. A Carin. 2009. *Teaching science as inquiry.* Boston, MA: Pearson/ Allyn & Bacon.

Hein, G. E., and S. Price. 1994. *Active assessment for active science: A guide for elementary school teachers.* Portsmouth, NH: Heinemann.

Martin-Hansen, L., and J. C. Johnson. 2006. Think-alouds in inquiry science. *Science and Children* 44 (1): 56–59.

National Research Council (NRC). 1996. *National science education standards.* Washington, DC: National Academies Press.

Peters, J. M., and D. L. Stout. 2011. *Science in elementary education: Methods, concepts and inquiries.* Boston, MA: Allyn & Bacon.

Sherwood, K., and B. Zavoral. 2011. "From Cookbook to Inquiry." Accessed January 18. *http://aimsnetwork.org/files/files/events/NI_Handouts/2007/From_Cookbook_to_Inquiry.pdf.*

Internet Resource

Contrasting Cookbook with Inquiry-Based Labs
www.phy.ilstu.edu/pte/312content/inquiry_vs_cookbook_lab.pdf

NSTA Connection
Download the complete set of steps for assessing inquiry skills at *www.nsta.org/SC1103.*

CHAPTER 28

Water Pressure in Depth

A Revamped Lesson on Water Gets Students Excited to Create Their Own Investigations

By Mary Jean Lynch and John Zenchak

How can a science concept be taught in a way that generates interest, gives students the opportunity to consider other possibilities, avoids one way of doing or seeing things, and gives them some ownership of their learning? Consider this scenario. We searched high and low for the perfect activity to illustrate a key concept for our partner teacher's fourth-grade classes: how depth affects water pressure (Figure 28.1, p. 150). We were excited because it actually worked and was student-friendly! Students understood that the lower the hole poked into a jug filled with water, the greater the water pressure. Unfortunately, their reaction was far from excitement: *OK, cool. Now what?*

The concept was so obvious that they weren't even curious. They didn't have to confront the idea or consider possibilities beyond the immediate situation. Did they really understand the relationship between depth and pressure? Many students believed that the amount of water in a lake affects water pressure in the lake. That is, a larger lake will have more pressure in it than a smaller lake. From the typical water pressure investigation, did they see that volume does not affect pressure? And did they understand well enough to avoid this common misconception about the topic? Probably not, because they had closure. This classroom experience was an endpoint, but it should have been the beginning of a more complete investigation leading to better understanding of the topic.

What we were seeking was a way to provide students with inquiry activities that encouraged them to identify and solve problems. Specifically, students needed a structure for problem-solving that was flexible enough to promote ownership of the process, which in turn, would lead to better understanding of the underlying concepts (Zenchak and Lynch 2011). To transform this activity into a real inquiry investigation, we included in our demonstration one variable—volume—that is commonly thought to affect water pressure, and not just the variable that actually affects water pressure—depth. With two variables, students had to use inquiry to determine which variable really matters.

Figure 28.1

How depth affects water pressure: A typical investigation

Materials:
An empty plastic jug (milk or juice), a nail (approximately one-eighth in. in diameter), water, a container to hold water, plastic packaging tape

Directions:
1. Use a nail to poke a hole in the side of the jug halfway up.
2. Poke another hole the same size above the first hole.
3. Poke a third hole (same size) below the first hole.
4. Cover the holes with packaging tape.
5. Fill the jug with water to approximately 1 in. from the top.
6. Place the container near the jug on the side with the holes to catch the water.
7. Remove the tape.
8. Observe the water streams.

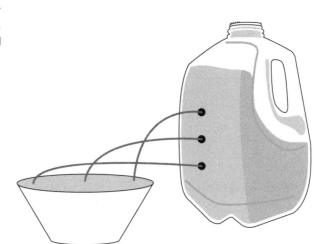

Results:
The stream of water from the bottom hole shoots out farther than the stream from the middle hole, which shoots out farther than the stream from the top hole.

Changing the Recipe to Inquiry

Our adaptation of the water pressure activity made all the difference (Figure 28.2). First, instead of using one jug, we used two jugs of different sizes (e.g., a half-gallon jug and a 1-gallon jug). Having two sizes allows you to include another variable (volume) in the activity. These materials are easy to obtain, and students enjoy reusing them for science. With a nail, poke one hole near the top of the half-gallon jug (4 in. down from the top) and one hole near the bottom of the gallon jug (2 in. from the bottom). Put a strip of packaging tape over each hole and fill the jugs with water to the same level (1 in. from the top of the jugs). Be sure to place a container at a lower level than the jugs to catch the water; then remove the tape. Students will see that water from the gallon jug shoots out farther than water from the half-gallon jug, but they won't know whether the difference was caused by the different volumes of water in the jugs or the different locations of the holes.

Now you have their attention and they begin to question: *What happened? What if you ... ?* They want to know which variable is responsible for what they saw. They are ready to explore and figure out what happened, rather than just copy your demonstration or something out of a book.

This is the perfect opportunity for students to learn how to design their own investigations.

A fair investigation has one variable that changes, whereas the other variables do not (they must be constants). If two variables change at the same time in an investigation and there are different outcomes, then it is impossible to know which variable caused the different outcomes. For the students to do a fair test to determine which variable caused what they observed, they must have materials available that allow them to focus on just one variable at a time. Therefore, additional gallon and half-gallon jugs allow them to change the variables independently.

Investigation 1

A fair test of water volume on water pressure uses two different-size jugs, but keeps the level of water above the hole constant. There are two possible fair tests for volume:

- A large and a small jug with the holes poked low in the jugs (same position as the low hole in the original demonstration); or
- A large and a small jug with the holes poked high in the jugs (same position as the high hole in the original demonstration).

Students can do either test; doing both tests is not necessary. As students prepare their investigation, have them mark where they want you (or a parent volunteer) to poke the holes. Teachers can do this after school. The results for each test should be the same—the water streams shoot out to equal distances—indicating that volume is not important.

Investigation 2

A fair test of hole location (depth) on water pressure changes the location of the holes, but keeps the size (volume) of the jugs constant. There are two possible fair tests for hole location:

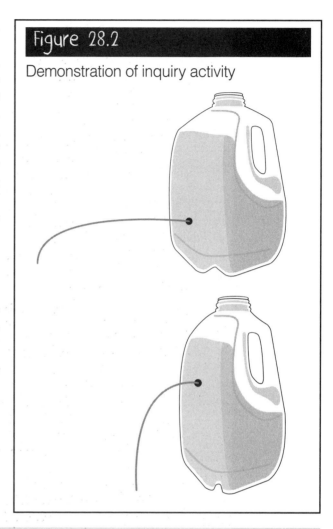

Figure 28.2

Demonstration of inquiry activity

Explanation of the Science

Pressure at any point in a liquid is determined by the depth (distance below the surface) at which the pressure is measured (Hewitt 1993). At any specific depth, pressure is caused by the weight of liquid above that point. In this activity, the farther (deeper) the hole is from the surface of the liquid, the greater the pressure is in the liquid at the level of the hole. Total volume of liquid does not affect pressure because only depth below the surface does. For example, pressure at the bottom of a very small lake that is 1 ft. wide and 10 ft. deep is greater than pressure at the bottom of a lake that is 1 mi. wide and 1 ft. deep because pressure depends only on the depth at which it is measured, and not on volume.

- Two large jugs, one with the hole higher and one with the hole lower (same positions as in the original demonstration); or
- Two small jugs, one with the hole higher and one with the hole lower (same positions as in the original demonstration).

For each test, the stream coming out of the lower hole should shoot out farther than the stream coming out of the higher hole. For either investigation, if the outcomes are the same, then the variable had no effect on water pressure. If the outcomes (the streams of water) are different, then the variable tested is responsible for differences in water pressure. Because the outcomes are the same in Investigation 1, water volume has no effect on the streams of water. In Investigation 2, the streams are different, so hole location (depth) is responsible for differences in water pressure.

Students are free to choose the specific constants for their investigations. Therefore, within the same classroom there may be two different investigations of each variable, depending on the students' choices. This inquiry method allows them to design their own investigations!

Student Assessment

Just as your activity does not have to be in a cookbook format, your assessments don't have to be either. We suggest a range of questions from traditional multiple-choice to more creative application.

At the beginning level, test student understanding of the science concept and process by asking students to recall what happened in the original activity.

1. Which variable caused the streams of water to shoot out farther from the sides of the jugs?

   a. Size of the jug
   b. Location of the hole
   c. Size of the hole
   d. Volume of water

   (The correct answer is *b*. Investigation 2 showed that hole location affected the stream length.)

At an intermediate level, see how well students can transfer their understanding of the same concept to a new situation.

2. According to an old folktale, a little boy in Holland saved his town from flooding when he stuck his finger in a small hole in the dam that separated the town from the North Sea. Based on what you learned about water pressure, where was the hole?

   a. The hole must have been near the top of the dam.
   b. The hole must have been near the bottom of the dam.
   c. The hole must have been in the middle of the dam.
   d. The hole must have been on the side of the dam.

Figure 28.3

Other examples of common demonstrations transformed into inquiry activities

Magnetism

Common Demonstration	Transformed Activity
"Which object does a magnet pick up?" Nail (steel) Penny	"Place a nail into each of two cylinders containing different liquids. Using a magnet on the outside of the cylinders, try to remove the nail. Which variable is important for removing it?"

	Setup #1	Setup #2
	Steel nail	Aluminum nail
	Water	Pancake syrup

Recycling

Common Demonstration	Transformed Activity
"See how one kind of packing peanut dissolves in water and one does not?" Styrofoam peanut Starch-based peanut	"Place a whole Styrofoam peanut and a starch-based peanut in pieces into water. Which variable is important in making a peanut dissolve?"

	Setup #1	Setup #2
	Styrofoam peanut	Starch-based peanut
	Whole peanut	Peanut in pieces

(The correct answer is *a*. Investigation 2 showed that the closer the hole is to the water surface, the less pressure there is; the boy should have been able to stop the stream with his finger if the hole in the dam was high.)

At the highest level, ask students to design an investigation when they are given only part of it. The content may be similar to the original activity or new, as in the question below, because the focus is on process.

3. You observe your teacher doing a demonstration with two identical yellow balloons. One balloon is blown to a large size, and the other is blown to a small size. Your teacher takes a nail and pokes it into the side of the large balloon, and it bursts. Then, the nail is poked into the top of the small balloon, and it does not burst. You are interested in testing whether the greater amount of air pressure in the large balloon caused it to burst. If the first setup of your investigation is a large balloon being poked on the side with a nail, draw the second setup needed to test for the effect of balloon size (amount of air pressure). Draw the second part of the investigation.

    (The correct drawing would show a smaller balloon with a nail in its side.)

For assessment questions such as 2 and 3, students may say that they didn't do those investigations. It isn't necessary for the students to have done the investigations before, because if they understand the concept and process, they can figure out the answer. If students can transfer their learning to other situations, then they truly understand the major concepts and are not just memorizing for the moment.

Empowering Students

In our approach to inquiry, students explore a science concept while directly confronting common misconceptions about it. Students may never understand that other variables have no effect if they only see how the important variable affects the outcome. Our format gives you, the teacher, an opportunity to embed in any activity variables that are at the heart of many science misconceptions. The key to transforming a common demonstration into one that promotes inquiry is to identify variables that people may think have an effect, check in advance to make sure they don't, and then include those "irrelevant" variables in the demonstration of the concept (Figure 28.3, p. 153).

Perhaps as important as confronting misconceptions is the students' ability to design their own investigations. This approach is an alternative to cookbook science and empowers students. With repeated engagement in the process, students learn to systematically solve problems and gain confidence in their abilities. They are excited to do science.

References
Hewitt, P. G. 1993. *Conceptual physics.* 7th ed. New York: HarperCollins College Publishers.

Zenchak, J., and M. J. Lynch. 2011. What's the next step? How to keep students engaged and on track when teaching inquiry skills during an experiment. *Science and Children* 48 (6): 50–54.

CHAPTER 29

What a Copper-Plated Nail Taught Me About Sharing Research Results

By Linda Shore

I was in elementary school the first time I ever shared the results of a science experiment. My teacher had assigned each student an experiment out of our science textbook, and my task was to electroplate an iron nail using a power supply, a piece of copper, and an electrolytic solution. The teacher helped us with our experiments, and in my case, even did it for me one day after school to make sure I knew how to connect the electrical wires properly and safely handle the chemicals. All I would have to do was precisely repeat the experiment in front of the class, get the same results, and accurately explain what happened using the chemistry principles we had learned that month. Students had one week to practice the experiments and prepare the class presentation.

I was nearly petrified when my turn came to present my science project. I had one chance to do the experiment correctly for my teacher and classmates, and to make matters worse, two students ahead of me had both failed to get their electricity experiments to work as they had expected and had to awkwardly describe what *should* have happened.

With my hands trembling badly, I poured the electrolytic solution into a glass container, connected the copper plate to the negative terminal of the power supply and the nail to the positive terminal, lowered both into the solution, switched on the power, and held my breath. To my immense relief, the power supply started making its familiar loud hum while the electrolytic solution bubbled vigorously. The students gasped with excitement. After a few minutes, I shut the power off, pulled the nail out of the beaker, and showed the class that what had once been an ordinary, dull iron nail was now plated with a fresh layer of shiny copper metal. The students cheered and applauded. My teacher smiled, nodded with approval, and gave me an A.

Although my electroplating "experiment" was a success, the experience left me, and probably my classmates, with serious misunderstandings about the nature of scientific research and the purpose of sharing research results with others. For many years that followed, I thought the purpose for doing science was to verify what was known and not to discover something unexpected or explore something new. It followed from my reasoning that if the goal of research was to verify science facts, then I concluded that the purpose of sharing work had to be to prove to others that you got the experiment "right."

Of course, my science project wasn't a research investigation at all, but rather a well-rehearsed demonstration involving little inquiry or critical thinking on my part. With a few changes, though, my teacher could have made the projects much more inquiry-rich and authentic—mirroring the ways that science research is actually carried out. For example, after doing the electrolysis experiment the way my text described it, the teacher could have asked me to change one of the variables, make a prediction based on my knowledge of the chemistry principles, and report what happened. I could have varied the voltage delivered by the power supply and observed how that changed if and how the nail got copper plated.

Sharing methods, data, findings, and conclusions—whether at conferences or through published articles—has been an essential part of my job for decades, starting as an astrophysicist and later as an education researcher. It actually took many years for me to abandon the elementary school notions that my colleagues were sitting in judgment of my work. I eventually discovered that my electrolysis presentation bore no resemblance to why or how research is shared. Unlike my teacher and classmates who witnessed my demonstration, my research colleagues do not know "the right answer." We are members of a community who are all equally in the dark and we share our work with each other so our research can be improved. Methods and findings are reviewed and debated vigorously. Research that survives the scrutiny of the community is accepted, moving the entire field of study a small step forward.

This kind of sharing is not unique to science. Experts in most professions rely heavily on peer discourse and review. Artists and musicians critique each other's techniques and performances. Physicians in hospitals go on morning rounds together to discuss their cases and review treatment plans. It is difficult to imagine any field of study that can progress without mechanisms for sharing, reviewing, and debating results.

This section of *Year of Inquiry*, devoted to how children can meaningfully share the results of classroom inquiry, could have provided my own elementary teacher with lots of ideas for incorporating discourse and peer review in meaningful, rich, and authentic ways. Perhaps my teacher could have divided the class into four or five research groups, each responsible for the same electrolysis experiment. We could have all started by copper plating the nail the way the textbook described it, then picked one of the variables to change, repeated the experiment, and observed the results. We could have informally visited each "research station" while the experiments were underway and shared strategies and ideas. Students having trouble with their initial experiments might have decided to adopt the successful techniques discovered by other groups. At the end of the project, we could have held a class "research symposium," shared our final results, and talked about what we learned. I think my classmates and I would have completed such a project with a far deeper understanding of the concepts and a more accurate conception of scientific discovery and inquiry.

It's amazing what a copper-plated nail can teach you.

CHAPTER 30

A Standards-Based Science Fair

A Revamped Fair Places Less Emphasis on Competition and More on Communication

By Peter Rillero

Imagine a science fair with hundreds of smiles, no problems recruiting judges, parent involvement at appropriate levels, and children engaged in rich discussions of their full-inquiry projects. These are just some of the benefits of the standards-based science fair.

In standards-based science fairs, children learn more about what they are interested in. They deepen understandings of how science works and improve inquiry skills—including the ability to communicate and share research results. Parents learn more about science inquiry and their child's science abilities.

The standards-based science fair builds on the strengths of traditional science fairs, but by having students compete against standards rather than against other students, the projects become more student-centered. The classroom format of this science fair features many opportunities for students to communicate about their full inquiry projects.

Science Fair Challenges

I have observed science fairs as a former science research teacher (where I had a special class for students to do science fair projects), as an evaluator for three Intel International Science and Engineering Fairs (ISEF), as a parent assisting with science fair projects, as a judge at elementary school science fairs, and last, as a science fair book author (Rillero 2000). In these roles, I have also observed challenges in elementary school science fairs, such as an abundance of volcanoes and solar system models. It is not clear why so many students build models when inquiry is not stressed. Perhaps they are thinking about their projects as museum displays or maybe their parents built models for their own science fair projects and guide them in this direction.

Many researchers consider children describing their work and research results with others as essential parts of inquiry experiences (Jennings and Mills 2009). However, elementary school science fairs often lack opportunities for children to communicate their work. When the children put their boards in the multipurpose room, because of supervision and idleness issues, it is often not practical to have them wait by their board for a few hours while judges make their rounds. Thus, at your typical elementary school science fair, judges judge boards; they don't talk to children. Children lose out on an opportunity to describe their work, answer questions, and receive verbal feedback and praise.

In a typical science fair, the judges' scores are typically not shared with children. Perhaps organizers don't want children to receive blunt criticisms of their work or they have concerns about low reliability among judges. This is a lost opportunity for children to receive adult advice for their project's improvement and their inquiry skill development.

Judges cannot discern what the child did versus what the parent did, because they never talk to the children.

Competition can help some students strive to higher levels of performance. At the elementary level, however, I believe student-against-student competition and declaring a few winners amplifies science fair problems and makes science seem elitist rather than an endeavor for all. There is a way to fix the problems with traditional science fairs, enhance the full inquiry benefits, and give students rich opportunities to discuss their work.

A student measures his plants at home.

An Important Change

One fundamental change fixes many science fair problems and creates new possibilities to enhance the inquiry experience and community of sharing: Shifting from children's projects competing against other children's projects to children, with parental help, competing against benchmark standards.

In norm-referenced assessments, students are compared to other students, providing information such as, "her science test score is better than 85% of the other U.S. students in fifth grade." Traditional science fairs are norm referenced; the few winners are selected because their scores are higher than other students.

Many problems are eliminated when the science fair shifts to a criterion-referenced approach, in which student achievement is determined with reference to established criteria or standards. The criteria for levels of inquiry achievement are set, and if children have enough points, they earn recognition. The criteria come from national and state inquiry standards. The term *standards* in the standards-based science fair is a double entendre as it refers to (a) the standard or criteria used and (b) the criteria that comes from state and national standards.

The shift to the criterion-referenced approach is powerful because a child's success is no longer based on the quality of other projects. When children and parents know what to do because they are given clear rubrics (Figure 30.1, p. 161), the majority of children will do full-inquiry projects, communicate their work, earn recognition, and feel great about their work.

The standards-based science fair establishes the idea that science isn't just for a few: It is for everyone.

In traditional science fairs, the problem with parent-centered projects is that other deserving students, with child-centered projects, may not earn recognition as a result. With the standards-based science fair, it doesn't affect the other students if another parent does way too much because student projects are not being compared. These other students (and their parents) don't end up feeling that they were cheated. Science fairs, as a result, seem much fairer.

Child-Centered Projects

With the standards-based science fair the goal is to redirect parent involvement so it is more appropriate for developing student inquiry abilities; projects should be child- not parent-centric. Ideally, the project should come from the child's interests. Safety note: Parents are still important to the process; they help to obtain needed materials and they ensure that the project is done safely. Children should not (a) work with hazardous, controlled, or regulated substances; (b) experiment on vertebrates; or (c) employ procedures that would place them in danger.

Teachers are also involved in making the projects child-centered. In-class full-inquiry activities give children an understanding of what they are going to be doing at home. Flannagan and McMillan (2009) have a useful four-question approach to facilitate inquiry. Students ask (a) Which materials are available? (b) What does X do and how does it act? (c) How can I change the materials to affect the action? and (d) How can I measure or describe the response of X to the change? Going through these questions helps students develop an experiment where a variable is changed.

In all science research, choosing a problem that is important and can be solved is the biggest challenge. To assist their work, children may be given some structure, such as a fill-in-the-blanks problem statement, such as "What is the effect of _____ on _____?" If children are interested in the growth of plants, they could investigate *What is the effect of coffee grounds on radish growth?* If they are interested in sports, they might investigate *What is the effect of temperature on the height of a bounce of a baseball?* The fill-in-the-blanks problem supplies the structure for students to develop a student-centered, clear, and answerable problem statement.

When assigning the projects, teachers should also give children dates for the submission of key parts of the project, such as problem statements and procedures, to make sure the projects are appropriate and progress is being made for completion on the due date.

Emphasis on Student Communication

Because the projects are done at home, children have to communicate what they were trying to find out, what they did, and what they found out to school audiences. The science display board and possibly materials from the investigation become props to promote communication and discussion. In the standards-based science fair, there are multiple opportunities for students to share their work. They can do a whole-class presentation and one-on-one presentations, and they can present to teacher, student, and parent audiences. For example, at Gavilan Peak Elementary School (which my two sons attend) a few days before the science fair, children present their projects orally with their display boards to the entire class and teachers use the rubrics to evaluate the projects as they are presented. On science fair day, each class displays their science fair boards in

Figure 30.1

Standards-based science fair rubric for grades 4–6

Standards-Based Science Fair Grades 4–6   Full Inquiry Standards Rubric

Student Name _____Teacher_____ Grade_____

Instructions to Scorer: For each item circle 0, 1, or 2. Do not leave any items unanswered.
0 = No   1 = Some Evidence   2 = Yes

	Evidence		
	No	Some	Yes
1. Is the investigation guided by a question?	0	1	2
2. Is a hypothesis proposed that gives a possible answer to the guiding question?	0	1	2
3. Are the procedures described in sufficient detail to allow easy replication by another person?	0	1	2
4. Is there evidence that a well-planned experiment was conducted? (*Note:* Experiments have comparisons, such as how plants grow under different conditions or experiments comparing different commercial products.)	0	1	2
5. Was appropriate equipment used (e.g., rulers, scales, thermometers, stopwatches, or magnifiers) to help collect data?	0	1	2
6. Did the student(s) measure and present quantitative data?	0	1	2
7. Are the data displayed in an easy-to-read graph and/or table?	0	1	2
8. Are the data analyzed to seek an answer to the guiding question or to evaluate the hypothesis? (For this item it is OK for the student to conclude that the results are inconclusive.)	0	1	2
9. Is the project presented in a manner that makes the purpose, procedure, and results clear?	0	1	2
TOTAL POINTS			

Circle the score below:
0–9   Falls far below inquiry standards
10–13   Approaches inquiry standards
14–17   Meets inquiry standards (Honorable Mention)
18   Exceeds inquiry standards   (Award for Exemplary Inquiry)

Additional Teacher Comments:

their classroom, with the child who did the project at the board so he or she can talk with visitors. Visits for other classes and parents are prearranged, so that children get many experiences describing their work and their projects. Many variations on the communication plan are possible. Larger schools might hold grade-level science fairs on different days. Some schools might hold their fairs in the evenings so more adults can attend.

Having a *classroom* science fair can help make the process more manageable. In traditional science fairs, students display their work in a large venue. Most schools have limited space, so projects have to be set up and taken down in a relatively short time to not affect other school functions. Instead, on science fair day children can set up their boards in the classroom and pre-arranged visits are conducted with other classrooms to learn about other projects and to communicate their work. These are designed to be like poster sessions at science conferences, where participants walk around, visit, and discuss the projects that they are most interested in. Children are given several blank "Kudos Cards" for the visits. When they like a project, they fill out the card and give it to the child as another way to say, "Way to go!" Parents are also invited to see the projects and this gives children another chance to communicate their problem, procedures, and results. On science fair day, the school community embraces the inquiry work of the children. There are hundreds of happy faces, and it is a celebration of science.

Teacher as Evaluator

Competing against standards as opposed to competing against other children means that only one person needs to judge each project. The most suitable person is the classroom teacher, who judges the project during the whole-class presentation prior to science fair day, using the rubric. As the teacher evaluates the projects, she or he gets firsthand data about the inquiry abilities of the students. Later, the completed rubric is given to the child, and the child's project is given a ribbon with the color representing the level of inquiry achieved. The child can then seek to improve his or her project for another science fair, or use what is learned to do a different project.

Unlike with external judges, the teacher-evaluator can use the score as part of the student's science grade. The teacher-as-evaluator eliminates the traditional science fair challenge of recruiting enough judges, and training the judges, which results in scores that are reliable and consistent.

Clear Rubrics

The assessment of inquiry is different than traditional assessments that focus on science content knowledge; inquiry assessment focuses "on examining the *processes* of engaging in scientific knowing and learning" (Duschl 2003). Rubrics can make expectations clear, which guide the children's work and the teachers' evaluation (Brookhart, Moss, and Long 2008). Clear and simple rubrics show the standards of inquiry that are expected in the standards-based science fair. Figure 30.1 is a sample rubric that can be modified to fit state and district standards and goals (see NSTA Connection for rubrics for grades 1–3 and other materials).

Depending on the criteria, children are evaluated with a 0, 1, or 2 for each item on the rubric. The rubric is constructed from the national, state, or district standards. In this way, the science fair is not only viewed as a tool for helping to achieve agreed-upon outcomes but it also provides a means for evaluating progress toward those outcomes. The rubrics help children, parents, and teachers know what must be done to achieve a high score. Plus, there is less confusion as to what a science fair project should be, because inquiry is the focus.

A Day of Celebration

Science fair projects can be a powerful tool to give children full-inquiry experiences fueled by explorations of their unique interests. The standards-based science fair has many improvements over the traditional science fair. Children discuss their work and answer questions, and ask questions about other children's work, turning science fair day into one of sharing and celebration of the accomplishments of all the children.

A student with her display board on science fair day.

Acknowledgments

The author would like to thank Principal Mai-Lon Wong and the teachers of Gavilan Peak Elementary School in Anthem, Arizona, for implementing the first standards-based science fair with all the children in the school.

References

Brookhart, S., C. Moss, and B. Long. 2008. Formative assessment that empowers. *Educational Leadership* 66 (3): 52–57.

Duschl, R. A. 2003. Assessment of inquiry. In *Everyday assessment in the science classroom*, eds. J. M. Atkin and J. E. Coffey, 41–59. Arlington, VA: NSTA Press.

Flannagan, J. S., and R. McMillan. 2009. From cookbook to experimental design. *Science and Children* 46 (6): 46–50.

Jennings, L., and H. Mills. 2009. Constructing a discourse of inquiry: Findings from a five-year ethnography at one elementary school. *Teachers College Press* 111 (7): 1583–1618.

Rillero, P. 2000. *Super science fair projects.* Lincolnwood, IL: Publications International.

NSTA Connection

For rubrics for grades 1 to 3 and other materials, visit *www.nsta.org/ SC1104.*

CHAPTER 31

Living or Nonliving?

First-Grade Lessons on Life Science and Classification Address Misconceptions

By Britt Legaspi and William Straits

I teach in a large urban area with a diverse student body. The diversity extends beyond ethnicities and languages to include a range of academic abilities and socioeconomic statuses. Once, a few years back, I asked my first-grade students the question "Is a rock a living thing?" To my surprise, several of them enthusiastically said, "Yes!" What seemed to be a simple enough question turned into more than just a teachable moment for me. It made me reevaluate the way I taught life science. During that moment, I struggled to keep myself from telling them the scientific truth. Instead, I tried to offer queries to challenge their logic. The following are some of my questions and the answers given by one of my seven-year-old students:

Q. Why do you think a rock is alive?
A. *Because it moves and drinks water.*

Q. Have you ever seen it move?
A. *No. But, I know it moves because at recess it's in one place and when I come back after lunch, it's in a different place.*

Q. Have you ever seen it drink water?
A. *No. But, after it rains there is a puddle under it. The puddle, it disappears because it drank it.*

Q. Well, how does it drink it?
A. *It sucks it up like a sponge.*

Q. Do rocks have babies?
A. *Yes, that's why we have little rocks.*

He was certain that a rock was living because all of his personal experiences thus far had taught him so. Although I have been teaching primary grade students for several years, I had never before given addressing alternate conceptions any serious thought. This incident prompted me to develop a series of lessons to help students practice their observation skills, ask questions, and articulate their own reasoning to others. In this article, I describe these lessons.

Looking for living, nonliving, and dead things

PHOTOGRAPHS COURTESY OF THE AUTHORS

Asking the Right Questions

Categorizing organisms as living or nonliving things may seem to be intuitive by nature. Yet, it is regulated by scientific criteria. The following are five of the most common scientific criteria used to define living things:

- ability to use energy;
- ability to reproduce (babies or seeds);
- ability to interact with its environment (external and internal);
- has cellular organization (single or multiple); and,
- ability to make waste products.

However, memorizing a list of scientific criteria does not make as lasting an impression as exploration can, especially for primary age children (grades K–2). In fact, at this early stage in their schooling, students' conceptual understanding has been shaped primarily by their personal and cultural experiences. Keeping this in mind, educators have some critical questions to ask themselves:

- What do our students come to school already knowing about living or nonliving things?
- What has influenced students' reasoning for believing whether something is living or nonliving?
- What might be developmentally appropriate responses and outcomes during related discussions or activities?

Just a Little Background

Students come to school with rules already in place. Their categorizing criteria have already been influenced by their personal experiences, also known as observations and inferences. Their intuitive sense has been coded by the observations and inferences gathered from their home culture (Caravita and Falchetti 2005). Jean Piaget's identified stages of cognition are well-known to educators and psychologists. His *Pre-Operational Stage* (2–7 years) is when children tend to see only their own point of view. They believe that all things are alive in

Figure 31.1

Living vs. nonliving classification rubric

4 (Advanced—Exceptional foundations in conceptual understanding for this age level)
- All things are classified correctly.
- Reasons for classification are consistent in logic and may even include scientifically recognized criteria.
- Reasons are based on at least three criteria.

3 (Proficient—Solid foundations in conceptual understanding to meet the standard)
- Most things are classified correctly.
- Reasons for classification are generally consistent in logic.
- Reasons are based on at least two criteria.

2 (Almost Proficient—Some conceptual understanding but not enough to meet the standard)
- Some things are classified correctly.
- Reasons for classification are inconsistent in logic.
- Reasons are based on one criteria.

1 (Not Proficient—Little or no conceptual understanding to meet the standard)
- Very few things are classified correctly.
- No reasons were given for classification.
- Reasons, if given, could not be based on any criteria according to the student.

some way or another—either it can move on its own, have feelings, or can think for itself. Piaget's *Concrete Operational* stage (7–11 years) is when young students use their experiences as a guide to how the world around them works (Bosak 1991). They can understand and develop rules. They also have the ability to think about and recognize that relationships exist between things. It is during the primary years that teachers help children to transition from the preoperational to the concrete operational stage.

Inspired by the conversations that I have had with my students, I developed a series of lessons to address the topic of living versus nonliving. In building these lessons, I maintained an awareness of the effect of their own cultural influences and developmentally appropriate responses for six- to seven-year-olds. The lessons I used in my classroom were designed to help my first-grade students develop their observational skills, their ability to articulate their own thinking to others, and the skill of asking themselves provocative questions.

Living, Nonliving, and Dead

Primary teachers are often asked to teach basic concepts about the characteristics of living things and life cycles. The National Science Education Standards charge us with helping students to delineate between living and nonliving things. However, in the course of my teaching, I have observed that my first-grade students experienced difficulty when they came across dead things. How can it be related to *living* things and *life* cycles if it's *dead*? In seeing this difficulty, I decided during classification activities to add a separate category labeled *dead*. I found this to be a useful way to scaffold the categorizing of living and nonliving things for the first graders. As the discussions and lessons continued, the "dead" column became a point of discussion leading to the redefining of this category as "once living." This distinction between living and dead is included in the activities described next.

Categorizing and Rationalizing

In Session 1, Part 1, my students practiced making an observation versus an inference. They stated observations and recorded them. Without prior discussion of the criteria for living, nonliving, and dead things, I assigned pairs to designated areas of our playground to find and illustrate the following: a living, nonliving, and dead thing. Safety note: Students were instructed not to handle things without teacher permission. Be sure to carefully examine the school grounds beforehand to identify and, if possible, remove any possible hazards (e.g., broken glass, poison ivy, unattended gardening tools).

Students were expected to give a rationale for classifying each item as a living, nonliving, or dead thing. They could jot down words, if they were able to write. Ultimately, they had to explain their reasons to a partner and to the class.

English Language Learner Tip: Elicit a word bank of objects that can be found on the playground from the students prior to sending them out with paper and pencil (adding simple illustrations next to the corresponding words adds clarity). When pairing students, place stronger English speakers strategically with those still acquiring the language.

For Part 2, the item name and rationales from Part 1 were written under the corresponding class-

A student illustrates what he's found.

generated list: living, nonliving, or dead. I then led a whole-group discussion on finding the commonalities amongst all the rationales. It was helpful to circle like terms in one color and

other terms in a different color. This made it easier to identify or isolate commonalities for discussion. I asked whether anyone would like to move any of the listed things to a different category. It was helpful to use sticky notes for this purpose. Some common elements stated by my students were *growth, ability to move, ability to think, ability to breathe, being made of metal, ability to grow seeds,* and *able to be killed.*

English Language Learner Tip: Though it added length to the discussion components, allowing students to participate in *pair-share*, a purposeful conversation between students in which dialogue may be directed for modeling correct grammar, gave them time to practice responses before sharing them with the whole class.

"Hmm, how do we categorize this?"

Discussing Criteria

In Session 2, Part 1, the class reviewed the categories and the commonalities in each of the three categories. We created a class set of criteria for living, nonliving, and dead things that reflected a few of the same items that are currently scientifically accepted (e.g., *eating and use of energy* for living things). The students evaluated and criticized reasons for their classification of things. During this session, my students were in a heated debate with me determining the difference between nonliving and dead things. They determined that both things did not breathe, did not have babies, and could not eat or drink. Just as we were at an impasse with reasoning, my wiggly and most inattentive student looked up. He cautiously raised his hand and said, "Um, the stuff that is dead was really once alive and the other stuff was never alive at all." Wow! He had made the connection that the others couldn't quite articulate! At this point, discussion followed with regard to changing the category title "dead" to "once living."

For Part 2, we reviewed the class-generated set of criteria. Next, I asked the following questions: "Where would you place _____ based upon these common criteria we have come up with? Why would you place _____ in that category?" *(rocks, bones, cars, eggs, and acorns)* I had students consult a pair-share partner for each item. I walked around asking guiding questions like "Is it alive? Is it living? Does it fit the criteria?"

English Language Learner Tip: If available, teacher should provide actual objects as visual aides (e.g., a real rock, replicas of bones, model cars, acorns).

Journal Reflections

In Session 3, we wrapped up our lesson with a discussion of observations recorded in journals. We also compared the rocks to humans using a chart. At the end of the discussion, we reviewed the pictures from Session 1. I asked students whether there were any changes they wanted to make to the list of criteria or move any pictures to other categories. I also asked whether any of the students would keep "rock" in the same category or move it to a different one. I allowed time for pairs to share their thoughts; this contributed to a more fruitful whole-group discussion.

Evaluation

I used a rubric (Figure 31.1, p. 166) to determine the level of students' conceptual understanding as part of Session 2, Part 2. My final assessment was to re-administer the classification activity from Session 1 and compare it to their initial classification skills. I allowed them to make observations for each category. First, they had to classify their original items and reclassify any or all of them. Second, they went back to the playground to find one new item to add for each category. They also had to make a list of reasons for their classifications. I took an overall look at the students' charts for growth in their conceptual understanding and for their level of developmental readiness.

As a result of the instructional plan, I found that most of the students (16 of 21) were using the key vocabulary (*living, nonliving,* and *dead*) correctly in both oral and written responses. For example, the students were able to explain that *living* things are those things that have needs (e.g., water and food). Most of the students stated that *soil* was something living things might need or that the ground (dirt) belonged under the list of dead things. Soil is a tricky item because it may consist of living, nonliving, and dead matter. This indicated to me that we needed to further explore the plant cycle and the role that soil plays as part of that cycle.

Another example is that most students were able to state that *dead* things were once alive but not anymore. They stated that dead things didn't move or eat anymore. In my personal research of the topic, I found that movement is a common element for children (9 months to 9 years old) and many adults as criteria for classifying something as living (Caravita and Falchetti 2005; DiYanni and Kelemen 2004).

Technology Tips

The lessons described previously can be easily infused with information technology. In lieu of illustrations, students can use digital cameras, camcorders, or document cameras. The digital cameras allow students to compare their factual observations with the images taken. The images can be put into a slide show and each student can share his or her thoughts. Teachers may want to create their own slide show of images collected from the internet, clip art, or other resources. During your slide show, you can ask the same guiding questions from Session 2, Part 2. Particularly useful is the ability to show multiple images on a single slide. The students can then compare and contrast those images. Cameras are also a nice alternative for students who have trouble with the fine motor skills involved in drawing but are capable of clicking a button on the camera. Camcorders can record thought process and reasoning as students wander around the playground. The document cameras offer the option of bringing things into the classroom to view much like a microscope. Some document cameras may offer a split screen on which students can compare or contrast two images simultaneously. All of these choices will require a projection unit, like an LCD projector or a television, for use with the entire class. Alternatively, a low-tech, low-cost version may be to print out the pictures and post them.

Final Thoughts

Opportunities for developing students' awareness of life as a series of interrelated processes need to continue beyond the primary grades. Teachers can provide a "push" or allow for the opportunity for students' conceptions to be challenged. This was just the case with my most wiggly and inattentive student who was able to make the distinction between nonliving and dead things during Session 2. Even though young children may not be developmentally ready to deal with challenging their intuitive senses, asking the right kind of questions and giving students multiple opportunities to challenge their thinking is still important. And, when the students are ready, then their experiences will provide a stronger conceptual foundation for them to build on as they move through their academic careers.

References
Bosak, S. V. 1991. *Science is…: A source book of fascinating facts, projects and activities.* Ontario, Canada: Scholastic Canada.

Caravita, S., and E. Falchetti. 2005. Are bones alive? *Journal of Biological Education* 39 (4): 163–170.

DiYanni, C., and D. Kelemen. 2004. Time to get a new mountain? The role of function in children's conceptions of natural kinds. *Cognition* 97: 327–335.

Internet Resource
Essential Science for Teachers: Life Science
   www.learner.org/resources/series179.html

CHAPTER 32

Claims, Evidence, and Reasoning

Demystifying Data During a Unit on Simple Machines

By Katherine L. McNeill and Dean M. Martin

A fifth-grade class is in the middle of a unit on simple machines. The teacher, Mr. Martin, asks his class, "Does a lever make work easier?" One student responds, "I think it makes work easier," another student disagrees stating, "I think it depends." Mr. Martin then responds, "Each of you has just stated a claim. By the end of our investigations today you will be able to provide evidence to prove which claim is actually correct."

Although students are enthusiastic when engaging in hands-on investigations, they can find it challenging to make sense of their data and to create explanations using evidence from their investigations. We spent a year designing and testing strategies in Mr. Martin's science classroom to better assist his elementary students in constructing and justifying their claims in both science talk and writing. Dr. McNeill collaborated with Mr. Martin to analyze students' writing and videotapes of classroom discussions to identify student strengths and weaknesses and to develop future lessons to meet their needs. Mr. Martin then tested those strategies in his two fifth-grade classrooms. In what follows, we describe the strategies we used to help students demystify data and share their results. We use examples from a unit on simple machines to illustrate the process, but the strategies and framework can be used in any science content area.

The Framework

The National Science Education Standards (NRC 1996) and reform documents (Michaels, Shouse, and Schweingruber 2008) include a focus on having students use evidence, construct explanations, and engage in argumentation. These meaning-making experiences, whether during classroom discussion or while writing, are essential for effective science instruction. To support students in communicating their explanations and engaging in argumentation, we developed a framework that simplifies these complex practices for students (McNeill and Krajcik 2011).

At the elementary level, we typically introduce the framework as consisting of three components: claim, evidence, and reasoning. The *claim* is a statement that answers a question or problem. *Evidence* is scientific data that supports the claim. The evidence can come from investigations students engage in firsthand or from research conducted online or in books that provide data. Last, *reasoning* provides a justification for why or how the evidence supports the claim. The reasoning often includes scientific principles or science ideas that students apply to make sense of the data.

As students gain more experience and expertise with the framework, we then introduce a fourth component—rebuttal. The *rebuttal* describes an alternative claim and provides counterevidence and counter reasoning for why the alternative claim is not appropriate. Typically, we have not introduced the term *rebuttal* until middle school, though elementary students can debate different claims and evidence in classroom discussions. The claim, evidence, and reasoning framework can support students in productive classroom discussions and science writing, because it provides them with a structure to communicate and justify their ideas.

Introducing the Framework

When first introducing the claim, evidence, and reasoning framework, Mr. Martin wanted to make the vocabulary accessible to his fifth graders, so he connected the language to his students' prior ideas and everyday experiences. In the introductory lesson, Mr. Martin began by asking whether anyone had ever heard of the words *claim, evidence,* and *reasoning* before. One student responded, "I saw a TV show that had police in it and they were looking for evidence." Another student said, "I know a reason for something like, the reason we come to school is to learn." Mr. Martin encouraged multiple students to share their ideas to develop a better understanding of their prior ideas about these terms.

Next, Mr. Martin posed a simple question to connect to their everyday experiences. He asked the class, "How was your weekend?" Clara replied, "I had a great weekend." Mr. Martin followed up by responding, "You did? Well you know something else you just did? You just made a claim." He then went on to explain to his students that a claim is simply an answer to a question. They make claims all the time in their everyday lives. In science class, we often make claims when we answer questions in our investigations. After discussing the term *claim,* Mr. Martin wrote the definition on a poster to provide a visual reminder for all his students (Figure 32.1).

Then, he asked Clara for proof that she had a great weekend. She responded, "I played with my cousins, we had a party, and we ate ice cream." Mr. Martin then explained that the proof that she just shared was evidence. *Evidence* is data that helps support your claim that

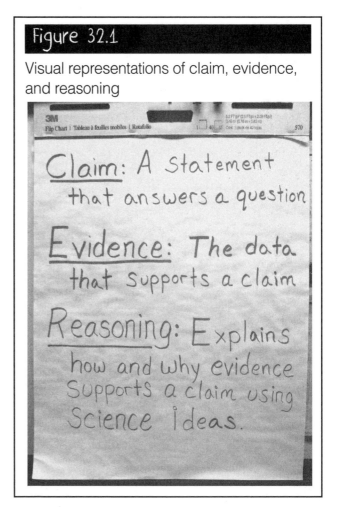

Figure 32.1

Visual representations of claim, evidence, and reasoning

Claim: A statement that answers a question

Evidence: The data that supports a claim

Reasoning: Explains how and why evidence supports a claim using science ideas.

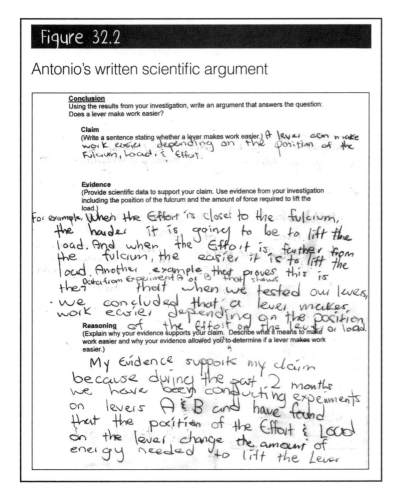

Figure 32.2

Antonio's written scientific argument

Conclusion
Using the results from your investigation, write an argument that answers the question:
Does a lever make work easier?

Claim
(Write a sentence stating whether a lever makes work easier.) A lever can make work easier depending on the position of the Fulcrum, Load, & Effort.

Evidence
(Provide scientific data to support your claim. Use evidence from your investigation including the position of the fulcrum and the amount of force required to lift the load.)

For example, When the Effort is closer to the fulcrum, the harder it is going to be to lift the load. And when the Effort is further from the fulcrum, the easier it is to lift the load. Another example that proves this is the Data from Experiment A or B that shows that when we tested our levers, we concluded that a lever makes work easier depending on the position of the Effort on the lever or load.

Reasoning
(Explain why your evidence supports your claim. Describe what it means to make work easier and why your evidence allowed you to determine if a lever makes work easier.)

My Evidence supports my claim because during the past 2 months we have been conducting experiments on levers A & B and have found that the position of the Effort & Load on the lever change the amount of energy needed to lift the Lever

you had a good weekend. After adding the definition of *evidence* to the poster, the class discussed other examples of evidence that would support the claim that they had a great weekend.

Last, Mr. Martin discussed the term *reasoning* by stating that reasoning helps you explain why or how your evidence supports your claim. He asked his class to brainstorm a list of things that answered the question, "What does it mean to have a great weekend?" The class discussed that having a great weekend means that you had fun and that you enjoyed yourself. Certain activities are often evidence that you had fun—like playing, a party, and ice cream—but not always. For example, you could eat too much ice cream and your stomach could hurt. So the reasoning needs to explain why or how the evidence supports the claim that you had a great weekend. Mr. Martin added the definition of *reasoning* to the class poster. He explained to his students that they would be using these three components—claim, evidence, and reasoning—when they needed to answer a question or explain the results from their investigations. They would need to support the claims they made in science class, just as they had supported the claim that Clara had a great weekend. The evidence would look different because it would come from their observations and measurements from their science investigations. The reasoning would look different because it would include science ideas. But their arguments would have the same structure.

In this case, the question "How was your weekend?" was used to introduce the framework. Other teachers we have worked with have used different everyday examples such as "Who is the best basketball player?" "How long should recess be at our school?" "What is the most popular song?" The examples the teachers used depended on the interests and backgrounds of their students. These everyday examples help students see that they already know how to construct a strong argument and that they can use similar strategies in science.

Designing Classroom Supports

After introducing claim, evidence, and reasoning in this initial lesson, Mr. Martin used the framework throughout the school year to support his students in making sense of and explaining the data they collected in their inquiry investigations, including with a unit on simple machines.

The fifth graders completed two lever investigations as part of the Full Option Science System (FOSS) module Levers and Pulleys (Lawrence Hall of Science 2005). In the investigations, Mr. Martin's students collected data around how the positions of the load and effort, relative to the fulcrum, affect the amount of effort required to move an object. Specifically, the investigations focused on the idea that a lever can make work feel easier, because a lever can reduce the amount of force required to move a load. The investigations did not focus on the idea that a lever may also reduce the required distance, though this would also be considered a mechanical advantage. In Lever Experiment A, the position of the load stayed constant, and the students changed the position of the effort. In Lever Experiment B, the position of the effort stayed constant, and the students changed the position of the load. In both investigations, as students manipulated the positions of the effort and load, they recorded the amount of effort required to move the load.

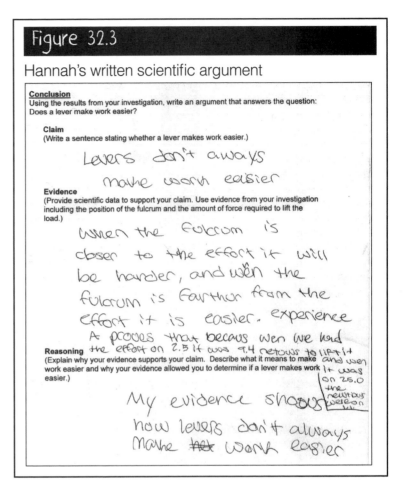

Figure 32.3

Hannah's written scientific argument

Conclusion
Using the results from your investigation, write an argument that answers the question: Does a lever make work easier?

Claim
(Write a sentence stating whether a lever makes work easier.)

Levers don't aways mahe work easier

Evidence
(Provide scientific data to support your claim. Use evidence from your investigation including the position of the fulcrum and the amount of force required to lift the load.)

When the fulcrum is closer to the effort it will be harder, and when the fulcrum is farther from the effort it is easier. experience A proves that becaus wen we had the effort on 2.5 it was 9.4 netous to lift it and wen on 25.0 the neutous were on

Reasoning
(Explain why your evidence supports your claim. Describe what it means to make work easier and why your evidence allowed you to determine if a lever makes work easier.)

My evidence shows how levers don't always mahe work easier

To help students make sense of and share the results from their lever investigations, we developed the student sheet in Figure 32.2. Specifically, we asked students to write an argument that answers the question, "Does a lever make work easier?" The student sheet includes writing prompts with *claim, evidence,* and *reasoning* to remind the fifth graders that they need to include these three components when they write a scientific argument. Students needed help learning how to apply the framework to different science ideas (e.g., biodiversity vs. simple machines). Consequently, we included in the writing prompts descriptions of what we were looking for in this specific investigation. For example, under Evidence the student sheet states, "Provide scientific data to support your claim. *Use evidence from your investigation including the position of the fulcrum and the amount of force required to lift the load.*" The first sentence provides a general definition of *evidence.* The portion that is in italics specifies what students should be using as data from their specific lever investigations. Including both the general and investigation-specific support in the writing prompts helped the fifth graders write the strongest scientific arguments by both reminding them of the framework and helping them see how to apply it to the specific investigation.

Using Rubrics

We developed a rubric to help us identify the strengths and weaknesses in the fifth graders' writing about the lever investigations (see NSTA Connection). For this specific example, we used the rubric to analyze the student writing to inform future instruction. In other lessons, Mr. Martin provided similar rubrics to his students to support them in evaluating their own writing and to help them revise their writing to provide stronger justifications for their claims. We used the claim, evidence, and reasoning framework to develop the three categories of the rubric and the content from the two lever investigations to develop the levels for each category (McNeill and Krajcik 2008a).

Using this rubric to examine Antonio's writing (Figure 32.2) helped us identify the strengths and weaknesses in the writing. Antonio provided the correct claim that a lever can make work feel easier but that it depends, so he received a 2 (on a scale of 0–2) for his claim. In terms of his evidence, he provided general statements about what occurred in his investigation, but he did not provide specific data or numbers. Consequently, he received a 1 (on a scale of 0–3) for evidence. This helped us understand that although he knew evidence was "Data from Experiment A or B," Antonio did not understand that he should use specific numbers. For reasoning, we gave him a 2 (on a scale of 0–3) for providing a generalization about levers stating, *The position of the effort and load on the lever change the amount of energy needed to lift the lever,* which articulates why he came up with the claim that it depends. Yet he did not talk about the idea of "work," which we had specifically included in the question and prompt to encourage students to talk about this scientific idea. Few students in the class actually discussed the idea of work, which suggested to us that they needed more support around including this science idea in their writing. Figure 32.3 (p. 173) includes an example from another student in the class, Hannah, who has different strengths and weaknesses. She also made a correct claim, but the evidence and reasoning she provides are different. We gave her a 3 for evidence, because she did include specific data (e.g., *when we had the effort on 2.5 it was 9.4 N*) to support her claim. We only gave her a 1 for reasoning, because she did not provide any generalization about levers or bring in the science idea of work.

The examples of student writing from these two students illustrate the challenges some fifth-grade students had with writing scientific arguments during the middle of the school year. Initially, introducing the framework helped the students be better able to provide a claim that specifically addressed the question and included some justification for why they came up with the claim. Yet they continued to struggle with including specific data as evidence to support their claim and providing reasoning to explain why their evidence supported their claim. Using rubrics helped us identify these challenges, provide students with feedback, and modify instruction to meet their needs. For example, based on the student challenges using evidence during the lever investigations, Mr. Martin facilitated class discussions during which students shared their evidence and had peers agree or challenge the quality of the evidence. This led to the class discussing and students recognizing the importance of including specific data (measurements) and specific vocabulary *(fulcrum, load, effort)* from their investigation in their evidence to support their claim.

Providing Support Over Time

Helping students develop strong scientific arguments during discussion and in writing takes time. After the lever investigation, we continued to provide students with writing prompts on their investigation sheets and Mr. Martin included a variety of teaching strategies in his instruction. He used instructional strategies such as modeling and critiquing samples of writing, connecting to everyday examples, and providing students with feedback (McNeill and Krajcik 2008b).

Reasoning was the most challenging component for his students to grasp. One strategy we used to help students understand what counts as good reasoning was to discuss examples of both strong and weak reasoning statements. For example, Figure 32.4 illustrates a multiple-choice task in which students had to select which reasoning statement was the strongest for an investigation focused on the question "Does friction affect the distance a car travels?"

Over the course of the school year, Mr. Martin provided his students with a variety of different supports. His fifth graders became better able to make sense of their data and appropriately share the results of their inquiry investigations in which they justified the claims they made with evidence and reasoning.

Figure 32.4

Does friction affect the distance a car travels?

Circle **ONE** of the following.

A. The data showed us that the car traveled the farthest distance on linoleum, a medium distance on sandpaper, and the shortest distance on the rug. That is why my evidence supports my claim.

B. Friction is a force that resists motion. The rug had the roughest surface so it had the most friction. The linoleum was smooth so it had the least friction. So the greater the friction, the shorter the distance the car will travel.

C. We had fun doing this experiment in class. The data showed that the greater the friction, the shorter the distance a car travels. All of the groups got the same results so that is how we know it is true.

References

Lawrence Hall of Science. 2005. *Full option science system: Levers and pulleys.* Nashua, NH: Delta Education.

McNeill, K. L., and J. Krajcik. 2008a. Assessing middle school students' content knowledge and reasoning through written explanations. In *Assessing science learning: Perspectives from research and practice,* eds. J. Coffey, R. Douglas, and C. Stearns, 101–116. Arlington, VA: NSTA Press.

McNeill, K. L., and J. Krajcik. 2008b. Inquiry and scientific explanations: Helping students use evidence and reasoning. In *Science as inquiry in the secondary setting,* eds. J. Luft, R. Bell, and J. Gess-Newsome, 121–134. Arlington, VA: NSTA Press.

McNeill, K. L., and J. Krajcik. 2011. *Supporting grade 5–8 students in constructing explanations in science: The claim, evidence and reasoning framework for talk and writing.* Boston, MA: Pearson Education.

Michaels, S., A. W. Shouse, and H. A. Schweingruber. 2008. *Ready, set, science! Putting research to work in K–8 science classrooms.* Board on Science Education, Center for Education, Division of Behavioral and Social Sciences and Education. Washington, DC: National Academies Press.

National Research Council (NRC). 1996. *National science education standards.* Washington, DC: National Academies Press.

NSTA Connection
Download the rubric at *www.nsta.org/SC1104*.

ASSESSING INQUIRY

CHAPTER 33

The Changing Landscape of Assessment

By Richard A. Duschl

"The times they are a changin'" Bob Dylan wrote in the 1960s. How very appropriate is that sentiment today in science education. The National Research Council (NRC) summary reports *Taking Science to School* (2007) and *Ready, Set, Science!* (2008) informed us that we have underestimated the science abilities of K–8 children. Children, even before kindergarten, are more capable than we ever thought—capable when accessible contexts are used and the classroom environment is geared toward the critique and communication of ideas and information. Surely, we have all noticed how a child's motivation, interest, and abilities can shift from one science topic to another. Our images of children need changing.

STEM policy reports like *The Opportunity Equation* (see Internet Resource) inform us of the need to align curricula, instruction, and assessments and to do so around core standards that are fewer, higher, and coherent. Our guidelines for selecting and sequencing what to teach within and across grades need changing.

A Framework for K–12 Science Education (NRC 2012) is organized around the coordination of three domains: practices, crosscutting concepts, and core ideas. The new *Framework* forms the core of the *Next Generation Science Standards.* An additional charge is that the standards be linked to learning performances. How we assess, what we assess, and when we assess need changing.

Assessing and evaluating science learning and the progression of learning is complex. Learning to do so effectively will require collaborations with classroom teachers and science educators like you. It is a complex problem. Sound classroom-level assessments by teachers are what keep learning on track. New technologies (cell phones, handhelds) and new tools (diagnostic assessment systems) provide teachers with information to guide learning and adapt instruction. Research has long informed us that the best learning environments—be they classrooms, homes, museums, or day care centers—monitor and mediate learning. Giving quality feedback on meaning-making and reasoning is what makes a great teacher. The research is telling us that teacher practices in regard to what is assessed and how it is assessed need changing.

In science, one important domain is assessing inquiry—monitoring and giving feedback on the knowledge meaning-making and the investigative and cognitive science practices that comprise the essence of science (namely, using evidence for building and refining explanations, models, and mechanisms). Although science involves doing investigations to obtain evidence, science is so much more. Our images of inquiry frameworks need changing.

Learning science, as we well know, is not simply learning facts and knowledge claims. Learning science is using facts and claims to pose, build, and refine explanatory models and mechanisms. As such, assessing inquiry is the keystone to good science instruction. I (along with others) have interpreted the essential features of inquiry (NRC 2000) as containing three transformations in scientific inquiry (Duschl 2003):

- Data to evidence, or determining whether data are anomalous or count as valid evidence;
- Evidence to patterns, or searching for patterns in and generating models for evidence/data; and
- Patterns to explanations, or developing explanations on the basis of the evidence/models selected.

Assessment of inquiry should focus on students making these transformations. Unpacking these transformations brings us to the central role of scientific practices. What the inquiry transformations signal is the need to make evidence problematic for students. Not something given but rather something that is obtained, evaluated, wrestled with, argued over, applied, represented, and communicated. What we want for children at all grade levels is to experiment for reasons and to reason about experiments. Our images of doing science need to change.

Taking Science to School (NRC 2007) tells us we need to move from science processes to science practices. Curriculum materials and instructional methods need to change from thinking about teaching general inquiry processes to thinking about teaching and having students engage in specific science practices. This is what the four Strands of Science Proficiency in *Ready, Set, Science!* (NRC 2008) are all about:

- Strand 1: *Understanding Scientific Explanations*—e.g., understand central concepts and use them to build and critique scientific arguments;
- Strand 2: *Generating Scientific Evidence*—e.g., generating and evaluating evidence as part of building and refining models and explanations of the natural world;
- Strand 3: *Reflecting on Scientific Knowledge*—e.g., understanding that doing science entails searching for core explanations and the connections between them; and
- Strand 4: *Participating Productively in Science*—e.g., understand the appropriate norms when presenting scientific arguments and evidence and to practice productive social interactions with peers around classroom science investigations.

So what does research tell us inquiry sounds like?

- *Planning investigations for data* is children deciding the selection of questions, tools, schedules for observation, and units for measurement.

- *Data collection to evidence* is children observing systematically, measuring accurately, structuring data, and setting standards for quality control.
- *Evidence to searching for patterns and building models* is children constructing and defending arguments, presenting evidence, engaging in mathematical modeling, and using physical and computational tools.
- *Patterns and models to generate explanations* is the sound of children posing theories, building and reporting conceptual-based models, considering alternatives, and generating new productive questions.

Fundamentally, assessing inquiry is all about making thinking visible through "Talk and Argument" and through "Modeling and Representation," Chapters 5 and 6, respectively in *Ready, Set, Science!* (NRC 2008). Assessing science inquiry begins with teachers and students learning how to listen for and respond to the core science practices involved with the critique and communication of science claims. The set of research and policy reports are strong evidence that we as teachers, science educators, and science education researchers have learned how to learn about learning. The answer isn't just "blowin' in the wind," now we have evidence!

References

Duschl, R. A. 2003. Assessment of Inquiry. In *Everyday Assessment in the Science Classroom,* eds. J. M. Atkin and J. Coffey (pp. 41–59). Arlington, VA: NSTA Press.

National Research Council (NRC). 2012. *A framework for K–12 science education: Practices, crosscutting concepts, and core ideas.* Washington, DC: National Academies Press.

National Research Council (NRC). 2000. *Inquiry and the national science education standards: A guide for teaching and learning.* Washington, DC: National Academies Press.

National Research Council (NRC). 2007. *Taking science to school! Learning and teaching science in grades K–8.* Washington, DC: National Academies Press.

National Research Council (NRC). 2008. *Ready, set, science!: Putting research to work in K–8 science classrooms.* Washington, DC: National Academies Press.

Internet Resource

The Opportunity Equation
http://opportunityequation.org

CHAPTER 34

Feed up, Feedback, and Feed Forward

How One Teacher Assesses Her Kindergarteners During a Unit on Conservation

By Douglas Fisher and Nancy Frey

M ention assessment and most people are likely to think about standardized tests and other formal methods for measuring what students know. But traditional paper-and-pencil tests inadequately describe what a child knows and still needs to learn because they come too late in the learning cycle. Children have a deep curiosity about the physical, biological, and social world, and they require an assessment system that fits with this science inquiry. In other words, they need a formative assessment system that feeds up, feeds back, and feeds forward. This assessment process, first described by Hattie and Timperley (2007), focuses on the ongoing information that is transmitted between teacher and student throughout the unit. Our experiences suggest that all three of these components are necessary for assessments to be of value, and on the plus side, none of them interfere with inquiry learning!

Feeding up establishes a substantive line of inquiry that compels learners to engage in investigation and inquire. It also forms the basis for the assessments that follow. Once students understand the purpose and begin to work, they receive *feedback* that is timely and scaffolds their understanding. Based on their responses, the teacher gains a sense of what learners know and do not know. These practices drive a *feed forward* system that informs the teacher about what needs to be taught, or what students need to experience, next. Hattie and Timperley (2007) described this as an "ideal learning environment or experience" that "occurs when both teachers and students seek answers to each of these questions" (p. 8). The dynamic nature of this inquiry-based assessment approach allows the teacher to make adjustments as students gain knowledge and skills and respond in a timely fashion when their learning stalls.

On the following pages, we describe how a kindergarten science teacher used this inquiry-based approach to assessment with her students during a unit on conservation of resources. She found that this approach to assessment allowed her to make adjustments in instruction and experiences as students needed them, rather than wait until the end of the unit. In addition, this formative assessment system complemented her inquiry approach and the information she collected about student understanding did not interrupt her students' investigation.

Feed Up: The Purpose of Assessment

Kindergarten teacher Debra Randall wanted to introduce her students to the principles of conservation using an essential question that would invite investigation and experimentation. In preparation for this unit, the students had filled two clear glass jars with soil the previous month. The soil in one jar covered a used plastic straw from one of the children's juice boxes, whereas the other covered an apple core from another child's lunch. A month later, she introduced the essential question to her students: "Where does trash and garbage come from, and where does it go?"

Safety note: The teacher (not students) should unearth the materials in front of students. Then place each item in a separate sealed plastic bag. This will prevent any exposure to potential microbes or fungi. Also have students wash their hands with soap and water once they are done viewing and handling the bag.

This provided the children with an overarching purpose for their unit of study. Each daily lesson included a statement of purpose that students used to guide their inquiry. For example, the students were told that "the purpose of this lesson is for you to use your observational skills to describe what you're finding out about what happened to the plastic straw and the apple. Each of you will draw what you're seeing and talk about it with your team." This purpose statement was an important and effective instructional routine to support her student's learning (Hill and Flynn 2006). It also focused her formative assessment of the lesson because it made clear how and what she would assess.

Ms. Randall distributed clipboards with observation sheets attached and then invited several children at a time to observe the two items. As they studied the contents of the two jars, the teacher modeled how she posed questions to herself. "I wonder how these two things have changed," she said, "and I'm thinking about what they looked like when we put them in the jars last month." As students returned to their tables to draw and discuss, she made notes on the observation behaviors of each child, and wrote down some of their questions, as when Araceli asked, "Why did the colored stripe on the straw change?"

Once all of the children had an opportunity to view the jars, Ms. Randall visited each table to gather further information about their budding understanding of decomposition. All the materials students had access to in this investigation decompose. However, the length of time required for each material's decomposition varied. The drawings each child completed gave Ms. Randall further information about their learning. Although Xiomara's drawing included wavy lines indicating that the jar containing the apple had an odor, Jorge's did not. Noticing these differences allowed the teacher to consider student understanding and how to facilitate additional learning experiences.

Ms. Randall was preparing students to construct and maintain a small composting heap outside their classroom and continued to build their understanding through shared readings of texts such as *Recycle!* (Gibbons 1996), *Diary of a Worm* (Cronin 2003), and *Earthdance* (Ryder 1999). At this time she introduced a simple rubric to her students based on "I can" statements so that the children could use this language in their conversations with their teacher as they reflected on their progress (Figure 34.1). This further reinforced the feed-up process of estab-

Figure 34.1

Rubric for kindergarten recycling unit

Our science goals	I can do this by myself!	I am learning how to do this.	This is new for me.
Using math in science	I can measure the amount of trash and garbage we generate and reduce it.	I know how much trash we generate, but I don't know how to reduce it.	I don't know how much trash and garbage we generate.
Using science every day	I can take care of our compost bin.	I can follow my teacher's directions for taking care of the compost bin.	I haven't used a compost bin before.
Using science to make the world a better place	I can sort trash and garbage for recycling and composting.	Most of the time I can sort trash and garbage correctly.	I don't know how to sort trash and garbage yet.
Using science to solve problems	When there is a problem, I can use my science knowledge to solve it.	I am beginning to use what I know about science. Sometimes the teacher solves it for me.	The teacher solves most of my science problems.
Communicating with others	I can work with others to offer, ask for, accept, and politely decline help.	Sometimes this is hard for me to remember to work with others, but I am doing this more often now.	It is hard for me to work with others, and I like to work by myself.

lishing purpose in the minds of the students. It also set the stage for Ms. Randall to provide feedback during the inquiry unit.

Feedback: How Am I Doing?

Several days later, Ms. Randall's students constructed a simple composting heap in the school garden, which was fenced in and used by multiple classes. Students also set up recycling bins in the classroom (see Internet Resource).

Safety note: The teacher needs to inspect all student items for the compost heap to make sure they are appropriate and will decompose (i.e., food scraps, paper containers, no meat or plastic). Hands must always be washed with soap and water after working with compost materials. A few individuals may be sensitive to some of the organisms (e.g., mold) in compost. The compost pile should not be stirred or disturbed when individuals who are susceptible to inhalation of allergens are nearby. Check with the school nurse and inform parents of this activity prior to having students do it.

PHOTOGRAPHS COURTESY OF THE AUTHORS

Making observations of fresh apples and a decomposing core (in bag)

Definitions

Feeding up: Establishes a substantive line of inquiry that compels learners to engage in investigation and inquire and forms the basis for the assessments that follow.

Feedback: When students understand the purpose and begin to work, they receive feedback that is timely and scaffolds their understanding.

Feed Forward: A system that informs the teacher about what needs to be taught, or what students need to experience next.

The students were going to investigate how much trash and garbage their class generates and find ways to recycle as much of it as possible. The teacher gave each team responsibilities for collecting, sorting, weighing, and charting their refuse. One team maintained the compost heap, another maintained the recycling bins, and so on. Ms. Randall provided the necessary materials, including earthworms and tools (such as shovels), as well as instructions for completing tasks safely (e.g., wear gloves when handling trash, properly handle and use tools). After the lunch scraps were gathered, sorted, and weighed, one group added the items to the compost heap and gently mixed it for the earthworms. The entire class observed the changes they saw each day and discussed it with their teacher, who chronicled their observations on chart paper.

Ms. Randall was interested in their content knowledge and the ways her students worked collaboratively. She collected observational data of her own about the way each team functioned using a narrative tool, with the following indicators: (1) Students are interacting with one another to build each other's knowledge. Outward indicators include body language and movement associated with meaningful conversations, and shared visual gaze on materials. (2) Students use accountable talk to persuade, provide evidence, ask questions of one another, and disagree without being disagreeable.

Ms. Randall's students know that she provides them with information about what they do well and what they still need to learn about working well together. Since the beginning of the school year, students worked on what Ms. Randall calls "the helping curriculum." She believes that a key life skill for all of her students is to learn how to ask for help, offer help to others, accept help, and politely decline help (Sapon-Shevin 1998). When she noticed that the composting group was having difficulty accepting help from one another, wanting instead to do everything alone, she recognized that this needed to be addressed. She knew this lack of collaboration would be a barrier to their science learning, so she met with the children, using the rubric (Figure 34.1) as a way to ground the discussion.

"When you were adding the lunch leftovers to the composting pile yesterday, I saw that you were tussling over who would throw them in, who would stir, and who would add the water. Can you tell me about that?" Over the course of several minutes, it became clear that the group had not agreed on whether one person a day should do all the work, or whether all three of them should work together each day. As Ms. Randall reflected on their concerns, the students began to realize that the job was

Learning what is recyclable

bigger than one person could handle, and would take too long. They agreed to try out the task together. "After you try it together tomorrow, let's talk about it again to see what worked and what didn't." In this case, Ms. Randall used feedback to develop opportunities for her students to make changes. By ensuring timely and actionable feedback and follow up, the children had a clear way to apply the feedback constructively.

Feed Forward: Where Do We Go Next?

An overlooked aspect of assessment is using the data collected to make instructional decisions. Assessments can be used as a tool for learning when teachers focus on the feed forward aspect and then guide students to additional learning experiences. As we have noted, it is not sufficient to simply provide students with feedback about their performance. Instead, we have to analyze the errors, misconceptions, and partial understandings that students have and plan next-step instruction to ensure that they gain a greater understanding. Feed-forward instruction does not mean that students are told the information they are missing, though, as that would violate the entire inquiry process. Rather, feed-forward instruction should involve additional experiences that help students clarify their understanding and can involve the teacher in questioning, prompting, and cueing learners. Unfortunately, when students make mistakes, their teachers can also err by re-assuming the cognitive responsibility in an effort to provide the missing information. Instead of directly explaining, teachers can guide students to greater understanding through the use of questions, prompts, and cues.

Questions should allow the teacher to check for understanding. These brief questions should not simply elicit recall or knowledge-level information, but rather should allow the teacher to uncover misconceptions or errors. Elaboration questions, which require that students explain their thinking, are particularly helpful in checking for understanding. When errors or misconceptions are unearthed, teachers can use prompts or cues to guide the learning. Prompts encourage students to engage in cognitive or metacognitive work, such as when a teacher prompts a student for background knowledge or a problem-solving heuristic. For example, when Ms. Randall prompted a group of students by saying, "How is it that items get sorted?" she was asking them to reflect on what they have learned to correct an error they have made. In addition, cues refocus students on an information source they are missing. There are a number of cues, including verbal, visual, gestural, physical, and environmental that all do essentially the same thing—invite the student to notice something that may help resolve the error or misconception. For example, when Ms. Randall followed up by saying, "Take another look at the poster we made," she was cueing students to notice the qualities that make an item recyclable. Further, this gives her insight into whether a concept needs to be retaught. Consider Ms. Randall's feed-forward efforts when the students in one of the groups attempted to compost items that did not belong in the bin (Figure 34.2).

Figure 34.2

Ms. Randall's feed-forward efforts

Ms. Randall: How do you know if something can go in the compost?

Brianna: *It has to be food.*

Eric: *Yeah, you gotta be able to eat it.*

Ms. Randall: All food goes in the compost?

Brianna: *Yeah, all the food.* [looking around the room] *Banana, sandwich, apple, watermelon, chips …*

Destini: *I like chips.*

Ms. Randall: I'm thinking about the kinds of foods listed on our poster. Remember the poster we made about food that can go in the compost?

Eric: *Yeah, it's right there, look.* [pointing to the wall]

Destini: *Not meat, no way. The worms can't have that meat. And it will make it smell.*

Ms. Randall: Right. I remember that, too. No meat for the compost because the worms can't eat it and it will just rot. And meat can attract rodents, which we really don't want, right? And what else? I'm seeing some things in your bin for composting that I'm not sure will work.

Brianna: [looking in the bin] *No meat.*

Eric: *Apple, watermelon, bread with peanut butter, peach …*

Ms. Randall: Pause right there. What was that?

Destini: *It's my peach.*

Ms. Randall: I thought you ate the peach.

Destini: *I did. It's the seed.*

Eric: *Like the apple seed.*

Ms. Randall: Take a look at the size chart next to the list of items for composting. What are you seeing?

Eric: *It's too big! We can't cut that up to the right size because it's too hard, so that shouldn't go in. The apple seed is small so it can go it, but not that watermelon part.*

Ms. Randall: It's called the rind. And you're exactly right. The peach pit, the seed from the peach, is too big and too hard for our worms. We can't put that in our compost. We can put the watermelon rind in, if we cut it up.

A Sophisticated Model

Taken together, feed up, feedback, and feed forward provide teachers and learners with a system of assessment that is consistent with inquiry-based learning. This system relies on teachers making instructional decisions by guiding their learners to additional experiences. This requires attention to the content and procedural knowledge that students are learning, as well as the investigative skills necessary for scientific thought. These often defy simple paper-and-pencil tests and are therefore overlooked in traditional assessments. However, by drawing from a more sophisticated model of formative assessment that reflects the inquiry-based nature of science, both content and investigation are afforded the attention they deserve.

References

Hattie, J., and H. Timperley. 2007. The power of feedback. *Review of Educational Research* 77: 81–112.

Hill, J. D., and K. M. Flynn. 2006. *Classroom instruction that works for English language learners.* Alexandria, VA: Association for Supervision and Curriculum Development.

Sapon-Shevin, M. 1998. *Because we can change the world: A practical guide to building cooperative, inclusive classroom communities.* Boston: Allyn & Bacon.

Resources

Cronin, D. 2003. *Diary of a worm.* New York: HarperCollins.

Gibbons, G. 1996. *Recycle! A handbook for kids.* New York: Little Brown.

Ryder, J. 1999. *Earthdance.* New York: Henry Holt.

Internet Resource

How to Make Classroom Compost Bins
   www.ehow.com/how_5566061_make-classroom-compost-bins.html

CHAPTER 35

Capitalizing on Curiosity

The Pursuit for Understanding the Science During Children's Inquiry Experiences

By Adam Devitt

Do your anxieties flair when a "well-thought-out" lesson goes awry? I planned what I thought to be an accommodating and appropriate lesson involving sinking or floating stations for our kindergarten, first, and second graders. They had an easy-to-read chart to record their collected data, with examples and pictures to help orchestrate what to do. I gave clear, concise directions using visuals. I asked for students to repeat in their own words what they would be doing during the exploration. I felt that this lesson would go smoothly, because I thought I had prepared a cognitively and developmentally age-appropriate lesson for these children, and had even anticipated possible difficult points.

Within moments, I noticed that few children were using their data sheets as requested. Others were trying to use the data sheet but could only produce scribbles. The noise level became uncomfortably loud and the children seemed to be playing around at each of the stations. I tried in vain to help many of the children at their stations. After a long, arduous cleanup at the end of class, I talked with a couple students to find out why they were "playing around" the entire class. One student, Tommy, soon looked confused and replied passionately, "No, we were working the whole time!"

Welcoming Holistic Inquiry

After school, Tommy's statement occupied my mind as I reflected about my day. I was a little upset that I did not capitalize on the chaos or recognize that wonderful scientific inquiries were being explored! It just looked different from what I had anticipated.

Scientific inquiry occurs when students make personal meaning of observed natural phenomena through which learning is shaped by students' prior knowledge and their own curiosities about natural phenomena (McDermott, Shaffer, and Constantinou 2000). Depending on various characteristics of the students, science investigations in the classroom will look different. For example, with younger children, you may observe what seems like random play with moments of surprise and nuance, some of which could be perceived as chaos. As students get older, you may see more systematic explorations involving overt student questions, explanations, and arguments. However, regardless of how students approach their explorations, they are still guided by their personal wonderings and attempts to make sense out of their own questions. This creates an authentic and meaningful learning experience because the motivation for learning is created through students' personal curiosities. Children need not be forced to learn how we want them to learn but rather be encouraged to develop their own ideas within settings we facilitate. By welcoming these new ideas, teachers can generate wonderful opportunities for students to share an investment in their own learning.

Students explore what sinks and what floats.

Assessing for Understanding

As one may anticipate, a traditional multiple-choice or question-and-answer format may not be the most appropriate informing tools for understanding children's learning. So what could formative assessment look like during children's inquiry experiences? When trying to assess the learning during science exploration, it is important to think about the content, process, and even the epistemic values considering the significance of matching methods of assessment to instruction (Taylor and Nolen 2008). Teachers can monitor student engagement with their explorations and listen to how they interact with other students. Because inquiry is student centered, teachers should facilitate organic learning that can be cultivated through open-ended and student-student questioning while students explore, process their observations, and synthesize understanding. This method of holistic, formative assessment will illustrate a vivid picture of student understanding of learned content and the learning process.

Facilitating the Inquiry Experience

On day one of teaching my lesson, I asked a child to stop "fooling around and clean up the mess" as he dunked an empty 2-liter bottle into a tub of water and caused water to overflow everywhere. I was responding to an unexpected behavior. What I saw as fooling around was really a student who did not understand directions, was not able to perform some of the tasks, and was not developed at the level of the demanded task.

To foster effective learning through inquiry, it is important to make conscious efforts to understand the science in children's thinking from careful listening and observing in the classroom (Hammer and van Zee 2006). Part of the assessment process of teaching science requires a keen awareness of how children develop personally meaningful understandings by connecting their "play" actions with their background knowledge and experiences. This does not mean that learning goals and objectives are obsolete. Teachers still need to have an agenda and can focus student inquiries through the materials they choose and asking provoking questions. On day two of this lesson with a new group the same age, I observed a different student trying the same experiment. This time my reaction was welcoming and thought-provoking. The student,

Denny, was pushing down a floating, 2-liter bottle into the tub of water, overflowing the tub. He stopped and cringed as I walked by.

> Teacher: No Denny, it's OK. What were you trying?
> Denny: *I wanted to see what would happen?*
> Teacher: … and what happened?
> Denny: *The water went over the side and made a big mess …*
> Teacher: I see that, but why did that happen? Why did the water overflow?
> Denny: *'Cause when I went like this* [pushing down on the water bottle]*, it [the bottle] took up lots of space and the water couldn't fit [in the tub], so it just overflowed.*

Reflecting about what happened on day one helped me prepare mentally for what might take place in the future. Luckily, I was given a chance to redeem myself and I capitalized on this "moment of chaos" to turn it into a positive and motivating teaching moment! By observing this student, I was able to make sense of what he was trying to do. Denny appeared to be asking, *What will happen if I push the empty bottle down in the water?* By testing his natural inquiry, he seemed to have gained the knowledge that empty bottles take up space and water will be displaced to make that happen when a force is applied. He clearly was able to define a *claim* based on an observation: *The water went over the side.* He further supported this claim by explaining that pushing down on the empty bottle caused the tub to overflow. Last, he reasoned that the bottle must be taking up space and that is why there was no room for the water in the tub.

Understanding How Children "Do" Science

Children come to school having a wealth of experiences ranging from playing in the backyard, watching their favorite TV shows, and even taking family trips to museums. The assessment process truly begins by understanding what ideas students are bringing to the classroom. Whether children come to the classroom with accurate representations or misconceptions of natural phenomena, they nonetheless hold personal ideas that are important to them (Hammer and van Zee 2006). By listening to children discuss their prior experiences and seeking to understand how they develop their current conceptions, we can learn starting points from which to devise explorations so that students make new observations and play with materials. Formative assessments can contribute by helping to make informed decisions about which new experiences would best fit.

During our exploration with sinking and floating, I had an intriguing conversation with a student. It was important to put into context what the child was saying, how she was saying it, and her actions. I came over to see what one student was doing. Tanya was throwing many different objects haphazardly into the bucket of water until she made a surprise discovery! The following conversation ensued:

> Teacher: Hey, what happened?
> Tanya: (shocked) *The wooden one floats!*
> Teacher: (pointing to the metal spoon) Well, what happened to that one?
> Tanya: *That one sank.*
> Teacher: Hum! So, why do you think that is?

Tanya: *That one is metal and metal is heavy!*
Teacher: What about this one? (pointing to the wooden spoon)
Tanya: *That one is not metal, so it floats!*

From the surprised expression on her face it seemed that Tanya anticipated, perhaps from prior experiences, that all spoons *should* sink. Maybe she had only experienced using metal spoons. She mentioned that the metal one sank, casually, as if that was the expected result. But when the wooden one floated, she seems to question her mental conception of spoons and whether wooden spoons should float, and for that reason she seems to reorganize her understanding of what floats into the categories of "metal" and "not metal." As a result of inquiring into the "chaos" that was occurring in the classroom, I was able to discover how these young minds created and pursued their own curiosities through the scientific process. By allowing the children, such as Tanya, to freely play, explore, and follow personal wonderings, I created a learning environment where students were motivated to make meaningful learning, and endeavor to make sense of what they were doing on their own.

Sinking experimentation was followed by reflection.

Safety note: As with any open-inquiry exploration, it is important that teachers anticipate and prevent many possible hazards like wet floors. Make sure to keep lots of clean-up tools on hand and talk with students about what it looks like to be safe in a science classroom before they set out on their explorations. Although students should be encouraged to continue their inquiries at home, they should do so with parent supervision.

Science Talks

The inquiry process should support the link between the scientific process and science content (Lehrer, Schauble, and Lucas 2008). Although this free exploration time is valuable, it is important to provide opportunities to refocus and reflect on learning to make students cognizant of not only new content knowledge but also how these new ideas are developing. Children can learn how to look back at what they did and extract what they feel is valuable to share with their classmates. To facilitate this experience, we have a science talk at the end of each class to hear what each child has learned, what new curiosities they still have, and allow for open discourse among students. During one of these talks, our sharing evolved into an occasion for students to practice communicating like scientists and have an argument.

Eli: *The pop bottle filled with water sank because of the water. My dad says water is one of the heaviest things on Earth.*
Jackie: *No, I don't think water is heavy. I think it is light.*

This beginning conversation opened the way for other students to give their ideas and explanations about the "weight of water." By listening to the students and seeing how they were forming a conceptualization about water from one another's ideas, I could respond by asking additional questions, prompting for more evidence, and providing future explorations to test their ideas to deepen and challenge their understanding. In addition, I recognized the value of having students think about new curiosities. Following the sinking and floating lesson, one of the kindergarten students, Christopher, said:

> *This weekend, I wanted to play more with sinking and floating. Me and my brother went home and filled up the bathtub and got a bunch of things from around the house and we threw them in the tub to see if they sinked or floated.*

I was delighted to hear that he was not only continuing to explore on his own, but he was sharing his learning with his family members in a free-choice setting. Because Christopher had some experiences in school he could re-create at home, he was motivated and capable to pursue his own inquiries. Isn't that one of our main goals for our young scientists?

Valuing Reflection

State and national standards have shifted what science learning should be from "plug and chug" formulas, to deep understanding of natural phenomena, competence developing ideas through the inquiry process, and even communicating scientific ideas among their communities (NRC 2007). By inquiring into my own teaching endeavors, I continue to value the reflection and assessment processes and recognize how they help me strive to cultivate improvements in my own learning toward being a more effective and competent educator. I do not suggest that teachers change their teaching to solely address newly mandated standards from higher powers, but many of the new standards are better representations of teaching and learning practices that address the needs of the whole child and ways to connect their classroom learning to the outside world. There is much to learn by listening to what children say and how they interact with one another and their environment. Supporting inquiry is a way to advance classroom instruction and prepare students to become better scientists in their own communities.

References

Hammer, D., and E. van Zee. 2006. *Seeing the science in children's thinking: Case studies of student inquiry in physical science.* Portsmouth, NH: Heinemann.

Lehrer, R., L. Schauble, and D. Lucas. 2008. Supporting development of the epistemology of inquiry. *Cognitive Development* 24: 512–529.

McDermott, L. C., P. S. Shaffer, and C. P. Constantinou. 2000. Preparing teachers to teach physics and physical science by inquiry. *Physics Education* 35 (6): 411–416.

National Research Council (NRC). 2007. Taking science to school: Learning and teaching science in grades K–8. Committee on Science Learning, Kindergarten Through Eighth Grade. Duschl, R. A., H. A. Schweingruber, and A. W. Shouse (Eds.). Washington, DC: National Academies Press.

Taylor, C. S., and S. B. Nolen. 2008. *Classroom assessment: Supporting teaching and learning in real classrooms.* Upper Saddle River, NJ: Pearson/Merrill/Prentice Hall.

Whoooo Knew?

Assessment Strategies for Inquiry Science

By Ellen Schiller and Jacque Melin

Who knew it would happen? Classroom assessment practices have shifted from a focus on checking for students' understanding of memorized material to examining their conceptual understanding as they engage in activities that involve scientific reasoning, inquiry skills, performances, and products. Inquiry-based science has shifted instruction away from teacher-centered, didactic teaching to student-centered, active learning. This shift is naturally accompanied by a need for formative assessment strategies that help students and teachers determine the learning that is occurring along the way.

The BSCS 5E Instructional Model (Bybee and Landes 1990) embeds assessment throughout the inquiry process:

- Eliciting prior knowledge before a lesson or unit,
- Checking for understanding throughout the unit, and
- Conducting summative assessment at the end of a unit to determine student learning.

Standardized summative assessment continues to garner the most attention, but science teachers know that it's critical to effectively evaluate student understanding *during* inquiry-based learning. We discuss several assessment strategies that you can use and adapt for inquiry-based science units, using the example of a weeklong fifth-grade unit about owls and owl pellets. These strategies, appropriate for middle to upper-elementary level students, actively involve students and provide them with the opportunity to self-assess their own learning.

Teachers need to check for understanding and offer feedback in every phase of the learning cycle so that students can conduct sound investigations, draw useful conclusions, and fully develop scientific ideas. To give effective feedback, all assessments should focus on predetermined learning targets. The results will supply information about how well each student understands science concepts and how effectively they use scientific process skills such as observing, interpreting, and communicating (Institute for Inquiry 2010).

Correlating Standards

Dissecting owl pellets is a common inquiry activity in elementary classrooms. Students enjoy pulling apart the pellets to discover what the owl ate. Safety note: Purchase commercially sterilized owl pellets and closely supervise students when using forceps or dissecting probes. We have found that plastic forceps work best, and dissecting needles are unnecessary. Students who are asthmatic or highly allergic to animal hair may need to be excused from dissecting real pellets. Pellets, Inc., offers the faux Perfect Pellet as an alternative (see Internet Resources). Students could also engage in virtual pellet dissection, which is a great follow-up extension for all pellet dissectors. Another typical follow-up task is to sort and identify the rodent bones found in the pellets. Often this is done as a "stand alone" activity, but owl pellet dissection can launch a full-fledged unit addressing learning targets related to food chains, food webs, animal adaptations, and predator/prey relationships. Assessments that link directly to the learning targets play a key role in any unit.

When developing sound assessments, begin by identifying clear statements of intended learning. These statements start with the science standards, but then the standards must be "deconstructed" and written as learning targets (i.e., objectives or goals) that can be shared with your students. Targets should be converted into student-friendly language through the use of "I can" statements. Shirley Clarke, a British teacher and author, recommends that "I can" statements be written to describe how well students have learned the targets and that they should be posted, not just shared verbally (Stiggins et al. 2009).

For our unit on owls, we deconstructed the relevant life science National Science Education Standards to determine our learning targets. Life Science Content Standard C, "The characteristics of organisms" is adapted into the "I can" statement: "I can describe the unique physical and behavioral characteristics of an owl." We address the following physical characteristics of owls: eyesight, hearing, silent flight, talons, beaks, and diet, as well as the owl's behavioral characteristics. Figure 36.1 shows how the learning targets were shared with students in this unit. Students were given individual copies of the targets and colored in each section of the owl as they demonstrated their mastery.

Making targets clear to students at the outset of a unit is the most important foundation to any assessment practice. Throughout the 5E model, students are engaged in hands-on explorations, investigations, and research, from which the teacher helps facilitate scientific understandings and explanations. As the teacher's role changes to one of facilitator, it's imperative that students understand the intended learning targets. Each of the assessment strategies we shared involves active student involvement and reflection on the learning targets.

Diagnostic Preassessments

Before beginning any science unit, it's important to engage students and elicit prior knowledge and possible misconceptions. Anticipation guides are a good method. Focused on key learning targets, anticipation guides list one to six true and false statements for grades 4–6 (one to four statements for primary grades, four to six for upper elementary). Lead your students through a discussion of the statements, having them share their rationale, prior knowledge, or current thinking about each statement before marking their predictions. You can use the predictions and discussion as tools for planning and revising unit lessons. After the learning targets have been taught, revisit the anticipation guide with your students and together check off which statements were true and false.

Figure 36.1

Learning targets

I can describe the energy flow in the food web of an owl.

I can describe what an owl pellet is and how it is made.

I can define *nocturnal, diurnal* and *crepuscular.*

I can explain the terms *predator* and *prey.*

I can draw a simple food chain showing the energy flow from the Sun to an owl.

I can describe the unique physical and behavioral characteristics of an owl.

I can classify the role of each organism in the food web of an owl.

Figure 36.2

Anticipation guide

Statement	Prediction		Findings	
	Agree	Disagree	True	False
1. Owls have an excellent sense of smell, which helps them locate prey in darkness.				
2. Owl pellets are owl poop.				
3. Owls are strictly carnivorous.				
4. All species of owls are nocturnal.				
5. Adult owls have few natural predators.				
6. It is a federal crime to intentionally injure or kill an owl.				

For the answer key, visit *www.nsta.org/SC1107.*

Although anticipation guides can also be completed individually via paper and pencil, we've found that the rich discussion that results when leading your whole class through the guide is more effective. Students enjoy sharing their opinions, background knowledge, and thought processes, along with casting their prediction votes and seeing whether they can convince classmates to vote their way.

Anticipation Guide

Figure 36.2 lists six sample statements about owls, all of which focus on the "big picture" unit learning targets. Make a copy to display on your document camera or overhead projector. Share with students that the anticipation guide lists six statements, some of which are true and some of which are false. Let them know that, during the inquiry unit, they will learn which are true or false through hands-on investigation, research, reading, and video clips (see Internet Resources). Next, read aloud each statement, allowing time for students to share their thoughts and predictions after each one. Although some students will share misconceptions, avoid commenting on students' ideas or sharing "correct" information at this early stage of the unit. We've found that students are more willing to share as the school year progresses, especially if you've created a risk-free learning community in which respect is given to students when they share ideas and questions with each other. After enough discussion time has passed for each statement (3–5 minutes is usually sufficient), take a vote and record the results on the chart. Students will now be engaged in the unit, ready to learn and find out whether they were right in their predictions.

We have used this anticipation guide many times and have found that it provides a great springboard to a unit on owls and predator/prey relationships. Note that the statements are written in kid-friendly language to help engage students. The statements also include some qualifying adjectives and adverbs, such as *strictly* and *all;* we've found that this helps to ensure a thoughtful discussion. At first blush, students may think that owls are nocturnal, but adding the qualifier *all* makes them think: *Are all owls nocturnal, or are there exceptions to this commonly held belief?* When constructing anticipation guides, it's also important to write statements that avoid trivial details. No one will know how many bones an owl has. Stick to the big picture learning targets and concepts.

Embedded Formative Assessments

Formative assessment that is embedded throughout the unit gives you valuable feedback about students' learning along the way. It allows you to intervene with struggling students, provide challenges for those who are ready, and adapt future lessons for more widespread achievement. Formative assessment also helps students monitor their own learning.

Think Dots

The "think dot" activity shown in Figure 36.3 could be used to help students share what they have learned about the unique physical and behavioral adaptations that allow nocturnal owls to hunt in darkness. Students enjoy the novelty of this activity as they formatively assess their

---

Figure 36.3

Think dots

Directions: Pairs of students are given a "think dot" sheet and a die. They take turns rolling the die to come up with a number that corresponds to a cell on the think dot sheet. For example, the first student rolls #3. The pair of students then discusses #3 (silent flight), including what they have learned about the physical appearance of the feathers and wings of the owl and how these characteristics help it to hunt prey at night. Each student then records this information in his or her science journal. Next, the second student rolls the die, and the pair follows the same procedure for a new number on the think dot sheet. Students continue to roll the die and report on their understanding until all six physical and behavioral adaptations are discussed and recorded. The teacher can collect the science journals and check for students' understanding of the physical characteristics of the owl.

Learning target: I can explain the unique physical and behavioral characteristics of an owl.

Eyesight	Hearing	Silent Flight
⚀	⚁	⚂
Talons and Beak	**Behavior**	**Diet**
⚃	⚄	⚅

Figure 36.4

Show-and-tell board

Learning targets:
I can classify the role of each organism in the food web of an owl.
I can explain the energy flow in the food web of an owl.

Task: Construct a food web with the owl at the highest trophic level. Be sure to include producers (green plants) and decomposers in your food web. Also include the Sun. The intermediate organisms should include the prey found in the owl pellets that you dissected in class. Label the role of all organisms and use arrows to show the energy flow between each organism. Finally, explain the flow of energy in the food web.

SHOW	Draw a **poster** showing a food web with the owl at the highest trophic level. Label the role of all organisms (consumer, producer, decomposer). Use arrows to show the energy flow between each organism.	Create a **PowerPoint** presentation showing a food web with the owl at the highest trophic level. Label the role of all organisms (consumer, producer, decomposer). Use arrows to show the energy flow between each organism.	Design a **brochure** showing a food web with the owl at the highest trophic level. Label the role of all organisms (consumer, producer, decomposer). Use arrows to show the energy flow between each organism.
TELL	Explain the energy flow in the food web by writing a **descriptive paragraph**.	Explain the energy flow in the food web by **writing a story**.	Explain the energy flow in the food web by **writing detailed sentences**.

understanding. Students report that they benefit from an activity that involves working with a partner to discuss and compare answers. They also like using the die, which makes this assessment more tactile.

Formative and Summative Assessments

Carol Ann Tomlinson (2006), an expert in differentiated instruction, states that assessments can be differentiated based on readiness, interest, and learning profile. However, it's critical that all variations of an assessment allow students to demonstrate what they've learned in reference to the learning targets.

Show-and-Tell Board

We created a show-and-tell board (Figure 36.4) for use as a differentiated summative assessment for some of the targets in this unit (Heacox 2009). Even though they have a choice of product, each student shows and tells what he or she knows about the same learning targets. After they read the task, students select a "show" from the top row of the show-and-tell board and a "tell" from the bottom row. For example, a student might choose to do a PowerPoint presentation to *show* the food web and write detailed sentences to explain (*tell*) the flow of energy.

Figure 36.5

Show-and-tell board rubric

Target	5	3	1
I can classify the role of each organism in the food web.	I have accurately illustrated and classified **all** of the organisms as either consumer, producer, or decomposer in the food web.	I have accurately illustrated and classified **some** of the organisms as either consumer, producer, or decomposer in the food web.	I have accurately illustrated and classified **very few** of the organisms as either consumer, producer, or decomposer in the food web.
I can explain the energy flow in the food web of an owl.	I have pointed **all** arrows in the correct direction of the energy flow and have accurately described the flow of energy in the food web.	I have pointed **some** of the arrows in the correct direction of the energy flow and partially described the flow of energy in the food web.	I have pointed a **few** of the arrows in the correct direction of the energy flow and have not described the flow of energy in the food web.

Rubric

The most common way to judge performance-based responses is through the use of a rubric. When designing rubrics, it's important to stay true to the learning targets being assessed. (Note that on the rubric in Figure 36.5, only the learning targets are scored.) Rubrics should be written in student-friendly language and help students understand what they must do to achieve a top-level score for a given target. Omit all trivial or unrelated features; criteria like neatness, attractiveness, color, artistic talent, effort, or design should not be included. You could give your students "work habits" feedback on these elements, but they should not be scored. If you are interested in developing your own rubrics, see Internet Resources.

RAFT and Think-Tac-Toe

Other types of differentiated choice activities that could be used as either formative or summative assessments include RAFTs or think-tac-toe boards.

A RAFT is an engaging strategy that encourages writing across the curriculum. It provides a way for teachers to encourage students to

- assume a **R**ole,
- consider their **A**udience,
- write in a particular **F**ormat, and
- examine a **T**opic from a relevant perspective.

An example RAFT writing choice board that could be used as an alternative to the show and tell board is shown in Figure 36.6 (p. 200). In this case, student choice is given through a choice of format used.

Figure 36.6

RAFT writing choice board

Directions: You will take on the role of an owl, explaining the owl's food web and how it connects to the owl's diet (topic), to prey (the audience). You have a choice of formats. Please see the RAFT choice board below.

Role	Audience	Formats (choices)	Topic
Owl	Prey	• a 3-minute speech with visual aides • a flowchart • an important e-mail • an interview between an "owl" and "prey" • a newspaper story	Explain my food web and how it connects to my diet.

Think-tac-toe choice boards play off the familiar childhood game. Typically, a think-tac-toe grid has nine cells in it like the tic-tac-toe game. Each cell contains alternative ways for students to express key ideas and key skills. It's important that no matter which choices students make, they must grapple with the key ideas and use the key skills central to the topic or area of study (Tomlinson 2003). In most cases, students choose to do three of the activities and form a tic-tac-toe (down, across, or diagonally).

Figure 36.7

Think-tac-toe choice board

Directions: Choose three activities in a row (down, across, or diagonally) to form a tic-tac-toe. For each choice, select a different physical or behavioral characteristic (eyesight, hearing, silent flight, talons & beak, behavior, diet).

Create a game for learning about the importance of **one** of the physical or behavioral characteristics of owls.	Create a PowerPoint presentation that could be used to teach students about the importance of **one** of the physical or behavioral characteristics of owls.	Write and recite a poem that shows the importance of **one** of the physical or behavioral characteristics of owls.
Make a flow chart to summarize important information about **one** of the physical or behavioral characteristics of owls.	Write an essay about the importance of **one** of the physical or behavioral characteristics of owls.	Plan and present a debate about which **one** of the physical or behavioral characteristics of owls is most important. Note: You may work on this with a partner; each take a different side of the debate.
Write and present an advertisement explaining which **one** of the physical or behavioral characteristics of owls is most important.	Write and perform a song or rap about the importance of **one** of the physical or behavioral characteristics of owls.	Write and illustrate a children's book explaining the importance of **one** of the physical or behavioral characteristics of owls.

An example is shown in Figure 36.7 of a think-tac-toe choice board that could be used as a formative assessment to determine what students know about the physical and behavioral characteristics of owls. This think-tac-toe choice board could be used as an ongoing formative assessment throughout the unit on owls. We've found that students are motivated by this differentiated assessment because they really enjoy having different product choices as they show us what they've learned.

Conclusion

Whether you are seeking to maximize learning while dissecting owl pellets, or searching for new ways to integrate effective assessment practices into your teaching, we hope these strategies will be valuable to you and your students as you use assessment to determine "Whoooo knew?"

References

Bybee, R., and N. M. Landes. 1990. Science for life and living: An elementary school science program from Biological Sciences Curriculum Study. *The American Biology Teacher* 52 (2): 92–98.

Heacox, D. 2009. *Making differentiation a habit: How to ensure success in academically diverse classrooms.* Minneapolis, MN: Free Spirit Press.

Institute for Inquiry. 2010. "Workshop 1: Introduction to Formative Assessment." Accessed December 8. *www.exploratorium.edu/ifi.*

Stiggins, R. J., J. Arter, J. Chappuis, and S. Chappuis. 2009. *Classroom assessment for student learning: Doing it right—using it well.* Portland, OR: Assessment Training Institute.

Tomlinson, C. A. 2003. *Fulfilling the promise of the differentiated classroom: Strategies and tools for responsive teaching.* Alexandria, VA: ASCD.

Tomlinson, C. A., and J. McTighe. 2006. *Integrating differentiated instruction and understanding by design.* Alexandria, VA: ASCD.

Internet Resources
Kidwings
   www.kidwings.com
Owl Cam
   www.owlcam.com
Pellets, Incorporated
   www.pelletsinc.com
Rubistar
   www.rubistar.com
Whoooo Knew
   www.whooooknew.com

Index

Page numbers printed in **boldface** type refer to figures.

A

A Framework for K–12 Science Education: Practices, Crosscutting Concepts, and Core Ideas, viii–xi, 178
Anticipation guides, **196,** 196–197
Assessment(s), 178–201
    based on learning targets, 193, 194, **195**
    changing landscape of, 178–180
    of Comet on a Stick! activity, 116
    of concept-based learning pond activity, 129–130, **130**
    for conservation unit, 181–187
    correlation with standards, 194
    diagnostic preassessments, 194, 196
    differentiated, 198
        RAFT and think-tac-toe, 199–201, **200**
        show-and-tell board, 198, **198, 199**
    of discovery box effectiveness, 122–123
    in 5E Instructional Model, 193
    formative, 53, 62–63, **63,** 94, 100, 130, **130,** 189, 198–199, 201
        embedded, 193, 197–199
        feed up, feedback, and feed forward model for, 181–187, **184, 186**
        think dots, **197,** 197–198
    in interactive reflective log, 58–59
    of investigatable questions, **74,** 78
    of lesson on water pressure in depth, 152–154
    for owl unit, 193–201, **195–200**
    purpose of, 182–183
    reflection and, 192
    of science notebooks, 46–47, 62–63, **63**
    of standards-based science fair projects, **161,** 162
    strategies for, 193–201
    of students' understanding, 188–192
    summative, 14, **14,** 62–63, **63,** 95, 130, **130,** 181, 193, 198–199
    of writing about lever investigations, 174
Asteroids, 116

B

Benchmarks for Science Literacy, viii, 2, 114
Bird vetch in Alaska, 91–96, **93–95.** *See also* Invasive plant study
Bloom's taxonomy, 82, **83**
Bonanza Creek Long Term Ecological Research Station, 92–96
Botanists, 16–22, 106
Bradbury, Leslie, 81–84
Brewer, Carol A., 32–36
BSCS 5E Learning Model, 10
Buoyancy predictions, 37–43. *See also* Sink or float activity
Bybee, Rodger W., viii, 134–136

C

California Science Center, 118
Camera activities, 81–84
    to classify living vs. nonliving things, 169
    generating questions for, 82–84
    to investigate rust, 84
    personal connections with, 84
    preparing for, 81–82
Caribou-Poker Creeks Research Watershed, 92
Cause and effect, teaching concept of, 6–8
Claims supported by evidence, 5–9, 88, 179
    definition of, 170, **171**
    introducing concept of, 171
Clarke, Shirley, 194
Cobb, Whitney, 113–117
Cognitive development, stages of, 165–166
Color variations in nature observations, 32–36
    assembling and sharing posters on, 35–36
    learning outcomes of, 36
    specimen collection for, 34–35
    student preparation for, 33–34
    teacher preparation for, 32–33
Comet on a Stick! activity, 113–117
    access to, 114
    alignment with national standards, 114
    background of, 113
    collaboration and modeling for, 114–115

continuation of, 116–117

evaluation of, 116

goal of, 114

information on comets for, 115

scientific discourse for, 115–116

Competitions between students, 159, 162

Concept-based learning pond activity, 124–131

developing understandings and essential questions for, 124–125, **126**

developing unit for, 124–125, **125**

ecology unit for, 127–130

five stations, 127–129, **128**

problem-based learning, 127

results and assessment, 129–130, **130**

sharing data, 129

introducing concept of change for, 126–127

reflection on, 130–131

Confirmatory inquiry, 143, **143,** 156–157

example of heat activity for, **144**

moving from structured inquiry to, 143–144, **144**

"Cookbook" labs, moving to inquiry from, 137–140

developing complex questions, 139

documenting and reflecting, 140

empowering students for, 154

for lesson on heat transfer and insulation, 142–147

moving from confirmatory to structured inquiry, 143–144, **144**

moving from guided to open inquiry for, 146–147

moving from structured to guided inquiry for, 145–146, **146**

for lesson on water pressure in depth, 149–154, **151**

assessment of, 152–154

demonstrations for, 150, **151**

investigations for, 151–152

vs. typical investigation, 149, **150**

listening to children's ideas, 138–139

subtle shifts leading to deeper engagement, 147–148

teachers' misconceptions about, 142

using standards as a guide, 139

using "thinking starters," 138, 140

Cooper, Sandi, 102–107

Coordinate graphs, 101

Creativity, 3, 46, 48, 118, 140, 152

Crissman, Sally, 97–101

Critical thinking, 5, 9, 26, 157

Curiosity, 26, 32, 42, 52, 66–68, 81, 82, 110–112, 123, 143, 149, 181, 188–192

D

Data. *See also* Evidence to support claims

claims, evidence, and reasoning framework for, 170–175, **171–173, 175**

collection and analysis of, 5, 88–90

for duck population dynamics study, 102–107, **104, 105**

for invasive plant study, 92–96, **93–95**

empirical, 3

observation/recording sheets for, 16, 17, **18**

using measure lines to represent, 97–101

visual representations of, 88–89

Dawn space mission, 116

Deaton, Benjamin E., 54–59

Deep Impact space mission, 113, 116

Density, **79,** 99

sink or float activity on, 37–43

Devitt, Adam, 188–192

Diagnostic preassessments, 194, 196

Diary of a Worm, 182

Dicots, 18

Discovery boxes for preschool activity on healthy food choices, 118–123

to capitalize on children's curiosity, 123

challenges and considerations for use of, 119–121

components of, **119,** 119–121, **122**

design of, 118–119

evaluating effectiveness of, 122–123

goals and objectives for, 118–119

implementation and student engagement with, 121

Discrepant events, 6–7

Diverse student population, 22, 93, 164

Drawings, 17–18

in science notebooks, 40–50, **50**

Duck population dynamics study, 102–107

beginning research for, 103–104

egg production and, 104, **104**

electronic communications with scientists for, **105**

finding other real-world learning opportunities, 106

integrating mathematics with, 104–107

learning outcomes of, 107

rationale for, 102

Duschl, Richard A., 178–180

Dyasi, Hubert, 112

E

Earthdance, 182

Ecologists

definition of, 34

observing natural color variations, 32–36

problem-based pond activity, 124–131

study of invasive plants in Alaska, 91–96, **93–95**

Ecologists, Educators, and Schools project, 32

Einstein, Albert, 69

Elementary Science Study (ESS), viii

English language learners, 22, 46, 49, 167, 168

EPOXI, 116

Evidence to support claims, 5–9, 88, 97, 134–135

cause-and-effect concept and, 6–8

communication/reporting of, 135, 136

definition of, 170, **171**

inquiry and, 24, 179, 180

introducing concept of, 5–6, 171–172

in lesson on sound, 10–14, **14**

making students' thinking visible about, **8,** 9

measurement of, 8

reasoning and, 171, **171,** 172

sources of, 170–171

for unit on simple machines, 170–175

variable control and, 8–9

Experimental questions, 76

Eye protection, 11, 129

F

Feed-forward instruction, 181, **184,** 185–186, **186**

Feedback to students, 9, 46–47, 89, 159, 174, 175, 178–179, 181, 183–185, **184,** 187, 193, 197, 199

by peers, 58–59

Feeding up, 181, 182–183, **184**

Finson, Kevin D., 27–31

Fisher, Douglas, 181–187

5E Instructional Model, 10, 193, 194

Flessner, Ryan, 137–140

Formative assessments, 53, 62–63, **63,** 94, 100, 130, **130,** 189, 201

embedded, 193, 197–199

feed up, feedback, and feed forward model for, 181–187, **184, 186**

think dots, **197,** 197–198

Four Question Strategy, 147

A Framework for K–12 Science Education: Practices, Crosscutting Concepts, and Core Ideas, viii–xi, 178

Frey, Nancy, 181–187

Friction, **175**

Froschauer, Linda, 46–47

Full Options Science System (FOSS), 51, 173

G

Gardening project, 16–22

goals of, 16, 21

learning outcomes of, 21–22

making observations for, **18,** 20–21

planting pea seeds for, 18–19

pre- and postproject writing samples for, **19,** 21

scientific drawing for, 17–18

sheltered constructivism approach to, 21–22

Goggles for eye protection, 11, 129

Gomez-Zwiep, Susan, 5–9

Goodman, Jeff, 81–84

Graphs of data, 88–89, 97

coordinate graphs, 101

for invasive plant study, **94,** 94–95, **95**

Gross, Lisa, 81–84

Guided inquiry, 26, 66, 137, 138, 145

moving from structured inquiry to, 145–146, **146**

moving to open inquiry from, 146–147

H

Hand washing, 18, 34, 75, 93, 106, 182, 183

Hands-on activities, viii, 24, 26, 37, 50, 51, 55, 67, 68, 84, 102, 111, 113, 134, 170, 194, 196. *See also* Inquiry

Harris, David, 5–9
Heat transfer and insulation lesson, 142–148
    moving from confirmatory to structured inquiry, 143–144, **144**
    moving from guided to open inquiry for, 146–147
    moving from structured to guided inquiry for, 145–146, **146**
Higher-order thinking skills, 9, 82
Holistic inquiry, 188–189
How People Learn: Brain, Mind, Experience, and School, 111
How Students Learn: Science in the Classroom, ix
Howell, Linda, 124–131

I
Inferences, 3
    to advance science, 31
    assumptions used when making, 30
    definition of, 28
    incorrect, 29–30
    influence of prior knowledge and experiences on, 30
    observations and, **27,** 27–31, **28**
Inquiry, 3, 134–136
    assessment of (*See* Assessment(s))
    books and, 26
    collaborative, 138
    confirmatory, 143, **143, 144,** 156–157
        moving to structured inquiry from, 143–144, **144**
    definition of, 24, 137–138
    empowering students for, 154
    to encourage students to think for themselves, 67–68
    essential features of, 25, 134–135, **135,** 179–180
    facilitating experience of, 189–190
    full inquiries, 111
        engaging children in, 136
    goal and method of, 26
    guided, 26, 66, 137, 138, 142, 145
        moving from structured inquiry to, 145–146, **146**
        moving to open inquiry from, 146–147
    through hands-on activities, viii, 24, 26, 37, 50, 51, 55, 67, 68, 84, 102, 111,
113, 134, 170, 194, 196
    holistic, 188–189
    inclusion in science practices, viii–ix
    integrating with core content, ix–xi
    judging quality of, 25–26
    levels of, **143**
    moving from "cookbook" labs to, 137–140
        developing complex questions, 139
        documenting and reflecting, 140
        for lesson on heat transfer and insulation, 142–147, **143, 144, 146**
        for lesson on water pressure in depth, 149–154, **150, 151, 153**
        listening to children's ideas, 138–139
        subtle shifts leading to deeper engagement, 147–148
        teachers' misconceptions about, 142
        using standards as a guide, 139
        using "thinking starters," 138, 140
    open, 67, 137, 138, 142
        moving from guided inquiry to, 146–147
    pathways to, 110–112
    personalized, 75–80
    as powerful approach to learning science, 111–112
    process skills and, 24–26, 137, 138
    role in *A Framework for K–12 Science Education,* viii
    safety notes for, 11, 18, 34, 35, 40, **56,** 75, **79,** 81, 93, 106, 121, **122,** 127, 129, 131, 145, 146, 156, 160, 167, 182, 183, 184, 191, 194
    Science and Children articles on, vii, viii
    science talks about, 191–192
    sharing results of, 129, 135, 136, 156–175
    sound lesson linking content, nature of science and, 10–15, **14**
    sparks that ignite, 66–68
    structured, 137–138, 142
        moving from confirmatory inquiry to, 143–144, **144**
        moving to guided inquiry from, 145–146, **146**
    teachers' questions about, 24

topics for (*See* Investigatable questions)

transforming demonstrations into activities for, 150, **151, 153,** 154

understanding how children "do" science, 190–191

using discovery boxes to promote, 118–123

what students should know about, 2

Inquiry continuum, 137–138

The Inquiry Project, 97–101

Institute for Inquiry, 110

Intel International Science and Engineering Fairs (ISEF), 158

Interactive reflective log (IRL), 54–59

    amplified assessment of, 58–59

    creation of, 54–55

    to develop reflective thinkers, 59

    making it interactive, 55, 58

    making it reflective, 55

    purposes of, 54

    sample of, **56–57**

    sections of, 54

Invasive plant study, 91–96

    age-appropriate data analysis for, **94,** 94–96, **95**

    classroom data collection for, **93,** 93–94

    field data collection for, 92–93

    noticing problem for, 91–92

    putting data into action for, 96

Investigatable questions, 66–84

    achieving awareness about, 74

    assessment of, 78

    Bloom's taxonomy and, 82, **83**

    cause–effect, **73**

    checklist for evaluation of, **74**

    descriptive, **73**

    Four Question Strategy for generation of, 147

    handling students' questions, 69–70, **71**

    identifying and refining, 72, 74

    literature-based, 76

    modeling and questions stems for, 72

    on natural phenomena, 70

    observations for generation of, 75–76

    for personalized inquiry, 75–80

    for photography activities, 81–84, **83**

    relational, **73**

    sparks that ignite inquiry, 66–68

    for standards-based science fair, 160

    student generation of, 69–74, 76–78, 82–83, **83,** 138, 139, 146–147

    "thinking starters" for generation of, 138, 140

    types of, **73,** 76

J

Jeffries, Carolyn, 118–123

Journals, **14,** 16–17, 70, 77, 84, 93, 96, 105, 168, **197.** *See also* Science notebooks

    interactive reflective logs, 54–59, **56–57**

Joyner, Valerie, 48–53

K

Kant, Immanuel, 46

Kim, Jenny, 37–43

Krajcik, Joseph, 88–90

KWL charts, 114, 116, 127

L

Lederman, Norman G., 2–4

Lee, Michele H., 10–15

Legaspi, Britt, 164–169

Leland, Katina, 54–59

Lener, Elizabeth, 60–64

Lever investigations, 170, **172, 173,** 173–175

Line plots, 97, 101

Literature, 17, 103, 124

Literature-based research questions, 76, **77**

Literature-research skills, 67

Living vs. nonliving things classification lesson, 164–169

    asking the right questions for, 165

    background for, 165–166

    categorizing and rationalizing for, 166–167

    discussing criteria for, 168

    evaluation of, 168–169

        rubric for, **166,** 168

    journal reflections on, 168

    learning outcomes of, 169

    living, nonliving, and dead categories for, 166

    students' misconceptions about, 164–165

    technology tips for, 169

    tips for English language learners, 167, 168

Lott, Kimberly, 142–148
Lowery, Lawrence F., 66–68
Lynch, Mary Jean, 149–154

M
Magee, Paula A., 137–140
Martin, Dean M., 170–175
Martin-Muth, Deana, 91
McBride, Brooke B., 32–36
McFadden, Lucy, 113–117
McNeill, Katherine L., 170–175
Measure lines, 97–101
    coordinate graphs and, 101
    definition of, 97
    developing criteria for, **99,** 100
    to investigate weight of very tiny things,
        100–101
    use in inquiry about the nature of matter,
        97–98, **98**
    what is indicated about data from,
        98–100
Melin, Jacque, 193–201
Merino, Barbara, 16–22
Minchew Deaton, Cynthia, 54–59
Misconceptions
    of students, 11, 120, 130, 149, 154, 185–
        186, 190, 194, 196
        about living vs. nonliving things,
            164–165
    of teachers, about moving to inquiry,
        142
Monocots, 18
Motivation of students, 58, 178, 189, 190, 191,
    192, 201
Motley, Tammy, 102–107

N
National Aeronautics and Space Administration
    (NASA), 113–114, 116
National Research Council (NRC), 2, 25, 178
National Science Education Standards, viii, 2,
    24, 25, 31, 32, 76, 78, 114, 118, 125, 134,
    137, 166, 170, 194
National Science Foundation (NSF), viii
Nature of science, 2, 10
Next Generation Science Standards, xi, 178
North American Waterfowl Management Plan,
    102

O
Observational studies, 76
Observations. See also Evidence to support
    claims
    definition of, 28, 34
    as essential feature of inquiry, 134, 136
    for generation of investigatable questions,
        75–76
    inferences and, **27,** 27–31, **28**
    of natural color variations, 32–36
    quality of, 28–29
Open inquiry, 67, 137, 138
    generating questions for, 146–147 (See
        also Investigatable questions)
    moving from guided inquiry to, 146–147
The Opportunity Equation, 178
Owings, Sharon, 16–22
Owl unit, assessments for, 193–201, **195–200**

P
Padilla, Mike, 24–26
Pareja, Enrique M., 10–15
Personalized inquiry, 75–80
    assessment of, 78
    beginning with observations for, 75–76
    of familiar topics, 80
    lesson 1: classifying questions for, 76, **77**
    lesson 2: generating questions for, 76–78
    lesson 3: series of stations for, 78, **79**
Photography activities, 81–84
    to classify living vs. nonliving things, 169
    generating questions for, 82–84
    to investigate rust, 84
    personal connections with, 84
    preparing for, 81–82
Piaget, Jean, 165–166
Pintail Partners project, 102–107
Plants
    gardening project, 16–22, **18, 19**
    invasive, 91–96, **93–95**
Preassessments, diagnostic, 194, 196
Problem-based pond activity, 124–131. See also
    Concept-based learning pond activity
Problem solving, 5, 21, 69, 104–105, 118, 120,
    145, 149, 154, 160, **183,** 186
    process skills for, 24–26
Process skills, 111, 191, 193
    inquiry and, 24–26, 137, 138

observations and inferences, **27,** 27–31, **28**
observing natural color variations, 32–36
for sink or float activity, 37–43
student responsibility for using, 111

R
RAFT writing choice board, 199, **200**
Randall, Debra, 182–186
Rankin, Lynn, 110–112
Ready, Set, Science!, ix, 178, 179, 180
Reasoning
    definition of, 171, **171**
    introducing concept of, 172
    strong vs. weak statements, 175, **175**
Recycle!, 182
Rillero, Peter, 158–163
Rountree-Brown, Maura, 113–117
Rubrics. *See also* Assessment(s)
    design of, 199
    for living vs. nonliving things
        classification, **166,** 168
    for recycling unit, **183**
    for show-and-tell board, **199**
    for standards-based science fair, **161,** 162
    for writing about lever investigations, 174

S
Safety notes, 11, 18, 34, 35, 40, **56,** 75, **79,** 81,
    93, 106, 121, **122,** 127, 129, 131, 145, 146,
    156, 160, 167, 182, 183, 184, 191, 194
Schill, Bethany, 124–131
Schiller, Ellen, 193–201
Science, Technology, and Society (STS) model,
    102
Science and Children, vii, xi, 32
Science Curriculum Improvement Study (SCIS),
    viii
Science fair. *See* Standards-based science fair
Science in Elementary Education: Methods,
    Concepts and Inquiries, 142
Science kits, 67, 111, 118, 125
Science notebooks, vii, 11–14, 46–64, 70, 72,
    93, 95, 103, 140. *See also* Journals
    assessment of, 46–47, 62–63, **63**
    benefits of, 46
    calendars and graphs in, 52, **53**
    drawing, dating, and labeling in, 40–50,
        50

focus questions for, 51, **51**
glossary in, 50
guidelines for, 61, **61**
guiding students in creation of, 46
"I wonder" questions in, 52
instructional goals for use of, 46
interactive reflective logs, 54–59, **56–57**
making predictions in, 51–52
retaining as reference tools, 60, 63–64
scaffolding entries in, 49, **49**
structure of, 48–49, 61, **61**
table of contents for, 50, 62, **62**
use of, 62
Science practices, viii–xi
    as essential elements of curriculum, x
    inclusion of inquiry in, viii–ix
    integrating with core content, ix–xi
Science talks, 191–192
Science terminology, 16, 17, 18, 49, 50, 58, 59,
    84, 113, 116, 129, 143, 168, 171, 174
Science—A Process Approach (SAPA), viii, 25
Scientific argumentation, x, 9, 21–22, 113, **135,**
    170, **172,** 172–174, **173,** 179, 180, 189,
    191. *See also* Evidence to support claims
Scientific drawing, 17–18
    in science notebooks, 40–50, **50**
Scientific explanations, 10–13, 15, 134–136,
    135, 143, 170, 179, 180. *See also* Evidence to
    support claims
Scientific investigations, 3, 111, 188–189. *See*
    also Inquiry
    assessing learning during, 188–192
    balance between structure and freedom
        in, 111
    data collection and analysis for, 5, 88–90
    determining cause and effect in, 6–8
    evidence supporting claims in, 5–9
    inquiry and essential features of, 25
    safety notes for, 11, 18, 34, 35, 40, **56,**
        75, **79,** 81, 93, 106, 121, **122,** 127,
        129, 131, 145, 146, 156, 160, 167,
        182, 183, 184, 191, 194
    stages of, 111
    students' thought processes in
        development of, **8,** 9
    topics for (*See* Investigatable questions)
Scientific knowledge, 2–4
Scientific literacy, viii, ix, 29, 31, 46, 88

Scientific method, viii, x, 2, 3
Scientists
    development of scientific knowledge by,
      2–4
    evidence to support claims of, 5–9
    gardening project to teach thinking,
      acting, and writing like, 16–22, **18, 19**
    sound lesson linking content, inquiry
      skills, and nature of science, 10–15, **14**
Seefeldt, Steve, 91
Sharing research results, 129, 135, 136, 156–175
    claims, evidence, and reasoning framework
      for, 170–175, **171–173, 175**
        designing classroom supports,
          172–173
        providing support over time,
          174–175
        rebuttal and, 171
        rubrics for evaluation of, 174
    of living vs. nonliving things classification
      lesson, 164–169
    methods and presentations for, 156–157
    science talks for, 191–192
    standards-based science fair for, 158–163
Sharkawy, Azza, 69–74
Sheltered constructivism, 21–22
Shore, Linda, 156–157
Show-and-tell board, 198, **198**
    rubric for, **199**
Sickel, Aaron, 10–15
Simpson, Patricia, 75–80
Sink or float activity, 37–43
    assessing students' learning during,
      188–192
    beyond process skills for, 37–38
    completed data chart for, 40, **40**
    developmental appropriateness of, 38–39
    learning outcomes of, 42–43
    lesson for, 39–42, **41**
    particulate model for, 37–38, **38**
Smithenry, Dennis W., 37–43
Sound, 5E Instructional Model lesson on,
    10–15, **14**
Spellman, Katie V., 91–96
Standards, 178, 192
    Benchmarks for Science Literacy, viii, 2, 114
    correlating assessments with, 194, **195**
    A Framework for K–12 Science Education:

      Practices, Crosscutting Concepts, and
        Core Ideas and, viii–xi, 178
    as guide for inquiry activities, 139
    National Science Education Standards,
      viii, 2, 24, 25, 31, 32, 76, 78, 114,
      118, 125, 134, 137, 166, 170, 194
    Next Generation Science Standards, xi, 178
Standards-based science fair, 158–163
    benefits of, 158
    challenges of, 158–159
    child-centered projects for, 160
    choosing topics for, 160
    criterion-referenced approach of, 159–160
    as day of celebration, 163
    emphasis on student communication for,
      160, 162
    evaluation of, 162
        rubrics for, **161,** 162
Stardust-NExt space mission, 116
Straits, William, 81–84, 164–169
Structured inquiry, 137–138, 142, **143**
    moving from confirmatory inquiry to,
      143–144, **144**
    moving to guided inquiry from, 145–146,
      146
Students
    assessing understanding of, 188–192
    competitions between, 159, 162
    critical thinking by, 5, 9, 26, 157
    curiosity of, 26, 32, 42, 52, 66–68, 81,
      82, 110–112, 123, 143, 149, 181,
      188–192
    diversity of, 22, 93, 164
    empowerment of, 154
    English language learners, 22, 46, 49, 167,
      168
    generation of investigatable questions by,
      69–74, 76–78, 82–93, **83,** 138, 139,
      146–147
    handling questions of, 69–70, **71**
    hands-on activities for, viii, 24, 26, 37, 50,
      51, 55, 67, 68, 84, 102, 111, 113, 134,
      170, 194, 196
    higher-order thinking skills of, 9, 82
    learning to think for themselves, 67–68
    listening to ideas of, 138–139, 192
    misconceptions of, 11, 120, 130, 149,
      154, 185–186, 190, 194, 196

motivation of, 58, 178, 189, 190, 191, 192, 201
Piaget's stages of cognitive development of, 165–166
providing feedback to, 9, 46–47, 89, 159, 174, 175, 178–179, 181, 183–185, 187, 193, 197, 199
with special needs, 22, 49
underestimating science abilities of, 178
Summative assessments, 14, **14,** 62–63, **63,** 95, 130, **130,** 193, 198–199
show-and-tell board, 198, **198, 199**

T
T-charts, 101, 114
Tables of data, 88–89, 101
Taking Science to School, ix, 178, 179
Think dots, **197,** 197–198
Think-tac-toe choice board, 199–201, **200**
"Thinking starters," 138, 140
Thomas, Julie, 102–107
Tomlinson, Carol Ann, 198

V
Variable scan, **71,** 72
Variables
changing/testing of, 7, 39, 42, **71,** 157, 160
for demonstrations, 147, 149–151, **153**
control of, x, 5, **8,** 8–9, 24, 67, 78, 147
dependent, 8, 89, 147
determining relevance of, 145, 149, 150–151, 152, **153,** 154
identification of, 25, **71,** 72, 147, 154
independent, 8, 39, 42, 89, 147

relationships between, **73,** 78, 89
Venn diagrams, 97, 101
Vibration, 10–13, **14**
Villano, Christine P., 91–96
Vocabulary, 16, 17, 18, 49, 50, 58, 59, 84, 113, 116, 129, 143, 168, 171, 174

W
Warner, Elizabeth, 113–117
Water pressure in depth lesson, 149–154
assessment of, 152–154
demonstrations for, 150, **151**
investigations for, 151–152
vs. typical investigation, 149, **150**
Watterson, Bill, 110
We Are What We Eat!, 121
Weed Wackers! A K–6 Educator's Guide to Invasive Plants of Alaska, 96
Writing
about lever investigations, **172, 173,** 173–174
gardening project for teaching of, 16–22, **18, 19**
in interactive reflective logs, 54–59, **56–57**
in journals, **14,** 16–17, 70, 77, 84, 93, 96, 105, 168, **197**
RAFT writing choice board, 199, **200**
in science notebooks, 46–64 (*See also* Science notebooks)

Y
Year of the Solar System, 116

Z
Zenchak, John, 149–154